The Pan-Afrikanis

(Part 3)

i

Pan-Afrikanism:

Material Based Concepts

Omowale Ru Pert-em-Hru

ISBN- 13: 978-1660041107

Published by
Omowale Ru Pert-em-Hru

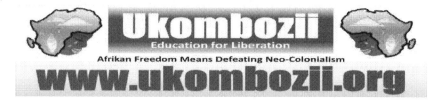

Ukombozii@gmail.com
00 44 (0) 7933 145 393

Pan-Afrikan Society Community Forum (PASCF) Ancestors:
Forerunner organisation to Ukombozii:

Brother Omowale

•*Brother Ras Lloyd* (aka Lloyd Johnson) the first *Chair of the PASCF* – Born 17th August 1956, crossed to meet the ancestors 20th December 2011;

•*Brother Oxalando Efuntola* (aka Andrew Navarro Smith) the first *Director of Communications* and *Organisational Priest* of the PASCF – Born 29th January 1957, crossed to meet the ancestors 16th September 2014; and

•*Sister Mawasi Bojang* (aka Patricia Presilla Chambers) the first *Deputy Chair of the PASCF*, who took up the role of *Chair of the PASCF* on the passing of Ras Lloyd – Born 8th February 1965, crossed to meet the ancestors 11th May 2016.

Though our comrades did not necessarily describe themselves as socialists, they were all ardent, committed and active anti-imperialists. They all gave selflessly to the struggle against capitalism and made important dedicated contributions to our people's advance towards socialism within the disciplined framework of organised resistance.

In part, this document comes out of their practical grounded work experience. We thank them for their contributions to the liberation of our people – each of them a solid rock in our struggle. They will always be remembered by the PASCF and Ukombozii.

Table of Contents

ACKNOWLEDGMENTS

To the Charles, Peltier, Emmanuel, Daniel, Lewis, Michel, Pascale, Bougyne, Ramey lines and all of our unknown ancestors right back to our origin in Afrika. Without all of you and each of you individually, our present day lineage could not exist; nor could anything that we've produced, including this book. Though I can never repay my debt to you, I can contribute to the recovery of Afrika by passing your gift of life to the next generation in a manner that will make us proud. Thank you for life and much, much more.

It is now 8pm on Wednesday 15th November 2017, the 19th anniversary of the passing of Kwame Ture. I worked with but never met him. He is one of my ideological fathers. The redrafting of this book will be completed tomorrow, the 47th anniversary of the passing of my father John Baptist Charles a.k.a. Agee, Kenagee or Senford. My debt to both fathers mentioned here is eternal.

.

Preamble

My Vision for Afrika and her people

Our capacity to create, produce and build as our contribution to a better world for humanity

I want every Afrikan person on earth to be an effective contributor to the technological advance of humanity and the production of ever more effective and efficient tools. What we are going to achieve with our mastery of new technology is beyond anything that we can currently imagine, but some of the indicators of our advance will include:

- The reproduction of ever healthier people symbolised by 100% live women and babies emerging from the birthing process and Afrikan babies born with an average life expectancy in excess of 100 years;
- The production of ever more intelligent/productive people symbolised by:
    - The understanding that Afrika – the richest land in the world – will remain under the exclusive sovereign control of Afrikan people at home and abroad collectively into eternity;
    - Afrikan children's complete mastery of the history/geography of Afrika and the world;

- o Afrikan children's complete mastery of the secrets of quantum physics;
- o Afrikan children's complete mastery of the ability to bring the past and future into the present and work on them to create an optimally better future;
- o Afrikan children's complete mastery of the languages and techniques of efficient and effective communication;
- o Afrikan children's complete mastery of managing our continent and the world for the greater good of humanity and Mother Nature;
- The production of ever higher and better technology i.e. tools in service of and in harmony with the best interests of humanity and Mother Nature, symbolised by an ever cleaner planet, in turn symbolised by the ability to produce and reproduce an abundance of:
  - o The purest and freshest possible air;
  - o The purest and cleanest possible water;
  - o The healthiest and most nutritious foods;
  - o The most robust travel vehicles facilitating the movement of Afrikan people through the universe at speeds faster than the speed of light;
  - o The most efficient and effective long and short distance communication tools;
- By living in a world where:
  - o We fully deploy the creative genius of Afrikan people to produce all that we need (and surplus) so effectively, efficiently and speedily that we create more time for us to respectfully engage with each other, Mother Nature and our ancestors; and
  - o The most advanced technologies flourish in service of Afrikan people as part of greater humanity and Mother Nature.

Driven by our capacity to govern a just society for Afrikan people
I want every Afrikan person on earth to understand that the most effective method for governing our homeland and people at this point in history means:

- Afrika, including her surrounding islands, must be united and governed as one continental-wide super-state, freed from all internal 'national' boarders;
- The super-state must be created by and be under the collective control of all Afrikan people – those at home and those abroad – and predominantly managed by women;
- The land and resources of Afrika must be under the exclusive sovereign control of Afrikan people at home and abroad collectively and used for the benefit of all Afrikan people in the first instance, making us the richest, most powerful people and humble leaders of the world for the greater good of humanity;
- We must develop a military capability sufficient to defend our homeland from any foe;
- Our continental-wide super-nation-state - the most powerful in the world - is constantly ready, willing and able to protect any and all of her children whether based at home or abroad;
- Our continental-wide super-nation-state is a means to a greater end. It is tasked with laying the foundation for a continent and by extension a world so supportive and in tune with the best interests of the people, Mother Nature and our ancestors, where truth, freedom, justice and peace are so inculcated into human existence, that all states become unnecessary, are removed from the world and become relics of history.

Driven by our capacity to build respectful relationships for the achievement of happiness
I want every Afrikan person on earth to understand, adopt and apply in the modern world the principles underpinning the tendency towards healthy relationships found typically in Afrikan village culture. Namely that:
- Human beings are fundamentally humble and respectful of other human beings, Mother Nature and their ancestors;
- Every human being is more important than property, money or profit and therefore an end in their own right, not a means to somebody else's end;
- The benefits to the 'we' are usually, but not always, prioritised over the benefits to the 'me' and when the benefits to the 'me' are given higher priority, that is decided by the 'we'; and

3

- Whilst all human beings are unique have differing qualities, attributes and abilities, we are all equal in essence;

Driven by a humble and respectful relationship with our environment for the achievement of higher understanding
I want every Afrikan person on earth to understand that:
- Mother Nature is composed of antagonistic opposites held in unison;
- The never ending engagement of opposites is the source of perpetual change in Mother Nature and everything in her;
- Mother Nature was there before us and gave us space within her;
- We are a part of Mother Nature;
- We are absolutely obliged to engage with Mother Nature;
- Spirit is inside Mother Nature;
- Spirituality is the process of connecting with spirit, achievable only through a respectful engagement with Mother Nature;

Agreement/acceptance with/of the above vision will form part of the criteria for membership of Ukomozii. It is to be recited twice daily (first thing in the morning and last thing at night) by all members and their families as a constant ongoing reminder of the future that unites us.

Omowale Ru Pert-em-Hru
19th January 2018

Foreword

In the space dimension all material has both essence and form – the essence being the form's contents. It is possible to know a thing by its form, but not know its essence. For instance, I know what a car is, but may not understand how it works. Similarly, it is possible to know the essence of a thing, but not its form. I know I want to be free, but don't know how.

In the time dimension it is possible to know a thing to be true and correct at one point only to later find that the thing has changed. What was known is no longer. The distinction between essence and form changes over time thereby giving life to the possibility of knowing and not knowing a thing at the same time. These contradictions expose weaknesses of concepts which are not real life, but at worst deliberate falsehoods and best abstractions from it. Pan-Afrikanism is Scientific Socialism. It is the particular form Scientific Socialism will take in Afrika. Scientific Socialism is the universal essence of the next phase of human history - Pan-Afrikanism is its Afrikan form.

This collection of essays expresses important aspects of Pan-Afrikanism conceptually: (i) the meaning of Pan-Afrikanism; (ii) history, culture and identity as tools of Pan-Afrikanism; and (iii) racism and sexism as realities to be overcome - The bias is towards form. It also uses imagery and diagrams to help convey conceptual points. These too have their limitations and should be treated merely as aids to assist assimilation of concepts.

There is a distinction between conceptual and real existence – conceptual is form, real existence essence. This means it is possible to have a conceptual understanding of reality, without truly understanding it. Also because concepts are a bit like photographs i.e. freeze frames of reality, even if they are correct, they are constantly in danger of becoming obsolete and cannot convey essence. In working with concepts and images, it is necessary to be fully cognisant of their limitations. They must be treated with caution and where used, continuously updated by reference to practice, for which they can never substitute. We cannot theorise our way to liberation.

Regardless of this range of weaknesses concepts are not valueless. In support of practice they can operate as powerful learning tools which heighten practitioners understanding of the situations in which they operate. Concepts and practice together enhance each other forming a unified whole, making better practice in turn informing theory, each correcting the other. Sekou Toure explains:

> "When a non-existent thing occupies the mind, only the result of our actions restores the truth that has not been perceived ... man does not create science, but he discovers it through progressive understanding of objective laws, which explains the impersonal character of science ... evolution of human conscience rests constantly on the practical knowledge and experience of men ... Theory postulates action and engenders and improves theory. The correspondence between human action and thought constitutes unity of opposites. In every existence, the unity of opposites is expressed ... " (Toure, No. 88, p. 53)

Critically important as they are, actions are not the only consideration. They must be supported by theory. The law of unity of opposites directs that, though at one level antagonistic opposites, revolutionary practice and ideas are inseparable and go together. The purpose of theory is not to replace practice, but the support, enhance and be improved by it. The essence of Pan-Afrikanism is defined by what practitioners do to achieve the objective. The role of these essays is to contribute to a theoretical framework that promotes clarity of thought among Pan-Afrikanists, current new or potential. The aim is to strengthen and assist practical actions.

Divisionism
Afrika's Enemy Within

Ukombozii
Education for Liberation
Afrikan Freedom Means Defeating Neo-Colonialism
www.ukombozii.org

Chapter 1

1 Divisionism: Afrika's enemy within
1.1 Divisionists are not Pan-Afrikanists
1.1.1 Divisionism exposed

Divisionists present as Pan-Afrikanists whilst advocating policies which actively oppose Pan-Afrikanism. Some are aware of their role in undermining and discrediting Pan-Afrikanism; many are trapped in an innocent, but wrongful belief that they are Pan-Afrikanists. For the latter, the likelihood is they haven't studied the history of Pan-Afrikanism correctly or sufficiently to notice the contradictions in the positions they advocate and if they have, haven't understood.

Divisionism presents a number of con tricks – the first being its relative anonymity. Perhaps the biggest is its advocacy of the boarders imposed on Afrika by European imperialism's Berlin Theft Conference held in 1884/5. Some Divisionists genuinely fail to understand that they cannot support the existence of enemy imposed artificial divides (i.e. boarders) and at the same time claim Pan-Afrikanism. Others have more sinister motives – they are active enemy operatives attacking Pan-Afrikanism 'from within'. It should be obvious that the first object of Pan-Afrikanism is the unity of Afrika and support for the enemy's divisions, anti-Pan-Afrikanists. This observation is not rocket science, but somehow Divisionists have managed to get away with it since the 1960's.

Hot on its heels is a second branch of Divisionism which conflates Anti-Arabism with Anti-Islam in a manner that appeals deeply to the divided emotions of Afrikan people. This branch is predicated on certain truths:

- North Afrikan lands are occupied and controlled by Arabs; and
- Arabs in North Afrika have a proven track record of ill-treating Afrikan people.

The problem is Divisionism offers no viable solution to these problems. On the one hand there are those who advocate a deadly confused permutation of race/religious wars to 'rid' the continent of Arabs/Islam. They seem blissfully unaware that nowhere in the history of Pan-Afrikanism has genocide ever been advocated as a solution to our problems, but persist all the same.

On the other there is a less blood thirsty branch which advocates division of Afrikan land south of the Sahara from the North. Yes, their solution is to reward Arab occupation by giving away the Northern section of the continent. We don't need to call our rocket scientists or brain surgeons from their duties to advise us that genocide and land giveaways are not Pan-Afrikanist policies. Our children can tell us such policies are Divisionist.

Divisionist Stances

Brother Omowale

A third strand is the many and varied more recently developed Divisionist arguments. They have in common the fact that they are targeted to trigger emotionally charged, often irreconcilable divisions among Afrikan people. They attack particular traits of sections of the Afrikan population, depicting them as 'un-Afrikan'.

Unity among Afrikan people is a precondition for Pan-Afrikanism. Understanding this, enemies of Pan-Afrikanism have cunningly slipped a number of Divisionist narratives into Pan-Afrikanist discourse designed to foster acrimonious divisions. These narratives attack people's personal choices and in some cases even biological make-up in a manner designed to elicit embarrassment, shame and most certainly negative reaction. These are perhaps best illustrated by scenarios, of which the following are a sample:

1. Narrative: *Christians are the problem; they can't contribute to Afrikan liberation.* If I am a Christian Afrikan man:
   a. How are you going to stop me being a Christian?
   b. How will you and I unite if I believe (rightly or wrongly) that you are attacking my religion?

2. Narrative: *Muslims are the problem; they can't contribute to Afrikan liberation.* If I am a Muslim Afrikan man:
   a. How are you going to stop me being a Muslim?
   b. How will you and I unite if I believe (rightly or wrongly) that you are attacking my religion?

3. Narrative: *If you have European blood, you're part of the enemy.* If I am an Afrikan man with a European mother:
   a. How are you going to stop me having a European mother?
   b. How will you and I unite if I believe (rightly or wrongly) that you are insulting my mother?

4. Narrative: *Homosexuals are an abomination in need of treatment.* If I am a homosexual Afrikan man:
   a. How are you going to stop me being homosexual?
   b. How will you and I unite if I believe (rightly or wrongly) that you are attacking my sexuality?

5. Narrative: *If you date outside the race, you're a traitor and can't be trusted.* I am an Afrikan man married to a European:
   a. How are you going to stop me being married to my wife?
   b. How will you and I unite if I believe (rightly or wrongly) that you are insulting my wife?

6. Narrative: *Anyone who bleaches is not an Afrikan.* If I am an Afrikan man that bleaches my skin:

    a. How are you going to stop me doing that to myself?

    b. How will you and I unite if I believe (rightly or wrongly) that you are insulting me?

7.   Narrative: *If you don't have natural hair, you're not really Afrikan*. If I am an Afrikan man who curly permed my hair and beard, dyed them a combination of red, white, blue and blond:

    a. How are you going to stop me doing that to myself?

    b. How will you and I unite if I believe (rightly or wrongly) that you are insulting me?

These and other Divisionist narratives have built-in, the fact that:

- They refer to personal matters – none of the business of the person launching the attack;
- The attacker cannot take any non-intrusive action to prevent the issue complained of – they're just making disruptive noises with little to no possibility of 'solution'; and
- The recipient will most likely be offended and respond by distancing themselves from the attacker and their perceived cause – turn their back on Pan-Afrikanism.

Some Divisionists get so caught up in the emotions of these arguments that they fail to appreciate their words/actions cause offence, pushing their impacted sisters and brothers further from them. They get caught in the trap of thinking they must 'correct' their fellows' 'un-Afrikan' personal traits before uniting with them. They fail to understand that:

- Their target might not want to change;
- History proves that unity is achievable without the need to change these traits; and
- By continuing to press their point, they wedge wider and wider divisions among affected Afrikan people.

'Successful' implementation of the destructive Divisionist narratives illustrated above is likely to result in the alienation of Christians, Muslims, Mixed race Afrikan people, Homosexual Afrikan people, Afrikan people in mixed relationships and Afrikan people who alter their skin or hair – Afrikan unity is therefore actively undermined from the grassroots. These narratives cannot be Pan-Afrikanist because of their divisive impact on relations between Afrikan people – they are

Divisionist.

At the base of these narratives is the realisations that when we publicly make negative issues out of other people's personal choices, an expected outcome is they will distance themselves from us and anything we claim to represent. This is why intelligence agencies promote such issues and target them to keep particular groups divided. If we're not careful, we end up doing the intelligence agencies job for them.

1.2 Divisionism's supplanting of Pan-Afrikanism
1.2.1 Modern origin of Divisionism - 1884/5 Berlin Theft Conference
The 1884/5 Berlin Theft Conference is a critical milestone in Afrika's history. Imposed on the continent and its people by external dictators (colonisors), it marks the modern origin of Divisionism[1]. Its geo-political dictates can be summarised as follows:
- Creation of artificial partitions in Afrika;
- Artificial division of Afrikan people on the continent;
- Linking partitioned areas to particular members of imperialism's colonising club;
- Granting sovereignty over partitioned areas to particular colonisers;
- Agreeing non-interference protocols between colonisers:
    - To prevent war; and
    - To prevent Afrikan uprisings;
- Mutual tolerance between colonisers:
    - To forestall war; and
    - To prevent Afrikan uprisings.

The fundamental task before Afrikan leadership during decolonisation (1950's/60's) was removal of Berlin dictates. Berlin's Divisionist agenda broke Afrika into jigsaw pieces and gave foreign dictators sovereignty over different parts. As independence loomed, the masses of Afrikan people vocally demanded unity as solution, whilst 'outgoing' colonisors quietly advocated Divisionism through its programme of unviably partitioned Afrikan 'independence'. Continental sovereignty is the

---

[1] Divisionism is the pretence of Pan-Afrikanism, whilst advocating policies which result in a divided Afrika – the opposite of Pan-Afrikanism.

linchpin of Afrikan political unity, as it determines ultimate loyalty and power. It also satisfied the people's demand. Leaders were therefore duty bound to unite Afrika and centralise its sovereignty under the control of Afrikan people *en masse.*

Instead they betrayed their people and did the opposite, entrenching Berlin's artificial boarders in the 1963 Oranisation of Afrikan Unity (OAU) charter, thereby transforming Afrika into a jigsaw puzzle of pretend sovereign states. During decolonisation, the 'outgoing' colonisors worked behind the scenes to garner support for Divisionism among an Afrikan leadership they had partitioned. Those they could persuade were persuaded; those they couldn't were replaced via assassinations, coups and other foul means. Divisionists became the majority in partitioned leadership circles and custody of Divisionism handed to them. They were secretly charged with responsibility for maintaining the enemy's boarders – against the will of their people.

The Afrikan masses wanted Pan-Afrikanism – the colonisors and their treacherous partitioned leadership, Divisionism. Pan-Afrikanism seeks the removal of Berlin's boarders, whilst Divisionism wants to enshrine them. On behalf of their masters, majority Divisionists 'leaders' set about destroying Pan-Afrikanism and with it, genuine independence by inculcating Berlin's boarders in the founding charter of the OAU. They reinforced the colonisor's blueprint established in Berlin almost 80 years earlier, incorporating non-interference and mutual tolerance protocols and all. Their decisions were so treacherous; they made Marcus Garvey's words from the 1920's appear prophetic:

> "We must realise that our greatest enemi[es] are not those on the outside, but those in our midst's, because when we can readily recognise the enemies on the outside and do not allow them to pass, we have those on the inside working with us to destroy us without our knowing." (Hill, 1987b, p. 108)

Whilst pretending to be Pan-Afrikanists, not only were Divisionists the enemy within, but actual Pan-Afrikanists ended up supporting them by playing along with their pretence. In a vein quest for unity, they made the error of acknowledging Divisionist enemy agents as Pan-Afrikanists. What would have been the correct action was explained by an enemy general:

> "In war, the enemy is plain and clear. In peace, a nation is confronted with a more insidious foe: the weakness within, from which alone great nations fall … the danger from within is always present and must be kept in subjection." (Montgomery, 2000, p. 19)

The 'outgoing' colonisors tactically implanted its chosen 'Afrikan enemy within', installing it as a majority of the 'leadership' in their unviably partitioned Afrika. As a result, from inception the allegedly Pan-Afrikanist OAU was dominated by Divisionists i.e. Afrika's weakness/enemy within, hell bent on carrying out their master's plan to prevent Afrika's unity and liberation. At the level of jigsaw puzzle governments, Pan-Afrikanist leaders were supplanted and marginalised. To this day, Pan-Afrikanism still has not recovered from that body blow with allegedly Pan Afrikanist Afrikan Union (AU) doggedly clenching Berlin's boarders.

Pan-Afrikanists failed to expose and keep 'in subjection' the internal Divisionist enemy, choosing instead to keep up the pretence that enemy agents were Pan-Afrikanists. They focused far too much on partitioned 'leadership', to the neglect of grassroots organising[2]. As a result, they rendered themselves separated from the Afrikan masses, outnumbered and out manoeuvred at the level of partitioned 'leadership'. In effect, they joined the Divisionist programme for handing the continent back to colonisors.

Dishonestly posing as Pan-Afrikanists, Divisionists derailed the decolonisation process by keeping the continent partitioned. Despite their treachery, Divisionists of that era are still labelled "Pan-Afrikanists" by many to the present. Worse still, their political descendents continue the same pattern of trickery and treachery on behalf of their masters. Divisionists fit precisely with traits identified by Marcus Garvey four decades before decolonisation. He explained how:

> "The traitor of other races is generally confined to the

---

[2] Nkrumah's All-Afrikan People's Conferences ceased by 1962.

mediocre or irresponsible individual, but, unfortunately, the traitors among the [Afrikan] race are generally to be found among the men highest placed in education and society, the fellows who can call themselves leaders.

For us to examine ourselves thoroughly as a people we will find that we have more traitors than leaders, because nearly everyone who essays to lead the race at this time does so by first establishing himself as the pet of some philanthropist of another race, to whom he will go and debase his race in the worse form, humiliate his own manhood, and thereby win the sympathy of the 'great benefactor', who will dictate to him what he should do in the leadership of the [Afrikan] race." (Garvey, 1986, p. 29)

The acid test of Pan-Afrikanism, is stance on Berlin's boarders. Those who advocate their removal are Pan-Afrikanists. Those who want to keep them are Divisionists – the enemy within to be 'kept in subjection'. The time has come to expose, uproot and contain them so that Afrika can move forward. That process begins with self-examination: Where do you stand on the Berlin boarders' issue? Do you want them gone or retained? Are you a Pan-Afrikanist or a Divisionist?

In addition we can look again at decolonisation history. With the benefit of hindsight we can identify the leaders that voted for retention of Berlin's boarders and out them as our Divisionists enemy within. It will be a painful task, as many alleged heroes will fall, but it will help us readjust and correct our path to liberation.

Thirdly, we can develop and roll out a simple mass education programme aimed at ensuring Afrikan people everywhere understand the nuances and distinctions between Pan-Afrikanists and Divisionists – the enemy within. Treacherous Afrikan leadership ought to be left with no hiding place so that we can contain them and move forward to liberation.

Furthermore, recognising the fact that a continental sovereign People's State of Afrika (PSA) will require local government structures, there's no intrinsic reason why we cannot set up a grassroots Local Government Boundaries Commission. As part of laying to rest the Berlin ghost, the

Commission can to map out how best to delineate the continent internally for the purpose of effective and efficient administration.

1.2.2 Divisionism's anti-Arab strand

Afrikan continental unity meant uniting with Arabs in the north causing considerable consternation, particularly among Divisionists pretending to be Pan-Afrikanists. Used by enemies of Pan-Afrikanism to generate internal splits, in some quarter's continental unity was presented as a departure from Pan-Afrikanism. The truth however, is Afrikan/Arab cooperation in political arenas is nothing new.

Arabs have been resident in north Afrika for well over a thousand years and it is this which enshrines them as Afrikan citizens with full rights of abode and security of tenure. However, there is a long painful history of Arab anti-Afrikan racism. Evidence is voluminous, but the very fact that Arabs engaged in anti-Afrikan slavery is sufficient to prove the case. Furthermore, the fact that this anti-human practice did not officially come to an end in Mauritania until recently entrenches the point:

> "On July 5th 1980, Mauritania officially abolished slavery, yet some 200,000 Afrikans a year still are captured and enslaved there and in the Sudan." (Anderson, 1995, p. 4)

Notions the official 'abolition' did not amount to an end, deepened schisms between Afrikan people and Arabs. Regardless of whether anti-Afrikan enslavement continues under the radar, there is no doubt that Arabic abuse of Afrikan people continues both in Afrika and Arabia. Through its undermining of Afrikan/Arab relations, Arabic abuses provide a playground for Zionism, which is strengthened by divisions between Afrikan people and Arabs. The possibility of it using the abuse to intensify acrimony, divisions and problems cannot be ruled out.

1.2.3 Divisionist 'dead ends' v Pan-Afrikanist solution

Given there is Arabic abuse of Afrikan people on the continent, the problem must be resolved. One strategic question is: (i) Should Arabs stay or leave? Flowing from this: (ii) If the leave option is chosen, should they be asked or forced? (iii) If they stay, on what basis should they remain?

If Afrikan people ask Arabs to vacate north Afrika, it is reasonable to assume they won't go. The only removal option is force. If force is pursued, what are the perpetrators going to do about the many Afrikan people who shout 'Jihad' and fight on the side of Arab Muslims. Are they to be killed? Expelled? If enough Afrikan people join Arabs, it could result in Arab victory and with it Arab domination over the entirety of Afrika. Whatever happens, the forced removal option divides Afrika at the level of people and citizens and leads to catastrophe.

Strategic Solution: Arabs in Afrika

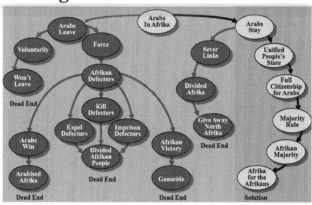

Brother Omowale

Imagine the perpetrators overcoming these massive problems and actually 'succeeding' in removing Arabs by force. It would require nothing short of genocide. Being perpetrators of genocide would put the 'victors' in the same category as other genocide practitioners i.e. Britain, France, US Satan, Australia, New Zealand, Zionist Israel etc. Their behaviour would be contrary to the core Afrikan principle - humanism. The forcible removal/genocide route is not an option – the Arabs stay.

Arabs remaining in north Afrika is a given. The only real question is, do Afrikan people break relations or include them? Severing relations amounts to a brand of Divisionism engineered by Afrikan people. It is an absurdity that results in giving away up to a third of the land in the richest continent in the world. It also isolates Afrikan people living in north Afrika. They, as a result become a permanently disempowered minority in their own land, with no protection from further abuse. Not only is dividing Afrikan land the anti-thesis of Pan-Afrikanism, severing relations amounts to a Zionist bolstering 'dead end'. Advocates of this route are not Pan-Afrikanists, they are Divisionists.

The only viable option is Pan-Afrikanism as advanced by Nkrumah – to unite thereby acknowledging the permanent citizenship rights of Arabs in north Afrika. This arrangement works for Arabs by guaranteeing them peaceful security of tenure. It is simultaneously to the advantage of Afrikan people provided two things are in place:

- Afrika is politically united under a single sovereign people's state:
    o This ensures all Afrikan citizens are:
        ▪ Protected by the state; and
        ▪ Subject to the same laws; and
- Universal suffrage i.e. one person one vote is the basis for electing Afrika's government:
    o Given Afrikan people are by far the majority in Afrika, Afrikan political control is assured regardless of the granting of citizenship to resident non-Afrikans[3].

A continental super-state combined with majority rule is the medicine ensuring Afrikan people cannot and will not be subjected to ill-treatment by minorities in their own land. It is a Pan-Afrikanist solution.

1.3 What Pan-Afrikanism is not
1.3.1 Defence of Pan-Afrikanism
For many, there is a lack of clarity as to what Pan-Afrikanism actually is. In part, this is to do with Divisionist[4] tendencies competing for the identity. Within that, a more sinister contributory factor is a dishonest attempt to associate Pan-Afrikanism with bigoted ideas, aimed at distorting its image and undermining its credibility. This section briefly addresses this contradiction with a view to demonstrating what Pan-Afrikanism is not, to clear the path for an honest explanation of what it is.

To its disadvantage, Pan-Afrikanism has become associated with attacks

---

[3] There are approximately 330 million Arab speakers (27.5%) in 2017 many of whom are indigenous Afrikan people. There are 6 million Europeans (1/2 of 1%) out of a 2016 estimated 1.2 billion (1,200 million) continental population.

[4] Divisionists advocate division of Afrika and her citizens whilst pretending to be Pan-Afrikanists

against people's religious beliefs, intimate sexual practices and even biological make up. This association is not only false, but cynically misleading. These are personal matters and Pan-Afrikanism does not intrude into people's personal likes or dislikes and does not tell them:

- How to manage their personal affairs i.e.:
  - o Which religion to follow or not i.e. it doesn't attack/condemn:
    - Christianity;
    - Islam;
    - Traditional Afrikan Spirituality;
    - Any other God related belief system; or
    - Atheism;
  - o Who to have intimate relationships with or not i.e. it doesn't attack/condemn consenting adults on the basis of their:
    - Racially uniform or mixed relationships;
    - Heterosexual or homosexual relationships;
- They are bad because of their biological make up i.e. it doesn't attack/condemn people because they are:
  - Afrikan;
  - Asian;
  - European;
  - American Indian;
  - Aborigine; or
  - A mixture of races.

None of the above groups are exempt from anti-Afrikan racism. Even Afrikan people can be guilty of projecting disdain towards each other. Racism fosters an environment where some Afrikan people can be seduced into a mode of reaction. This can ignite emotionally charged counter-attacks against others. In some cases it is a genuine reaction against Anti-Afrikan racism, but nonetheless can lead to unsavoury, even insulting exchanges between affected individuals and groups.

Rather than descending into an exchange of insults, the progressive question for Pan-Afrikanists is 'what is our plan for uniting with our sisters and brothers in these categories?' Since no sensible general goes to war without building alliances, they ought to also answer 'what is our plan for building effective alliances with progressive non-Afrikan elements in these categories?' Actively answering these questions helps overturn emotive/reactionary responses. It also reduces the likelihood of being distracted into counter-productive dead end red herring debates.

Where attacks of this kind are launched and projected as Pan-Afrikanism, trickery and deception are at play and an audience is being manipulated. Trickery can include agent provocateurs set up to be mistaken for Pan-Afrikanists. They are engaged to publicly rant highly intrusive, bigoted sentiments and positioned, so that Pan-Afrikanism can be perceived as the source and pick up blame. Pan-Afrikanism then becomes tarnished, with even its own community alienated and confused about what it is.

Such processes undermine Pan-Afrikanism – on the face of it 'from within' and not wanting to be associated with bigotry, its natural constituency, dissociates and becomes increasingly unreceptive to its message. This underhand dishonest process is designed not only to distort Pan-Afrikanism, but to make it so unpopular, discredited and disrespected in the eyes of Afrikan people and potential allies, that it is rendered useless as a liberation tool.

1.3.2 Religious beliefs are personal

When Pan-Afrikanists engage with issues, one of the first questions to be asked is, 'what can we do about it?' We also need to clarify whether our cause will be better or worse off as a result. If somebody is a Christian, Muslim, Traditional Believer or Atheist and we for some reason don't like it, 'what can we do about it?' and if we make an issue of our personal dislike 'what will be the impact on Pan-Afrikanism?'

I don't have the power to compel my adult children to follow/not the religion of my choosing/dislike. They will choose/dismiss whatever religious beliefs they see fit and there's nothing I can do to prevent it. It follows that if I cannot compel my adult children, then I cannot compel adults in general. Arguing with them is a waste of their time and mine – neither altering their belief nor transforming them into Pan-Afrikanists. This is precisely what Marcus Garvey was alluding to when he warned:

> "Man's religion is something that we cannot eliminate from his system or destroy in him, therefore it is folly for any man to go about attacking another man's religion,

because to him it is fundamental". (Sons of Garvey Press Association, 1990, p. 24) ... [and] "... any man who gets out and attacks religions, thinking he can convert men to the organisation by doing so is not helping the organisation. He is doing more harm than good." (Sons of Garvey Press Association, 1990, p. 24).

If somehow we develop the power to impose our religious will and use it, we've fully entered the realm of bigotry. It is an objective abuse of power to impose our will on somebody else's personal affairs and even if we do they can simply practice their personal preference secretly, whilst publicly pretending to accept the 'order' we've created. Again our time and energy would be wasted and antipathy towards us increased.

If we recognise we can't impose our religious beliefs/dislikes on others but nonetheless attack them on the basis of theirs, we create an argument with them over something we know in advance will hurt them deeply without producing a positive tangible outcome. In fact the reverse will be "achieved" as they react against Pan-Afrikanism. We are therefore wilfully creating pointless acrimony in the knowledge that:

- Belief systems are often so deeply ingrained that we're extremely unlikely to change practices; and
- Our behaviour will generate a dislike of us and our cause i.e. creating the basis for permanent deep rooted conscience level divisions between Pan-Afrikanists and religious groups.

Nkrumah specifically warned against divisions at the level of conscience, saying:

> "The three segments of Afrikan society ... the traditional, the Western and the Islamic co-exist uneasily ... the two other segments, in order to be rightly seen, must be accommodated only as experiences of the traditional Afrikan society. *If we fail to do this our society will be racked by the most malignant schizophrenia*." (Nkrumah, 2009, p. 78 – *author's emphasis*)

The role of Pan-Afrikanism is to bring religious groups into the liberation process on the side of justice – an approach critical to the recruitment

22

approach of Marcus Garvey and the UNIA. Pan-Afrikanism must therefore make space for religious diversity. The last thing Pan-Afrikanists want is to cut themselves off from Afrikan people. As a form of division, this stands in open opposition to a critical component of our objective - Afrikan unity.

It follows that wherever you find religious bigotry dressed up as Pan-Afrikanism i.e. Divisionists pretending to be Pan-Afrikanists whilst conducting fruitless, counter-productive personal attacks based on religious beliefs, the hand of capitalism's intelligence agencies is at work. The proponents may be either innocent unsuspecting members of the Afrikan community seduced by a false line of reasoning or actual operatives in the field. Regardless, they are Divisionists, actively propagating capitalism's divide and rule agenda in the Afrikan community and actively undermining Pan-Afrikanism.

1.3.3 Intimate lives are private
This same analysis holds true for people's personal practices in intimate relationships i.e. whether those targeted practice same/mixed race or hetero/homosexual relationships. Attacks in this area amount to an attempt to police people's intimate relationships. They attempt to tell people who and how they should love. Put crudely, they amount a campaign aimed at telling adults where to put/not their genitals.

Worse still is the attempt to assign superior/inferior status based on where consenting adults privately decide to put their genitals. Arguing with people in these areas is a breach of their personal boundaries and is guaranteed to offend. It is objectively worse than a waste of time; it is a catalyst for mutual animosity, contradicting our objective of winning Afrikan practitioners over.

In all likelihood we are going to live our entire lives without ever seeing or having contact with each other's genitals. They are private, ownership of them is conclusive and their use is not ordinarily the business of strangers. It should be obvious that we cannot enforce a system that proscribes to consenting adults where in private they can/not 'legitimately' put their genitals. These activities are, in the main, nothing to do with outsiders.

Furthermore, if we managed to obtain the power to officially compel strangers to put their genitals where we decide, they'd put their genitalia where they want when they're in a situation we can't detect. Since these intimacies happen in private anyway, they would only be marginally inconvenienced, but at the same time highly resentful, with a correspondingly negative impact on our mutual relationship. All of the arguments applied to religion above also apply to absurd attempts to police adult's intimate consensual relationships/practices.

1.3.4 Ancestry is unalterable

Attacks on people based on their race is even more absurd, since race is an unalterable given. Afrikan people can't help being Afrikan people; Arabs can't help being Arabs, Chinese can't help being Chinese, South Asians can't help being South Asians, American Indians can't help being American Indians, Aborigines can't help being Aborigines etc. Nor can people who are racially mixed help that – we are all biologically the unalterable outcome of our ancestry.

Attacking people based on their biological make up essentially amounts to condemning them based upon where their parents and fore parents put their genitals some years earlier – something which we cannot go back and undo even if we wanted to. Furthermore, the individuals under attack have absolutely nothing to do with decisions around placement of the particular genitalia that directly or indirectly brought them into being. Arguing with them on these issues goes well beyond wasting time to actively and wilfully insulting them and their lineage.

Such attacks are counter-productive absurdities which lead nowhere constructive, because those targeted can't change themselves biologically even if they want to. The end result can only be acrimony. They alienate, rather than transform them into friends or supporters of Pan-Afrikanism. Again with the exception of secrecy, all of the arguments applied to religion above also apply to nonsensical attempts to attack people on the basis of their unalterable biological make up.

1.3.5 Private matters - not for public consumption

Your private business is none of my concern and vice versa. Pan-Afrikanism does not therefore condone the practice of thrusting or imposing intimate and private matters on public situations. In much the same way that we are aroused upon exposure to a blue movie, discussion of private, particularly sexual matters can elicit an arousal of emotions. Furthermore, heightened emotions can override rational thinking, making behaviour increasingly volatile and unpredictable, which in turn creates fertile ground for exchange of deeply hurtful insults.

Engagement in public discussions of private matters can reveal inappropriate things that should never be brought to public attention. Publicly spotlighting personal 'weaknesses', is not only out of context, but parcels out shame causing offence and inviting counter-offensives. It sows seeds for intensely bitter disagreements. Deep rooted divisive acrimony is an inevitable consequence of broadcasting intimate private weaknesses. This outcome 'achieves' the opposite of Pan-Afrikanism's unity objective.

Individuals have a right to personal opinions, including on private/moral practices. However, if those opinions cannot compel change in others and are at the same time objectively offensive, it may be tactically unhelpful and unwise to make a public show of them. If an ill-disciplined 'Pan-Afrikanist' nonetheless does so, the onus is on her/him to make clear they espouse their personal position which has nothing to do with Pan-Afrikanism. Pan-Afrikanism is not dogmatic.

1.3.6 Hidden hand undermining Pan-Afrikanism
The philosophical tactic used to undermine Pan-Afrikanism is the 'straw man' approach. It involves analysis of genuine Afrikan/Pan-Afrikan positions to manufacture undermining distortions to be associated with Pan-Afrikanism for the purpose of damaging it:

- Imperialism used Christianity as part of its tool kit to steal and subordinate Afrika. A distorted portrayal implying Christianity stole Afrikan people and land is used to spread division between Pan-Afrikanists and Afrikan/non-Afrikan Christians;
- A shortage of Afrikan men has a detrimental impact on Afrikan women when significant numbers of Afrikan men marry outside their race. Distortions asserting Afrikan people marrying outside their race are 'traitors' to be ostracised, creates acrimonious divisions between those in mixed and non-mixed relationships and their off-springs; and
- Afrikan culture is traditionally resistant (not hostile) to homosexuality. Distortions designed to encourage bigoted anti-

homosexual attacks, encourage deep rooted wedges between Pan-Afrikanists and Afrikan/non-Afrikan homosexuals.

In process terms, intensely disturbing personal attacks are manufactured and engineered by intelligence agencies. They are then targeted for inappropriate public consumption and pumped into the Afrikan community through pseudo-liberation groups[5]. Their purpose is to ignite and sustain deeply emotive, acrimonious, divisive and most of all circular i.e. never ending arguments within the community to destabilise internal relations. Success for them leaves us entrenched/lost in a range of never ending deep rooted disagreements which we can't solve precisely because we can't compel others to conform to their personal likes/dislikes to ours. The result is no change in behaviour, whilst protagonists remain deeply buried in emotively charged sectarian self-hatred.

These publicly projected acrimonious personal attacks are designed to be emotional triggers that cloud our judgment, foster internal disdain and keep us in a permanent state of division, fuelled by internal self-hatred. Furthermore, by falsely and misleadingly attributing these attacks to Pan-Afrikanism, they produce permanent irreconcilable barriers between genuine Pan-Afrikanists and Christians, Muslims, Arabs, other Asians and other racial groups, homosexuals and our people in, or the product of racially mixed relationships.

The underlying aim of attacks is to turn the natural constituency of Pan-Afrikanism against it, by making it appear bigoted. The object is to make Afrikan people and potential allies dismissive of and even hate Pan-Afrikanism so that the majority of Afrikan people never adopt and carry out its self-liberating agenda. In this way, it creates and maintains a permanent rift between Afrikan people, impeding our objective path to liberation. Afrikan unity is absolutely crucial to liberation. By entrenching divisions among and between us and potential allies, the enemy ensures liberation is blocked before it gets off the ground.

---

[5] Pseudo-liberation groups are Divisionist entities pretending to be Pan-Afrikanist.

1.4 Correcting Divisionist Intrigues
1.4.1 Anti-thesis disguised as thesis

Pan-Afrikanism is the unification and liberation of Afrika under Scientific Socialism. It is an objective and its achievement represents the solutions to Afrika's current political and economic problems. Neo-colonialism is the anti-thesis of Pan-Afrikanism and Divisionism the anti-thesis of its unity element. Intentionally or inadvertently, Divisionists adopt political positions, which ultimately mean division of Afrika or her people.

Brother Omowale

Divisionists create confusion by misleadingly calling themselves Pan-Afrikanists. They are sometimes mistaken for Pan-Afrikanists, but fail its political test of **UNITY** through their advocacy of either a divided Afrika or divided Afrikan people. Since one of the tactics of neo-colonialism has been to disguise itself as Pan-Afrikanism, clarity of definition is crucial for correct identification. Clarity eliminates confusion and distinguishes Pan-Afrikanism as solution from Divisionism's 'dead end' distractions.

During decolonisation Divisionists used carefully crafted 'sugar coated' language to confuse the world and present themselves as Pan-Afrikanists. Pan-Afrikanism was usurped by Divisionists posing as Pan-Afrikanists. Divisionists came in a number of forms including:

- Those wanting to retain the Berlin boarders and dictates;
- Those wanting to formalise division between 'North Afrika' and 'Afrika south of the Sahara'; and

- Those deploying emotionally charged subjects to irreparably divide Afrikan people's internal relations.

Those attacking people based on religious beliefs, sexual practices or biological make up are the most recent manifestation of Divisionists dressed in 'Pan-Afrikan' clothing. There is an endless array of emotive personal topics used by Divisionists to sow division. They must be: (i) personal, emotive – attacking the targets sense of worth, so as to put their backs up; (ii) none of the attackers business; (iii) something the attacker stands little to no chance of changing; (iv) something leaving those targeted feeling publicly embarrassed; and (v) something which turns those targeted into an adversary of the attacker and their alleged cause – to stifle Pan-Afrikanism and its unity objective.

Afrikan people not fitting a supposed 'ideal type' such as skin bleachers and those with unnaturally hair are also subjected to ridicule and insult. When we make a negative public issue out of other people's personal choices, the likelihood is we push them away. This is why Divisionists promote such issues and target them to keep particular groups away from liberation organisations.

1.4.2 Our solution is to join hands
At the level of principle Divisionism is a brand of individualism aimed at separating Afrika and her people. As Pan-Afrikanists we are guided by our principles: humanism (people before money), collectivism (we before me) and egalitarianism (we're all equal in essence), which are inculcated into our objective. Unity is a sub-category of collectivism and a just social system demands people are treated equitably (egalitarianism) and humanely (humanism).

Our cardinal principle is humanism. It requires we treat fellow human beings with the upmost dignity based on nothing more than the fact that they are human beings. Each human being has inner worth. This means even the murderer ought to be treated with basic human dignity despite their wrong. How then can we treat another less favourably based on religion, sexual practices or biological make up, which are not even crimes.

Religious beliefs, sexual practices or biological make up are neither among the objectives nor enemies of Pan-Afrikanism, nor do they guide it. Our beliefs can be right or wrong, correct or incorrect. They are not necessarily based on facts and do not provide an objective basis for liberating an oppressed people. Even if provable, they are only relevant to Pan-Afrikanism if they fit with our objective and principles. If they don't they are a potential source of distraction and confusion. At worse/best they are de/motivational.

For practical guidance a helpful question is 'Do we want fellow Afrikan people to give up religious beliefs/sexual practices that we don't like, before we'll unite with them, or will we unite regardless?' The acid test is whether uniting moves us away from or closer to the greater objective. It obviously moves us closer and unity - a part of the Pan-Afrikan objective - which is a precondition for liberation, whilst agreement on religious beliefs and sexual practices are not. The principled Pan-Afrikanist must subordinate her/his personal opinions to the greater objective and unite regardless. Uniformed religious beliefs/sexual practices are not a requirement and biology can't be changed.

Pan-Afrikanists want to win support for our cause. This involves recognising Afrikan people and their friends can contribute to the Pan-Afrikanist objective regardless of religious beliefs, intimate practices of consenting adults or those of their fore parents. An individual's private religious beliefs and personal sexual preferences pose no intrinsic obstacle to them making a contribution to the Afrikan part of worldwide revolution. The revolutionary objective of Pan-Afrikanism is not advanced by personal attacks based on religion, sexual practices of consenting adults or biological make up - they retard it.

We must win our people and citizens over to the greater objective and act in unison to achieve it. This requires putting aside squabbles and building practical working relationships with fellow Afrikan people and citizens who hold different (even opposite) positions on personal issues. Unity which is absolutely crucial is not the same as unanimity – we don't have to agree on everything. We merely need to agree to conscientiously work jointly towards the greater objective.

Whatever our personal opinions on religious belief, sexual preferences and biological make-up, they should not cause a breach of our principles or distract us from the greater objective of Afrikan unity, liberation, development and the creation of a just social system that guards our humanity and equality. It is also blatantly obvious that dividing Afrikan land, whether on Berlin or anti-Arab lines is a departure from Pan-Afrikanism's principles and objective. Our principles and objective combined mean we cannot reject any Afrikan person/citizen on the basis of these criteria or give up an inch of Afrikan land.

Divisionists are and must be distinguished as an example of Afrika's weakness/enemy within. In addition to undermining the credibility of Pan-Afrikanism, their role is to confuse Pan-Afrikanists and stakeholders alike in order to supplant. Pan-Afrikanism is not to be confused with any of the above Divisionist approaches. Pan-Afrikanism requires as a prelude to liberation, political unity of:

- Afrikan people the world over;
- Afrikan citizens throughout the continent; and
- The entirety of Afrikan land and surrounding islands.

Any deviation from this three point unity agenda is proof conclusive that proponents are NOT Pan-Afrikanists.

Chapter 2

2 Pan-Afrikanism
2.1 Milestones in Pan-Afrikanism's development
2.1.1 The 3 origins of Pan-Afrikanism

There are differing perspectives on what constitutes the origin of Pan-Afrikanism. There are those who see it as coming into being as a result of activities surrounding first Pan-Afrikan conference organised by Henry Sylvester Williams in London in 1900. Others link its origin to Afrikan people's resistance to alien incursions into our continent; and yet others argue that it is as old as humanity and part of the organic development of Afrika into a continental scale society. The truth is all three tell an important part of the story of Pan-Afrikanism – they are all critical milestones. Together they provide a framework for defining Pan-Afrikanism and outlining its historical development.

2.1.2 The natural progression towards Pan-Afrikanism

Afrika was organically developing on its historical path towards continental unity. Certainly in the initial phases there were no outsiders, meaning it was free from external domination. Its principles and social systems were broadly just in that they were not based on exploitation. Communalism, the longstanding dominant social system was developing into the early phases of feudalism in some parts.

As part of that process, Afrika was developing larger and larger political, economic and social aggregates. It developed from family to clan to tribe to nation and even 'empires'. Examples include: (i) Ghana; (ii) Mali; (iii) Songhay; (iv) Zimbabwe; and (v) Monomatapa. These were all signs of its organic progression towards a kind of continental unity. The organic development of Afrikan people into greater and greater aggregates is the **unity element** of Pan-Afrikanism.

2.1.3 The disruption of organic Pan-Afrikanism

The resistance aspect of Pan-Afrikanism began at the point at which people from outside of Afrika invaded and stole our land. From that time onwards Afrikan people have continually resisted, with our purpose being the retrieval of every inch of our stolen land.

Afrika's development towards unity was interrupted by external invasions. The first documented 'successful' invasion was by the Hyskos via Egypt in 1783BCE. It might be representative of this versions 'starting point' for Pan-Afrikanism. That said, the notion of resistance might incorporate those attempted invasions which were successfully resisted dating back much further.

More recently there were the Arab incursions in the North of the continent dating from 642CE and European colonialism's invasions from around 1441CE. As a result of these events Afrika suffered enslavement of its people by Arabs and Europeans; colonisation of its land by Arabs and Europeans and the current neo-colonisation of its resources by European imperialism.

Arab imperialism was just as brutal and wicked to Afrikan people as European imperialism. However, it never managed to subdue and dominate us to the same extent that European imperialism did. Where Arabs currently control parts of our Afrikan soil, they do so under the hegemony of European imperialism. Resistance to external incursions is the **liberation element** of Pan-Afrikanism.

2.1.4 'Organised' Pan-Afrikanism

Another milestone/origin of Pan-Afrikanism comes in the form of formal conferences/congresses – what some have referred to as 'organised' Pan-Afrikanism. Du Bois' Pan-Afrikan congresses (started by Henry Sylvester Williams in London 1900), together with Garvey's UNIA conventions (of the 1920's and 30's) and Padmore's Pan-Afrikan Federation (of the 1930's) were modern attempts to achieve continental wide structures for Afrika's governance.

The pinnacle of their activities was the 5th PAC, which brought together those 3 competing tendencies. WEB Du Bois was present and played an active role. Marcus Garvey had by this time passed, but his first wife Amy Ashwood Garvey participated and chaired part of the activities and his second wife Amy Jacques Garvey was intimately involved in the planning and participated through the Jamaican branch of the UNIA. George Padmore was the joint secretary of the Congress.

It was this congress that spearheaded the process of Afrikan independence – what the imperialist enemy called 'the wind of change'. During that congress Pan-Afrikanism formally declared its anti-imperialist and socialist credentials. The movement towards continental governance coupled with the chosen political direction explains the **scientific socialist element** of Pan-Afrikanism. **The outcome of the 3 components is an objective which is: the unification and liberation of Afrika under scientific socialism. Pan-Afrikanism is an objective**.

2.1.5 Pan-Afrikanism world wars and liberation
During WWI Russian people rose up in a revolutionary confrontation with the state, won and launched the Socialist Soviet Union. Similarly, as a result of WWII, India partially broke away and declared independence in 1947. Two years later the Chinese made a more decisive move by taking firm control of their land through socialist revolution. They cut away from imperialism, creating breathing space for socialist internal development. This approach was critical to their current economic success.

By contrast, the Afrikan liberation process was slower, partly because Afrikan people had been divided geo-politically by artificial boarders and imperialism could not afford to lose control of the richest continent in the world. The underlying pattern of world wars weakening imperialism is clear, but the proliferation of nuclear weapons means another World War will almost certainly destroy the planet. Is Afrika as a result eternally trapped?

Another World War will not cause Afrika's liberation, though it may assist - Pan-Afrikanism will achieve it. External factors such as World Wars provide the conditions of change by contributing to the climate of revolution. However, the factors of change are internal. Momentum for the Afrikan revolution will come from Afrikan people and their struggles, wherever located.

What follows is an indicative timeline outlining some important milestones in Pan-Afrikanism. It gives a sense/summary of some of the main historic struggles impacting Pan-Afrikanism. It is a summary of actions, not mere concepts. The role of concepts (which must be learned from past actions to be useful) is to guide people's current and future actions. The liberation of Afrika requires concepts that guide actions towards Scientific Socialism.

The timeline below is an incomplete attempt to summarise liberation struggles i.e. Afrikan people's actions pushing for liberation over time and incidents impacting them. It should be treated as a starting point rather than a completed effort, providing references for more comprehensive historical study. It is indicative of the bare minimum historical knowledge needed by Pan-Afrikanists. The grounding of Pan-Afrikanism and its concepts/theory comes from its historical material.

2.1.6 Incidents in Pan-Afrikanism - Selected timeline
1. Homo Sapien Sapien (100k – 200k BCE)
2. Hyskos (1783 – 1550 BCE)
3. Arab invasion (642)
4. First Portuguese enslavement of Afrikans (1441)
5. Treaty of Tordesillas (1494)
6. Establishment of Freetown (1787)
7. Haitian Revolution (1791 – 1804) and other rebellions and acts of defiance
8. Liberian Independence (1847)
9. Europe's anti-Afrikan colonial wars (1800's – 1914)
10. Berlin Theft Conference (1884-5)
11. Congress for Afrika (1895)
12. The Afrikan Association (1897)
13. 1st Pan-African Conference (1900)
14. Niagara Movement (1905)
15. UNIA established (1914)
16. World War I (1914-18)
17. Russian revolution (1917)
18. 1st Pan-Afrikan Congress (PAC) (1919)
19. 1st UNIA Convention - (1920)

20. 2nd UNIA Convention - (1921)
21. 2nd PAC (1921)
22. 3rd UNIA Convention - (1922)
23. 3rd PAC (1923)
24. 4th UNIA Convention - (1924)
25. 4th PAC (1927)
26. 5th UNIA Convention - (1929)
27. Invasion of Ethiopia (1935)
28. 6th UNIA Convention - (1936)
29. Caribbean Uprisings (1397)
30. 7th UNIA Convention - (1937)
31. 8th UNIA Convention - (1938)
32. World War II (1939-45)
33. Atlantic Charter (1941)
34. Bretton Woods Conference (1944)
35. 5th PAC (1945)
36. West Afrikan National Congress (1946)
37. Ibibio Women's War (1947)
38. Armed struggle in Madagascar (1947)
39. Indian Independence (1497)
40. Chinese Revolution (1949)
41. CPP elected – Nkrumah First Minister (1951); PM (1952)
42. Egypt Independence (1952)
43. Bandung Conference (1955)
44. Imperialists Massacre UPC supporters (1955)
45. Pan-Afrikan Women's Day (1955)
46. China provides aid to Afrika (1955)
47. Sudan Independence (1956)
48. Suez crisis (1956)
49. Ghana independence – Nkrumah President [Independence meaningless unless it is linked to total independence of the Afrikan continent - constitution] (1957)
50. Treaty of Rome – Formation of European Union (1958)
51. Guinea-Conakry [PDG] – no vote (1958)
52. 1st Conference of Independent Afrikan States (1958)
53. All-Afrikan People's Conference (1958)
54. Ghana – Guinea Union (1959)
55. PACA formed (1959)
56. Sanniquellie Declaration (1959)
57. Cuban Revolution (1959)

58. Ghana – Guinea – Mali Union (1960)
59. National Congolese Movement [LMC Lumumba government and secret pact] (1960)
60. 2nd Conference of Afrikan Independent States (1960)
61. Wind of Change – Rolling independence (1960s)
62. Brazzaville group – French [Keep with France] (1961)
63. Casablanca group [Political union] (1961)
64. Monrovia group [mutual trading, Commonwealth & Francophone] French & British (1961)
65. Colonisation Continuation Pact (1961)
66. Organisation of Afrikan Unity (OAU) – 32 independent states (1963)
67. Kenya independence – Land & Freedom Army (1963)
68. Organisation of Afro-American Unity (OAAU) (1964)
69. Black Panthers (1965)
70. Passing of Nkrumah (1972)
71. Guinea-Bissau Liberation - PAIGC (1973)
72. Fall of Salazar's Government (1974)
73. 6th PAC (1974)
74. Mozambique Liberation - FRELIMO (1975)
75. Angolan Liberation - MPLA (1975)
76. Creation of G5 (1975)
77. Creation of G7 (1976)
78. Black Consciousness Movement/AZAPO (1977)
79. The New Jewel Movement (1979)
80. Zimbabwean independence (1980)
81. Battle of Cuito Cuanavale (1988)
82. Namibian Independence (1990)
83. The Battle of Mogadishu, Somalia (1992)
84. Removal of Apartheid (1994)
85. Russia joins G8 (1994) formalised 1997
86. China Afrika Forum (2000)
87. Afrikan Union Formed (2001) Launched (2002)
88. Africom (2007)
89. G20 leaders' Summit (2008) Finance Ministers met from 1999
90. Obama Presidency (2009)
91. Russia Suspended from G8 (2014)

2.2 Context foundations and principles of Pan-Afrikanism
2.2.1 Pan-Afrikanism comes out of philosophical materialism
Pan-Afrikanism is a philosophical materialist concept that recognises the existence of both material and **matspiritual**[6] aspects of reality, treating the material as primary. This means when we engage with apparently abstract concepts such as 'philosophy', 'principles', 'ideology', 'culture', 'history' and 'identity' we are bound to make material our starting point and reference for checking accuracy. They must be grounded i.e. developed from a material base in order to be correctly understood and applied in the real world.

That material base is land – the platform upon which much of life resides and at an even deeper (internal) level, it is atoms – the building blocks, which are found in massive quantities deep within all material things. This essentially means all of these and similar concepts need to be derived from either the material base or the building block (or both) in order that we can correctly and precisely identify them. We must be able to demonstrate how concepts are derived from nature to establish their correct use and interpretation.

Afrika's traditional approach of having nature as starting point and proof is the essence of what it is to be scientific. Science is essentially process/methodology i.e.:
- Making a clear statement of premise;
- Testing and proving/disproving that premise both scientifically and philosophically, using nature as base reference;
    o The main methods/techniques are observation and experimentation;
- Once proven, establishing the meaning/significance of proof;
- Implementing/applying the proven premise to improve circumstances.

This approach underpins the philosophical approaches of Afrikan culture

---

[6] **Matspiritual** denotes Afrikan culture's nature based approach to "spiritual" matters. "Spirits" come from nature, are inseparable from it and cannot exist independently of it. All "Spirits" have material as their base. "Spirit" is anchored in and by material.

and the next phase history – Scientific Socialism.

2.2.2 Human motion in space-time: The 3 motion tool

Any motion generated by the human brain has at least 3 distinct, but inseparably related outcomes: in nature the result is movement; in society activity; and culture idea. Physical motion occurs in nature; physical expression of motion in society; and mental expression in culture. From this vantage point, people are the core ingredient of nature; their activities the core of society; and their ideas the core of culture. Nature is material and primary, society and culture *matspiritual* and secondary. Nature does not depend on society and culture for its existence, but there can be no such thing as society and culture unless they are in nature. *Matspiritual* dimensions are therefore dependent upon material, but not the other way round. This is the basis for the *3 motion analytical tool/Matter Motion Chain* (Pert-em-Hru, 2017c, p. 284/5).

Human Activity Categories

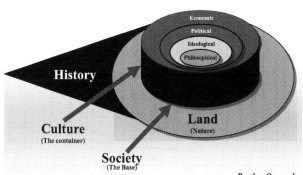

Brother Omowale

As people interact with people in nature, their activities produce politics in society whilst their ideas, ideology in culture. As people interact with nature, they produce economics in society and philosophy in culture. Land the base of nature is also the fundamental base of society and culture. Nature is the base of society and society the base of culture. Culture is specifically the people's ideas, but since neither ideas and actions, nor culture and society can be separated, its general expression is as the container for the sum total of people's activities and ideas, with society as the container's base. The movement of the container and contents through space deposits history in time.

2.2.3 Conflicting principles of humanity and their atomic source

At the same time, the manner in which people interact with other people and nature produces *matspiritual* forces impacting and altering the material world at many levels. Application of the *Matter Motion Chain Analytical Tool* (Pert-em-Hru, 2017, p. 284) reveals how at the societal level individuals have conscience within and groups, ethics. At the cultural level these translate into powerful ideological and philosophical forces directed from inside by principles and dialectics respectively; they drive all individual and group activity at societal level. Ideology and philosophy are deep internal drivers – principles and dialectics are deeper and determine their direction. At the same time, individual and collective will are internal drivers, with deeper level conscience and ethics determining their direction. All of this occurs in the context of nature with its inbuilt natural laws.

Material changes translate into people's actions and changes occurring generally in nature. Nature impacts the *matspiritual* forcing change, which in turn is driven and directed by *matspiritual* forces. Conscience directing will within people; ethics directing collective will within groups; principles directing group ideology; dialectics directing group philosophy and natural laws directing nature are internal *matspiritual* behavioural guides. Though they are *matspiritual* they direct movement in the material realm. Their differing combinations and permutations have a qualitative impact on material producing variable outcomes. These powerful *matspiritual* forces are interrelated, but operate at different levels i.e. individuals, society, culture and nature.

At the centre of culture are people's philosophical and ideological ideas. They occur inside society's individual and group activities, driving them. This entire combination occurs inside nature – in the specific location within which people reside. At the level of *matspiritual* behavioural guides, the outcome is: (i) universal laws are inside and driving dialectics in nature; (ii) dialectics is inside and driving principles in culture; (iii) principles are inside and driving ethics in society; (iv) ethics are inside and driving conscience in individuals. At the same time the reverse is true: (v) individual conscience is inside and driving ethics in groups; (vi) group ethics is inside and driving principles in society; (vii) principles are inside and driving dialectics in culture; and (viii) dialectics is inside and driving universal laws in nature.

At **matspiritual** source i.e. material, people are inside nature and nature is inside people. More precisely at the macro level most of nature is outside people, meaning people are inside it; at the micro level the rest of nature i.e. part of nature fills them. People are nature in microcosm. All of the above mentioned **matspiritual** activity simultaneously occurs inside and outside people. As they interact with nature, its universal laws operate as constraints on people's consciences, ethics, principles and dialectics. They experience external universal laws, dialectics, principles and ethics internally as conscience. Through conscience, they have a deep:

- Sense of right and wrong; and
- Connection with everything occurring in nature around and within them.

Their will is their **matspiritual** driving force; their conscience gives direction to that force – in the context of their material and **matspiritual** environment. Their interactions are fundamentally impacted by local environment, meaning all people do not interact with nature in the same way. Peoples in a hot environment for instance will interact in a manner different from people in freezing cold (Diop, 1991, p. 16-20). Material differences have corresponding **matspiritual** manifestations.

Natural Law in Logical Types

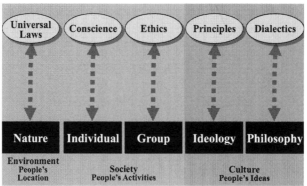

Brother Omowale

At the cultural level, their interactions produce variations in societal behaviours, which in turn produce variations in particular people's methodologies and principles, philosophies and ideologies in culture. If they interact on the basis that they own other people and nature, they produce mystical methodologies and exploitative principles; if they interact on the basis they, other people and nature are ends in and of themselves and not means to somebody else's end, they produce scientific methodologies and humanist principles. The calibre or quality of produced methodologies and principles determine the basis upon which the society operates.

Methodologies and principles in the societal arena translate into philosophy and ideology at level of culture and vice versa. Therefore the calibre of a people's behaviour is the source of theirs and their society's philosophy and ideology. There is a causal link between a people's behaviour and their ideology and philosophy. As people interact with nature they also produce ideas and emotions (Toure, No. 88, p. 133) and since ideas and emotions are the centre of culture, they produce culture and since culture is the outcome of history (Cabral, 1979, p. 142), they produce history.

Remembering that nature is composed of thousands, millions, billions, trillions, quadrillions, quintillions, sextillions, septillions, octillions, nonillions, decillions ... centillions + ... of atoms, there is a microcosmic reflection of all of this going on deep within. Our ancestors told us to look deep within and the atom is a physical/material manifestation of that which is deep within virtually everything. At the core of each atom there are neutrons which are negative and protons, positive. Neutrons exude a contracting force, pulling inwards toward the core, whilst protons' expansive forces move away. Forces are so great, if protons succeed in getting away the result is nuclear explosion. This means every single atom has within it nuclear scale dialectical forces, held in tension by contracting and expanding forces of neutrons and protons respectively.

Forces which hold atoms together when multiplied millions ... centillions + of times translate into humanist principles and scientific methodologies driving and directing society and culture. Similarly, forces which propel the atom towards destruction translate to exploitative principles and mystical methodologies. The sum total of those forces codified into principles at societal and cultural levels become grouped into social classes composed of people, their ideas and emotions, manifested in their actions and feelings – they are competing/antagonistic social classes, with equally antagonistic methodologies. Tension of nuclear scale forces in atoms massively multiplied translate to struggle between classes at societal level. Social classes are driven by opposing sets of principles in a manner similar to conflicting forces in atoms driving neutrons and protons in opposite directions.

If exploitative principles 'win', the result is destruction of the particular society – mimicking the atom's nuclear explosion. The historical task facing humanity is to ensure humanist principles 'win'. If we fail, we are informed by atoms, the outcome is catastrophe i.e. destruction of humanity. Whatever we do nature will of course continue, the issue for humanity is do we want to be present in its next phase. This for us is the central lesson of dialectics – the key issue in this phase of history. If we fail to grasp it – humanity is no more. If we learn and apply it humanity not only survives, but thrives in a new massively superior phase of history – Scientific Socialism.

On the surface humanity's choice is between capitalism and socialism. However, since capitalism unchecked ultimately leads only to destruction of humanity, the real underlying historical choice is between human extinction and Scientific Socialism.

2.2.4 Survival of atoms and implications for humanity

There is no number large enough to describe the number of atoms in nature. That number is infinite; there are an infinite number of atoms; nature is infinite. This means there are an infinite number of nuclear scale forces in nature each capable of producing a nuclear explosion. Despite this, they are incredibly rare. Nature does not easily allow such explosions, preferring instead to change form at the point when it can no longer contain the atom's conflicting forces.

Therefore on the face of it, humanity is safe since Mother Nature will not allow proton expansion forces to 'win' thus preventing nuclear scale explosions i.e. she will not allow exploitative principles at the societal level to 'win', preventing the extinction of humanity. Except, nature has no greater need for human beings than it had for dinosaurs or doe does – it changed form and rid itself of these creatures and is easily capable of continuing without human beings.

What's more, human beings have learned how to interfere with nature's capacity to contain nuclear explosions. By firing foreign particles directly at neutrons, they weaken their contraction forces thereby allowing protons to release themselves at nuclear force, resulting in a massive overpowering explosion. On 6th and 9th August 1945, driven by their exploitative principles, maniacs in control of US Satan even used this knowledge to deliberately destroy tens of thousands of innocent unsuspecting human beings in Hiroshima and Nagasaki respectively. These same maniacs are in charge of many thousands of nuclear warheads – a nuclear arsenal large enough to destroy the earth many times over.

Aware that exploitative maniacs have nuclear capacity and a proven willingness to kill with it, others have felt the need to similarly arm themselves, making the prospect of nuclear war ever more real. Humanity has a survival crisis and this is even before we take account of the environmental damage exploitative principles are inflicting on nature's air, water and soil. Exploitative principles left unchecked will destroy humanity in one way or another. All of this is merely an indication of the magnitude of the survival problem confronting humanity. In much the same way contracting neutron forces of the atom must contain proton expansion forces to ensure survival of atoms, humanism must 'win' at the level of principles in order for humanity to survive.

More can be deduced, but from the forgoing we can conclude:
- Concepts must be traceable back to nature in order to prove their correctness;
- Interaction between people and nature produces economics and philosophy;
- Interaction between people and people produces politics and ideology;
- Where the manner of these interactions are respectful of people and nature as ends, humanist principles and scientific methodologies are produced;
- Where people and nature are used as a means to a sub-group's ends, exploitative principles and mystical methodologies are produced; and
- The battle for survival of humanity requires triumph of humanist principles.

Having established these points, it is necessary to further explain and clarify opposing sets of principles.

2.2.5 Opposing principles, ideologies and philosophies in nature and society

Land is the natural base so far as human activity is concerned. When people interact on the basis that other people and nature are ends in and of themselves, no one claims preferential 'ownership' of land and everybody shares produced wealth. Everyone has equal access to land so nobody needs to trick anyone else to get more. Engagements are therefore honest and methodologies for explaining nature, driven by the pursuit of truth, are scientific.

Three *humanist principles* come into being: firstly, the welfare of people is treated as more important than individual 'ownership' and becomes society's highest priority, generating the principle of *humanism [People before property]*. Secondly, as people work together, they each gain more than if they work by themselves, generating the principle of *collectivism [We before me]*. Thirdly, since adults are generally not dependent on other adults, everybody recognises they are neither superior nor inferior i.e. each equal in essence generating the principle of *egalitarianism [We're all equal]*. These 3 are core humanist principles.

When humanist principles are dominant in a pre-industrial setting, the social system created is called *communalism*. All human societies, without exception, were originally communal societies. Every section of the human family started off in this way. *Communalism*, with its humanist principles was the social system of Afrika before the invasion of alien cultures. Even after, *communalism* didn't disappear, instead it retreated to the countryside to Afrikan villages (Afrikan Information Service, 1973, p. 49). *Communalism* does not stand as an isolated system; it is part of a family of social systems which includes *socialism* and *communism*. They have in common operation on the basis of humanist principles (and materialist methodologies) – *Afrika's principles are humanist*.

By contrast, when a sub-group interacts on the basis that they own other people and land, it selfishly claims everybody else's wealth as its own. The sub-group steals common wealth from others and not wanting to be caught out, lies to justify its theft. Knowing lying to be wrong, it covers up and justifies its behaviour through trickery via the deployment of **mystical** 'explanations' of nature.

Three **exploitative principles** develop as a result: firstly, the more landless people produce, the wealthier 'owners' become, who begin to value wealth more than other people, producing the principle of **exploitation [property before people]**. Secondly, they think of personal wellbeing before that of the group, generating the principle of **individualism [me before we]**. Thirdly, non-owners became dependent on 'owners' causing 'owners' to view them as inferior, producing the principle of **elitism [I'm better than you]**. These **exploitative principles** are core **principles** of: **slavery, Sexism, Racism, feudalism, colonialism, settler-colonialism, Zionism, neo-colonialism, capitalism and imperialism**.

Opposing Principles

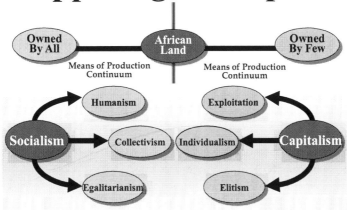

Brother Omowale

Where mystical methodologies and exploitative principles are dominant in a pre-industrial setting, the result is slavery or feudalism. Where the territory under consideration is pre-industrial in a world where industry exists in territories elsewhere, the result is colonialism, settler-colonialism or neo-colonialism. Where the territory under consideration is industrialised, the result is capitalism. Imperialism is the physical expansion of exploitative principles. In the current phase of world history – where industrialisation has been achieved in some territories, the two most relevant systems are capitalism and socialism.

Humanist and exploitative principles are totally incompatible; they are diametric opposites; they are the anti-theses of each other; to support one automatically means to destroy the other; where one dominates, the other must fight for its survival. In the industrial setting, humanist principles produce socialist ideology in the first instance, whilst their exploitative counterparts produce capitalism. Socialist and capitalist ideologies are locked in a battle for domination. In the capitalist centres that battle is more ideological than physical because socialism and capitalism occupy different phases in history, meaning their relative strengths vary according to time. The industrialised nations are relatively powerful enough to export their physical battles to Afrika and other pre-industrial parts of the world and do. In pre-industrial Afrika those battles are bloody costing millions of Afrikan people's lives.

We are currently in the capitalist phase of world history and capitalism, though weakening is still strong; socialism with its mishap in the Soviet Union is still in its birthing phase, having hardly established a secure foothold in the world. As capitalism weakens further and socialism strengthens, a point will be reached where they can be expected to be locked in a physical confrontation in the capitalist centres in a revolutionary clash. If capitalist ideology 'wins', it spells the end for humanity; if socialist ideology triumphs, humanity survives and has in place the foundations to thrive. Socialism will then lay the foundations for the next historical phase – communism (Pert-em-Hru, 2017c, p. 234).

2.3 The battle for Afrika
2.3.1 Afrika arrested
Afrika traditionally operated through a communal system, with a materialist i.e. scientific methodology/philosophy and humanist principles/ideology. Afrika was invaded by European imperialism which brought with it its idealist mystical philosophy/methodology and exploitative principles/ideology. However, Afrika was not totally subsumed by its enemy's alien philosophy and ideology. The alien system sat on top of the largely intact Afrikan society and culture. The capitalists created capital cities to do their bidding and Afrikan culture retreated to the villages (Cabral, 1979, p. 148).

Afrika suffered 80 to 90 years of colonial oppression under which the above contradiction prevailed, before being defeated and the enemy transforming into neo-colonialism. Capitalism remains dominant in Afrika in its neo-colonial form and continues to curtail Afrika's development. Despite this, Afrika's true philosophy and ideology remain in place, essentially ready for socialism.

Pan-Afrikanism is a revolutionary objective aimed at improving the quality of life of the masses of Afrikan people. That improved quality will require the liberation of Afrika and her people from capitalist exploitation. It will create the conditions for a free and self-determining Afrikan people to map their path to improved living standards, which will be ushered in through:

- Reinforcement of Afrika's traditional nature based scientific approach to solving the problems of Afrika and her people;
- Reinforcement of traditional Afrikan principles, underpinning its culture;
- Unification of the entire Afrikan continent under one state, governed by the masses of Afrikan people in their interest, whilst offering protection to Afrikan people in the Diaspora. Capitalism divided Afrika into more than 50 non-viable jigsaw puzzle pretend states, which must be eradicated; and
- Full scale industrialisation, incorporating all of the latest technologies managed and deployed in a manner consistent with rather than antagonistic to nature. Industrialisation is some 150 years old. The only nations that are not industrialised are those prevented. When Afrika achieves political self-determination, the blockages to mass production will be removed and the achievement of Scientific Socialism in sight.

2.3.2 Faces of socialism and capitalism in Afrika

The world level battle going on between capitalism and socialism is also being carried out in pre-industrial Afrika. This presents a major contradiction because industrialisation and a strong state are requirements for both capitalism and socialism and Afrika is pre-industrial, with non-viable jig saw puzzle pretend 'states'. In the pre-industrial setting of Afrika, both capitalism and socialism are impossible. Their battle is therefore carried out by proxy. The current face of capitalism in Afrika is neo-colonialism – this is the method by which capitalists outside Afrika use small groups of handpicked Afrikan traitors as surrogates to carry out their exploitative bidding, against the interests of the Afrikan masses.

The role of Pan-Afrikanism therefore is to advance Afrikan people to the next i.e. better phase of history where they can flourish and prosper. Afrika's next historical phase is socialism, which conveniently is driven by the same nature based scientific methodology and humanist principles as Afrikan culture and Pan-Afrikanism – *Afrikan, Afrikan communalist, Pan-Afrikanist, Socialist and Communist principles are identical – they are all humanist i.e. they all respect nature and people – Afrika, Communalism, Pan-Afrikanism, Socialism and Communism stand on the same side of the battle*.

There is only one Pan-Afrikanism – Revolutionary Pan-Afrikanism. It has as its outcome the achievement of Scientific Socialist Afrika. This in turn is part of a wider global revolutionary movement. The purpose of revolution is to advance humanity from one phase of history to the next i.e. from its current backward phase to a future, better one. On the world level that current backward phase is capitalism, with the future better one being socialism (Pert-em-Hru, 2017c, p. 149-236). In Afrika the current backward phase manifests as neo-colonialism, whilst socialism is the future better phase - the destination Pan-Afrikanism.

Communalism, Socialism & Communism Compared

Philosophy + Ideology = Culture; Economics + Politics = Society
Afrikan Culture intact; Afrikan Society in a mess   *Brother Omowale*

The face of socialism in Afrika is Pan-Afrikanism. Pan-Afrikanism arises naturally from the culture of Afrikan people in defence of socialism, because like Afrika's ideology and corresponding culture it is founded on humanist principles. Afrikan communalism has exactly the same methodology and principles as Pan-Afrikanism and socialism, meaning they are already inculcated in Afrika, her people and Pan-Afrikanism. There are therefore two major stumbling blocks separating Afrika and her people from achieving socialist development: (i) a continental wide super-state for effective governance; and (ii) industrialisation for effective production and Afrika's development. These form the core of the objective of Pan-Afrikanism, with the super-state being the most urgent (Nkrumah, 1998, p. 216-222).

Socialism is a scientific formula in the realms of ideas, practices and material. Its ideas are fixed, but practices vary within certain parameters according to specific peoples operating in specific environments, impacted by specific histories. This gives socialism slightly different forms according to people, location and time. Variations in form are not by chance or haphazard, but rather rooted in scientifically explainable differences between specific peoples in time and space (i.e. historical material and physical environment):

- In the realm of ideas – philosophically it is materialist and ideologically humanist – ideas are the centre of culture;
- In the realm of practice it requires state machinery for governance (politics) and industrial production (economics) – practice is the manifestation of culture;
- In the material realm – it requires specific peoples in specific environments operating on the basis of specific historical material, giving it specific forms in specific times and places – all cultures are inside nature and unique.

Materialism, humanism, state machinery and industrialisation are its higher level ingredients. Specific peoples, their environments and historical material comprise its lower level ingredients. Socialism's fixed ideas are integrated with variable material conditions producing different forms in the realm of practice. One such form is Pan-Afrikanism which achieved, is scientific socialism in the Afrikan setting.

The emergence of socialism in Afrika threatens the very existence of neo-colonialism. Neo-colonialism is therefore bound to do everything in its power to prevent its emergence. Politically is does this by:

- Maintaining Afrika's assemblage of jig saw puzzle pretend 'states', to prevent her unification;
- Denying stolen Afrikan people in the Diaspora citizenship rights;
- Constantly harassing and attacking Afrika's suffering people to prevent them organising to take power and with it, their freedom;
- Attacking, undermining and destroying all vestiges of Pan-Afrikanism under its sphere of influence;
- Disguising neo-colonial outfits as Pan-Afrikanist in order to confuse and fool Afrika's suffering people on route to murdering them;
- Aspiring to and accepting junior positions in capitalism's clubs such as the UN and G20.

At the economic level it:
- Bankrupts Afrika's pretend 'states' by accepting loans that can never be repaid;
- Give's away Afrika's natural resources and other valuable assets at prices so 'knocked down' that Afrikan people are poorer after the 'deal' than before it;
- Actively prevents self-help initiatives created by Afrikan people to benefit Afrika's masses;
- Awards at extortionate rates, contracts to foreign trans-national companies to build things that Afrikan people don't need – in some cases whilst Afrikan people starve.

At the military level it:
- Invites foreign armies to set up bases on Afrika's soil so they can more easily murder and contain Afrika's suffering people;
- Assists foreign invasions in neighbouring areas of Afrika;
- Pays foreign mercenaries to come to Afrika and murder Afrikan people;
- Provides soldiers as cannon fodder for capitalism's proxy wars in Afrika and in some cases outside as well;
- Assists coups in the part of Afrika where it is resident, also assisting in other parts when called upon;
- Pays foreign military advisors to tell it how 'best' to murder fellow Afrikan people;

These lists are illustrative and by no means exhaustive.

2.3.3 Afrika's solution: The Pan-Afrikanist route to socialism
Bringing the atom back into the equation, neo-colonialism through its expansive principles is representative of its destructive proton expansive forces. Pan-Afrikanism driven by Afrika's humanist principles is representative of neutron contracting forces. Neo-colonialism is trying to rip Afrika apart; Pan-Afrikanism is resolutely trying to hold it together. If neo-colonialism 'wins', Afrika effectively explodes into pieces, each controlled by a different set of outsiders eventually rendering Afrikan people extinct.

The signs are already written all over Afrika. It was revealed that Afrikan babies are dying at a rate of 200,000 per annum i.e. 2 million per decade (Pert-em-Hru, 2017d, p. 216). Proxy wars have been raging all over Afrika in recent decades, with death tolls running into 10's of millions (Pert-em-Hru, 2017d, p. 218/9). Added to this are epidemics of Aids, Ebola and other forms of chemical warfare including implanting of dead seeds which produce no off-spring. Life expectancy in some parts has fallen to little more than 40 years.

The atoms inform us that the only way for Afrika to survive at the societal level, is for scientific methodology/humanist principles to triumph. In the modern setting it means socialism is Afrika's only hope – its one and only chance to survive. The triumph of Pan-Afrikanism automatically means the death of neo-colonialism, signalling the imminent death of the entire capitalist system. It is the key not only to Afrika's survival, but to its successful development as well.

As neo-colonialism nears its death, we can expect that its source – the capitalist system – will come to its aid, if only to save itself. In order to meet this challenge and win, the whole of the Afrikan masses will need to come forward and organise in defence of socialism via its Pan-Afrikan route to effectively defend Mama Afrika and achieve victory.

2.4 Milestones of Pan-Afrikanism – Scientific Socialism
2.4.1 Revolutionary transition: Pan-Afrikanism means Scientific Socialism
The achievement of Pan-Afrikanism is simultaneously the updating of Traditional Afrikan Culture and achievement of socialism in Afrika.

Scientific Socialism is a phase of history as well as a socio-political-economic system. It is the next phase of history for the whole of humanity. The longer it takes to reach, the more protracted will be humanity's suffering. Its achievement requires the following fixed higher level (**Matspiritual**) ingredients:

- Materialism – **respect for nature** at the philosophical level;
- Humanism – **respect for people** at the ideological level;
- State structures – **centralised continental power, controlled by the sovereign masses i.e. a people's continental state** at the political level; and
- Industrialisation – **advance technology owned by the sovereign masses i.e. people's nature-friendly industry** at the economic level.

This must be developed and utilised in a manner that complements rather than antagonises nature. These higher level ingredients are applied to its lower level (material) ingredients, namely:

- Specific peoples – (people);
- Operating in their specific environments – (space/nature);
- Driven by their specific history – (time).

Socialism Matrix

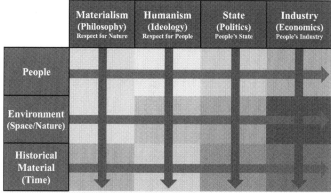

Brother Omowale

The application of the higher level (**Matspiritual**) ingredients of Pan-Afrikanism to (material) Afrikan people in (material) Afrikan environments (nations/communities) produces Scientific Socialism. Traditional Afrikan Culture, Pan-Afrikanism and Scientific Socialism are imbued with the same philosophy and ideology. Pan-Afrikanism and

Scientific Socialism adapt the politics and economics of Traditional Afrikan Culture to meet the challenges of modern living. They represent the updating or modernisation of the outer layers of Afrikan culture, whilst keeping its core intact. Pan-Afrikanism is Scientific Socialism. It is the particular form Scientific Socialism will take in Afrika. Scientific Socialism is the universal essence of the next phase of human history - Pan-Afrikanism is its Afrikan form. Pan-Afrikanism will be briefly assessed against the *4 Dialectic analytical tool* as a guide to explaining its expected outcomes.

2.4.2 Further clarification of the Pan-Afrikan objective
The *4 Dialectic tool* provides a framework for analysing the status of any nation's high level societal ingredients (Pert-em-Hru, 2017c, p. 202). It measures Afrika's current societal condition as a combination of: (i) materialism at the philosophical level i.e. respect rather than disrespect for nature; (ii) the principles humanism, egalitarianism and collectivism at the ideological level i.e. respect rather than disrespect for people; and (iii) balkanised states i.e. non-viable jig-saw puzzle states and pre-industrial production methods i.e. simple agriculture at political and economic levels respectively.

4 Dialectic Analysis

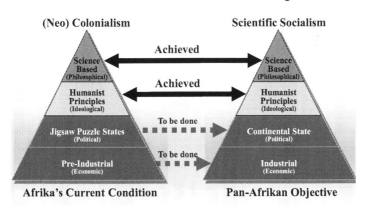

Brother Omowale

At the same time it illustrates the Pan-Afrikanist objective for Afrikan society as a combination of: (i) materialism i.e. respect for nature at the philosophical level; (ii) the principles humanism, egalitarianism and collectivism i.e. respect for people at the ideological level; and (iii) the mechanisms of a unified state plus industrial production under the control of Afrikan people worldwide at the level of political and economic or cultural instruments (Pert-em-Hru, 2017c, p. 205). Therefore, Afrika currently has materialism as it philosophy; humanism as its ideology, both of which need to be maintained for the achievement of socialism. However its assemblage of jig saw puzzle pretend states operationally directing its patchwork politics; and its largely pre-industrial economy must make way for a continental wide unified state and rapid coordinated industrialisation. These are the key changes required for a modern Afrika equipped to look after its people's needs worldwide.

As neo-colonialism becomes stronger in Afrika and our material conditions worsen, the very fabric of our materialist philosophy becomes undermined as our people rush to notions of God somewhere outside themselves for deliverance from evil. Neo-colonialism is using this development to its advantage by setting up fake brands of Pan-Afrikanism (i.e. Divisionist brands) devoted to cussing Christianity and Islam as a means to fostering deep divisions among Afrikan people. Garvey saw this trend developing a century ago and gave advance warning:

> "Man's religion is something that we cannot eliminate from his system or destroy in him, therefore it is folly for any man to go about attacking another man's religion, because to him it is fundamental ... [also] ... any man who gets out and attacks religions, thinking he can convert men to the organisation by doing so is not helping the organisation. He is doing more harm than good." (Sons of Garvey Press Association, 1990, p. 24).

It also creates pseudo churches and mosques as religious tools targeted against Afrikan liberation and antagonistic cussing opponents in its artificially created split between Pan-Afrikanism and religions followed by Afrikan people. Neo-colonialism's intention is to make Afrikan people schizophrenic at the philosophical level so that we remain acrimoniously and permanently divided, thereby better facilitating its domination. Nkrumah explained one part of the approach to preventing these artificial divides taking hold:

> "I have stressed that the two other segments [Christianity

and Islam], in order to be rightfully seen, must be accommodated only as experiences of the traditional African society. If we fail to do this our society will be racked by the most malignant schizophrenia." (Nkrumah, 2009, p. 78)

We cannot and must not try to reject Christianity and Islam, because to do so would entail the rejection of our own sincerely devoted sisters and brothers. This in turn seals deep permanent divisions between us. Garvey indicated a practical approach to holding us together whilst maintaining our materialist philosophy:

"Make your interpretation of Christianity scientific – what it ought to be and blame not God, blame not the white man for physical conditions for which we ourselves are responsible." (Garvey, 1986, p. 33)

His words are generally applicable not only to Christianity, but Islam and other religions also. Our philosophical task is to maintain and heighten our longstanding respect for nature and scientific engagement with her.

At the ideological level our natural tendency to put the welfare of people first has been substantially undermined by neo-colonial intrigues, particularly neo-colonial proxy wars on our soil. Afrikan people are now being killed by fellow Afrikan people on a massive scale in Afrika and around the world. The ideological objective of Pan-Afrikanism is to put an urgent end to these wars at source to create space for the recovery of the Afrikan personality (Nkrumah, 2009, p. 79; Pert-em-Hru, 2017c, p. 218).

In capitalist centres wars are fuelled by the drug economy it imposes on us. It is increasingly using fake Pan-Afrikanist groups to sell drugs to Afrikan children as part of its anti-Afrikan genocide programme. Divisionists attempt to justify their crimes through the dishonest guise of 'raising funds to support Afrika's liberation'. The objective of Pan-Afrikanism in this instance, is to thoroughly extricate Afrikan people from this source of death by self-destruction.

At the political level, neo-colonialism inherits the jig saw puzzle of nations created at the Berlin conference in 1884/5, which it has transformed into pretend 'states'. Land is material and therefore fundamentally real. Society – a mental construct – is **matspiritual** and not 'fundamentally real', but because we have come to believe it, we act to make it 'real'. This means the artificially created boarders (which are **matspiritual**) are not fundamentally 'real'. Afrikan people have come to believe them to be 'real' and have made them 'real' by giving them material substance.

At official border crossing points there are real buildings and other structures, staffed by real people, examining real passports (where available), taking real money to facilitate crossings. This is further backed by real pretend 'states' with sufficient power to punish those who fail to observe their rules. Yet local people make a mockery of 'official reality' on a daily basis. Ten minutes from official crossing points, they go about their business passing through boarders many times a day with no reference to officialdom. This fundamental reality is true for a large percentage of all land passable border crossings.

Pan-Afrikanism's political objective is to dismantle these artificial boarders and install one continental wide unified state governing the whole of Afrika. The creation of one continental wide unified state out of Afrika's assemblage of neo-colonial jig saw puzzle pretend 'states', against the will of those who control them is Pan-Afrikanism's political sub-objective. To prevent this Divisionism has seized control of what should have been the linchpin of Pan-Afrikanism – the Afrikan Union (AU), using it instead to maintain the artificial boarders and destroy Pan-Afrikanism at the highest structural level. To achieve its political objective, Pan-Afrikanism has to create a strong desire amongst Afrika's masses for continental unity or more precisely, enhance the existent strong desire to levels where it becomes impossible to contain, making achievement inevitable.

At the economic level, Pan-Afrikanism's objective is the urgent industrialisation of Afrika. However, unless the Afrikan masses have genuine political sovereignty, this will amount to putting Afrika's industry straight into the hands of foreigners, whose interests are not the same as ours. Under these conditions, industry will be further used to cripple Afrikan people.

2.4.3 Strategic Pan-Afrikanism

Careful study of actions and words of Marcus Garvey, Kwame Nkrumah and Malcolm X forms a solid basis from which a strategy of Pan-Afrikanism can be derived (Pert-em-Hru, 2017c, p. 31-146). Garvey laid the strategic foundation and in the following generation Nkrumah led the strategy, co-opting Malcolm X to lead the Diasporan element.

All three placed heavy emphasis on Afrikan people organising in their localities. Real life campaigns aimed at bettering the lives of Afrikan people were deployed as means of recruitment. The building of robust local self-help organisations was the bedrock. Central to their development was education alongside campaigning to equip members for their revolutionary roles.

Strategic Pan-Afrikanism

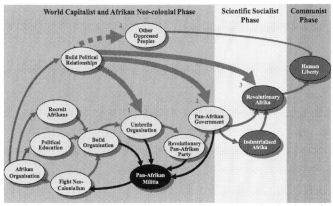

Brother Omowale

The next stage was to bring disparate local campaigning organisations under an umbrella structure to rationalise, co-ordinate and synchronise efforts. For Garvey this was the UNIA, Nkrumah the OAU initially and later the AAPRP and for Malcolm X the OAAU. Umbrella organisations contained both political and military wings.

The paramilitary character of Garvey's UNIA was influenced by its birth during World War I. Nkrumah's military wing developed as a result of armed struggle for Afrikan liberation during the 1950's, 60's and beyond. Nkrumah strongly advocated the need for an Afrikan High Command. In the case of Malcolm X he was assassinated before developing a Diasporan military wing, but the Black Panthers would later take up arms. They all saw need for a strong military to defend Afrika's gains.

The objective of umbrella organisations was retrieval and control of Afrika's stolen land to bring justice to its dispossessed people. Its higher level purpose was to bring justice to the whole of humanity and for this they worked in solidarity with non-Afrikans willing to reciprocate. Garvey, Nkrumah, Malcolm X and the Black Panthers recognised the crucial importance of alliance building for a liberated Afrika.

To meet the challenge of running a nation, the umbrella organisations were to transform into governing political parties. This was clearly the intention of Garvey's UNIA which by electing officers into paid ministerial positions even before returning to Afrika had created an Afrikan government in waiting. Similarly Nkrumah tried to institute the OAU as Afrika's continental government, but was undermined by Divisionists.

After achieving governmental power (the first stage to Scientific Socialism), the second stage was industrialisation. Garvey declared his intention in this regard by building factories even before returning to Afrika. Diasporan factories were practice pending return. In Nkrumah's case a mass industrialisation programme was already under way in Ghana pending Afrikan unity. It included: a damn large enough to power a substantial section of West Afrika; laying the keystone for Ghana's nuclear plant; the building of a motorway even before Britain built its M1; and a host of mega factories producing all kinds of goods relevant to Afrikan people's needs – including bikes for instance. Industrialisation – the stage that ushers in Scientific Socialism - was unquestionably their intention.

2.5 Glimpse of Pan-Afrikanism achieved
2.5.1 Unification milestones
At the philosophical level unification translates into nature being one unified whole comprising all its material and *matspiritual* properties – all that there is comes from nature. It brings with it the requirement that Afrikan people must live as one with nature. Industrialisation is inevitable for Afrika's survival. Under capitalism the world has experienced it as destructive and polluting. Afrika's industrialisation programme must not harm nature and should aim to contribute to

nature's rejuvenation powers.

At the ideological level it is collectivism, the recognition that the collective gives life to, is superior to, is more powerful than, has greater longevity than and is wiser than the individual manifested through putting 'we before me'.

At the political level it is the recognition that Afrikan people must actively and purposefully organise to achieve unity; that the highest expression of unity is state power; and to express that highest level Afrikan people must overthrow its externally imposed jigsaw puzzle state structure, replacing it with a single unified continent wide state structure under the sovereign control of Afrika's agricultural and industrial workers at home and abroad. That state will provide:

- One unified political system
- One unified economic system
- One unified foreign policy
  - One unified/common diplomatic policy
- One unified military defence strategy (Nkrumah, 1998, p. 216-222)

At the economic level it means Afrika's land, resources and other elements of its means of production are centrally organised under the exclusive structured democratic control of Afrika's agricultural and industrial workers at home and abroad. They will develop, manage and direct: (i) a common industrial policy; (ii) a common monetary and banking system based on Afrikan resources; (iii) a common market with open trading internally and barriers externally; and (iv) a common policy for overseas trading.

2.5.2 Liberation milestones

At the philosophical level liberation means the recognition of Mother Nature as an end in and of her own right, requiring Afrikan people and others to live in harmony with her and her universal laws and recognising her as the source of all. This implies bringing to an end all industrial and other nature polluting activities in Afrika's sphere, to be replaced by 'nature friendly' ones.

At the ideological level it is the triumph of humanism over exploitation.

The advance of humanity to a social environment where, not only are people more important than money, profits and property, but are treated as worthy ends in and of their own right for no reason other than the fact that they are human beings.

At the political level it is a single unified Afrikan continent wide state structure under the sovereign control of Afrikan agricultural and industrial workers at home and abroad. Amongst its components will be a union government for processing political decisions democratically and an Afrikan High Command for the protection of Afrika and her people.

At the economic level it is Afrikan agricultural and industrial workers at home and abroad regaining exclusive control of Afrika's land and resources, utilised in their interest. When Afrikan people around the world assume their legitimate control of Afrika (the richest land in the world), Afrikan people will become powerful and **Capitalist corporations** will: (i) cease to be the most powerful entities; (ii) cease dominating Afrikan people and resources; and (iii) become dependent upon Afrikan people for vital resources.

All other nations will then have to trade fairly with Afrika. **Neo-colonial** mechanisms i.e. the **capitalist corporations**, the **World Trade Organisation (WTO)**, the **International Monetary Fund (IMF)** and **the International Bank for Reconstruction and Development (IBRD)** colloquially referred to as the **World Bank** will all become redundant.

2.5.3 Indicators of ongoing Development
At the philosophical level it is the recognition of the equality of the material and **matspiritual** properties of nature and humanity's balanced approach to them, deploying the material as its starting point for scientific engagement. It is the invention and adoption of the most up to date technologies for improved quality of life, applied with the welfare of nature and people as highest priorities.

At the ideological level it is recognition of egalitarianism i.e. all human beings, being made of the same matter are equal in essence as the base from which we move forward to achieve ever increasing levels of happiness for Afrikan people and others.

At the political level there will develop a system of laws, mores, conventions and practices based on Afrikan history and culture that will enshrine scientific methodology and technological innovation founded on the protection of people and nature. The extent of the people's health, education, wealth and happiness will be the measure of our success at the people level. Land, air and water quality will be the measure at the level of nature.

At the economic level there will develop a centrally planned coordinated programme of industrialisation utilising Afrika's resources at a predetermined rate focused on going beyond satisfying our people's needs to delighting them. The resources of the richest land in the world being put into service to improve the quality of life of Afrika's agricultural and industrial workers will be the starting point of Afrika's true development.

Industrialisation will spread across the continent, planned in the best logistical interest of the continent as a whole. Production will be focused on catering for the needs of Afrikan people across the entirety of the continent and where necessary support for those abroad. It will be organised in a manner that helps rather than harms nature. There will be heavy investment in health and education services aimed at promoting and heightening the people's physical and mental wellbeing. A healthy and well educated people will repay that investment multi-fold.

Indicators of Afrikan Freedom

Milestones/ Indicators	Matspiritual Categories			
	Philosophical (Respect for Nature)	Ideological (Respect for People)	Political (Continental state)	Economic (Advanced Industry)
Unification	Spirit in Nature / People & Nature Are One	Collectivisn Defeats Individualism	Afrikan Union Government	Afrikan People Own Afrikan land
Liberation	Nature Before Spirit / People Respect Nature	Humanism Defeats Exploitation	Sovereign Afrikan People	Production Meets Needs of Afrikan People
Development	Nature/Spirit Equal / People in Harmony with Natural Law	Egalitarianism Defeats Elitism	Afrikan High Command	Afrikan People Produce Best Quality

Brother Omowale

There will be an Afrikan common market where Afrikan products will be traded in Afrika in the first instance to cater for the needs and wants of Afrikan people. There will be no tariffs or trade barriers between Afrikan people or regions. Employment will be of Afrikan people in production and service organisations collectively owned by Afrikan people for the benefit of Afrikan people at home and abroad in the first instance. Excess produce will be made available for external trade at the discretion of Afrikan people.

Afrika's economy will be managed and directed through: (i) a common industrial policy; (ii) a common monetary and banking system based on Afrikan resources; (iii) a common market with open trading internally and barriers externally; and (iv) a common policy for overseas trading.

2.6 One billion revolutionary Pan-Afrikanists required
2.6.1 What is the purpose of Afrikan revolution?
Pan-Afrikanists do not engage in revolution for fun, revolution's sake or as a religious type commitment. Engagement is because there is something seriously and fundamentally wrong in Afrika and the world. The essence of the wrong is Afrikan people and others are being *exploited* - they want to right that wrong and end *exploitation.* The aim of the Afrikan revolution is to *improve the quality of life of the masses of Afrikan people as a contribution to greater human happiness*. Initially, the masses of Afrikan people need an end to: (i) genocide being carried out against us; and (ii) the destruction of Afrika's land and environment. In addition, we need to create for ourselves:
- Clean and easily accessible drinking water;
- Safe nutritious food;
- Quality clothing;
- Quality shelter and housing;
- Quality sewerage facilities;
- Quality healthcare services; and
- Quality education services.

If the Afrikan revolution does not provide this in the first phase of reconstruction, then it will have fallen short of properly serving Afrikan people. In the medium to longer term the assessment of revolutionary success will be based on the level of self-determined improvements in Afrikan people's quality of life. As economic conditions improve, production will be geared towards the majority of the people's needs

and away from profit maximisation for the few:
- Heavy industry will proliferate;
- Health services will improve with expanded availability:
  - Disease will reduce;
  - Life expectancy will increase;
  - Safe birthing processes will be standard;
- The quality and quantity of food production will improve;
- Construction quality and availability of housing will increase;
- The people's consciousness will rise:
  - Availability of education services will expand;
  - Syllabuses will be designed for the benefit of Afrika's majority:
    - They will emphasise the priority of people and nature over money making;
  - Literacy rates will increase; and
  - Media will promote the interests of the masses of Afrikan people, emphasising the priority of people and nature over money making.

2.6.2 Embrace our bright future

Despite a plethora of negative oppressive experiences, Afrikan people's future looks bright. There are three key signs. Firstly, Afrika is the richest continent in the world:

> "Each of the seven continents of the world has diverse natural resources. Africa has the richest concentration of natural resources such as oil, copper, diamonds, bauxite, lithium, gold, hardwood forests, and tropical fruits. It is estimated that 30% of the earth's mineral resources are found in the African continent. Additionally, Africa has the world's biggest precious metal reserves on earth." (Sawe, 2018, *World Facts*) ... [Furthermore] ... "Whosoever controls Afrika (the richest continent in the world) become the richest and most powerful people in the world. It is this realisation, coupled with the greed and quest for power that were motivating factors for European imperialism's orchestrated campaign of theft, lies and genocide against Afrikan people. It is their 'success' in stealing Afrikan people's land that made Europeans the richest and most

powerful people in the world. It was the loss of the most valuable territory in the world, right from under their feet that condemned Afrikan people to being the most disorientated, disorganised and disrespected paupers in the world – Afrikan people were not in charge of anything of importance, not even their own home – they became the laughing stock of the world." (Pert-em-Hru, 2017d, p. 24)

When we recover control of our land, we become the richest most powerful people in the world.

Continental Populations & Ages

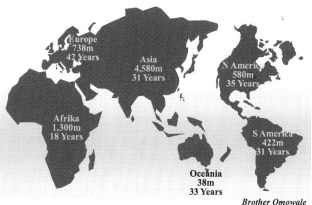

Brother Omowale

Secondly, there is a large growing Afrikan population. We have been decimated by Aids, Ebola, mass sterilisation programmes, infant mortality at a rate of one death every three seconds, internal proxy wars killing millions etc. Instead of becoming extinct, our numbers have multiplied fourfold from 400 million a hundred years ago to 1,600 million. The Afrikan Diaspora is as large now as Afrika's entire world population 100 years ago - in Garvey's time. This proves that even at our weakest our vicious enemy cannot exterminate us. It follows that when we're at our strongest, no force on earth will be able to contain us. *1.6+ billion Afrikan people properly orientated and organised cannot be prevented from retaking control of Afrika and becoming the most powerful people in the world.*

Thirdly with a median age of 18, Afrika has by far the youngest population of any continent. Furthermore, it is projected that by the year 2100, half of the world's 0-4 year olds will be Afrikan people. In a world of rapidly changing technology, it is the young who are most adaptable. *Our 'tech savvy' world majority children will consolidate Afrika's position as the most highly developed continent in the world.*

2.6.3 Pan-Afrikanist or not? What are you?

There is no possibility of achieving revolution i.e. Pan-Afrikanism without the support of the substantial majority of Afrika's 1.6 billion Home and Diaspora population. They must be urgently transformed into Pan-Afrikanists. This possibility is assisted by the fact that Afrika has the youngest population of any continent. The critical first step is education programmes aimed at helping Afrikan people understand the absolute necessity of unity as a means to achieving it. Unifying and organising Afrika and her people is the first indispensible great milestone. This means: (i) unifying our land —Afrika; (ii) unifying our state structure; and (iii) through political organisation, unifying Afrikan people worldwide.

Every Afrikan person should be conversant with neo-colonialism, capitalism, Pan-Afrikanism and socialism and act on that knowledge. Neo-colonialism is Afrika's most dangerous ever enemy, its death nail if left unchecked. When we were oppressed under slavery and colonialism our ancestors knew they had to remove them to be free. *Now we live in the neo-colonial phase and most of us don't know or understand it. If we don't understand it, we can't consciously challenge and get rid of it; if we can't get rid of it, we'll remain stuck, Afrika won't be liberated and we will be destroyed.*

Neo-colonialism v Pan-Afrikanism

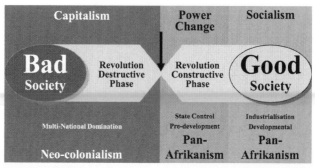

Brother Omowale

The critical task is to raise our collective consciousness of neo-colonialism and how to defeat it. This means joining a genuine revolutionary Pan-Afrikanist organisation - the first physical step towards becoming part of Afrika's and the world's solution. Pan-Afrikanism is the revolutionary objective of Afrika and her people. Its purpose is to rapidly move Afrika into the next phase of history - Scientific Socialism. Any Afrikan organisation without this as its objective, is neither revolutionary nor Pan-Afrikanist.

Socialism as objective marks the dividing line between revolutionaries and counter-revolutionaries; and Pan-Afrikanists and neo-colonialists. It matters not how radical sounding individuals or groups may be, if their activities are not geared precisely towards the achievement of socialism, they are neither revolutionary nor Pan-Afrikanist. If they actively oppose capitalism/imperialism whilst falling short of having socialism as their objective, they are not revolutionary, but are nonetheless progressive; and if they actively oppose or decry socialism as the objective/desired outcome, they oppose history and are counter-revolutionary and neo-colonialist. Such organisations should be avoided by any and all Afrikan people seeking to make an honest contribution to the Afrikan revolution – which doubles as the achievement of the Pan-Afrikan objective.

To be a Pan-Afrikanist is to be a revolutionary; to be a revolutionary is to contribute to advancing humanity to its next phase of history – socialism; to be a revolutionary Pan-Afrikanist is to contribute to advancing Afrika and her people to the next phase of history – socialism; to be a revolutionary Pan-Afrikanist is to destroy neo-colonialism as a stage to destroying its source capitalism; to be a revolutionary Pan-Afrikanist is to save Afrika and her people from extinction; to be a revolutionary Pan-Afrikanist is the save the world and humanity from extinction.

These things can only be accomplished through achieving the next phase of history - socialism. The most crucial task of revolutionaries in this phase of history is to advance humanity from capitalism to socialism. The desire to achieve socialism is therefore a precondition for all revolutionaries in the current historical phase. If you are not for the achievement of humanity's advance to socialism, you are neither revolutionary nor Pan-Afrikanist. To oppose socialism is a counter-revolutionary neo-colonialists act – it is to oppose historical progress and advancement of humanity.

If you stand against achievement of Scientific Socialism (in Afrika and the world), you are a neo-colonial counter-revolutionary, actively or passively contributing to the destruction of Afrika and the world. If you are actively contributing to the achievement of Scientific Socialism in Afrika (and the world), you have the foundations of a revolutionary. This is the essence of a Pan-Afrikanist. *What are you?*

History
For Revolution

Chapter 3

3 History for revolution
3.1 Human history in context
3.1.1 History - driven by nature and its contents

Quoting Engels, Nkrumah emphasises the primary as opposed to sole reality of material aspects of nature:

> "According to the materialist conception of history, the *ultimately* determining element in history is the production and reproduction of real life ... if somebody twists this into saying that the economic is the *only* determining one, he transforms the proposition into a meaningless, abstract, senseless phrase ... people sometimes lay more stress on the economic side than is due to it ... " (Nkrumah, 2009, p. 1)

Material is the fundamental driver of nature, but does not operate alone; there is more to the universe than material. Economics is fundamental to society, but cannot by itself explain it; there is more to society than economics. Philosophy is fundamental to culture, but cannot alone explain it; there is more to culture than philosophy. There is more going on in the universe than the physical relationship between people and nature. Although people and nature are fundamental drivers of history, that relationship alone is inadequate to explain it. Material alone cannot explain history, but it is impossible to explain history without it.

3.1.2 The 9 Dialectic analytical tool

People and nature are material. Their relationships and quality are **matspiritual**. As they interact in the material realm, people and nature produce outcomes in the **matspiritual**. History is driven forward by a series of dialectics in both. The universal dialectic is between material and **matspiritual** aspects of nature – the universal philosophical dialectic. In the material realm there are three overarching dialectics between its ingredients people and nature:

- People and people;
- People and nature; and
- Nature and nature.

These are nature level dialectics – fundamental, but not total drivers of history. With land as their base they form society, its surround and in turn the base from which historical and dialectical materialism spring. It is important to recognise that although analysis starts in material, it doesn't end there. As people and nature interact each of the material dialectics produce societal level properties:

- People and people produces politics;
- People and nature produces economics; and
- Nature and nature produces ecology.

Politics and economics are the summation of human activities of society, with ecology inside and surrounding them. Inside each of these material properties, there is a principal societal level dialectic:

- Politics   – no state or state
- Economics   – industry or pre-industry
- Ecology   – life or death[7]

Interactions between people and nature are not all the same. They each have a particular quality about them and contribute to the formation of particular types of society. These can be good or bad for particular people and nature. The quality of these interactions produces properties of material properties and the pattern of these

---

[7] Where organisms are composed of a multiplicity of elements, life is dominance of active over decaying elements at the microscopic level and death vice versa.

cultural level 'properties of properties' are derived from societal principles. Societal principles derived from:

- People and people interactions (politics) produce particular ideologies;
- People and nature interactions (economics) produce particular philosophies;
- Nature and nature interactions (ecology) produce manifestations of Nature's intelligence;

Ideology and philosophy are the summation of human ideas at the level of culture, with nature's intelligence inside and surrounding them. Intelligence inherent in the movement in matter causes it to encroach at the level of ideas, providing the basis for nature's intelligence at the boarder of societal and cultural levels. Nature's intelligence is a 'property of property', but since nature is not alive (trying to survive), it is not ideas. Inside each of these 'properties of properties' there is a principal cultural level dialectic:

- Ideology   - Humanism or exploitation
- Philosophy   - Science or mysticism
- Nature's intelligence - Known or unknown.

These 9 dialectics: 3 operating at the material level, 3 societal and 3 cultural, 10 if the universal philosophical dialectic is included are all inside nature forming one unified whole driving history forward. Culture is the outcome of history. The material dialectics are primary, give life to societal and cultural dialectics, which in turn come back to reshape material. Despite the immense power of society and culture, they are fundamentally dependent upon material, whilst material does not depend on them. Nature can survive without people and societies, neither of which can exist without nature.

3.1.3 Nature: its material and matspiritual contents
People are an inseparable part of nature. People are nature, meaning their interactions are varieties of nature and nature with qualitative differences. This means people, nature, politics, economics, society, ecology, ideology, philosophy, nature's intelligence and culture are inseparable, forming one unified whole with nature as its container. Material operates at the level of nature; 'properties of material' at the level of society; and 'properties of properties' at the level of culture,

each related and inseparable from the others. Everything is inside nature - there is no possibility of being outside.

Nature is infinite, meaning no matter how much we know, we can never know all. One aspect of nature's intelligence occupies the unbridgeable gap between what is known and what there is. It is in one manifestation the movement within the unknown and is beyond rational thought. Philosophy, the highest level of human thinking is unable to explain it, merely contrasting it with material. The next level below is ideological (Nkrumah, 2009, p. 56). Philosophical and ideological thinking are manifested i.e. put into societal practice through ideological instruments (Nkrumah, 2009, p. 59). The overarching ideological instruments are politics and economics. Within and between them are contained all other ideological instruments.

History Culture & Logical Types

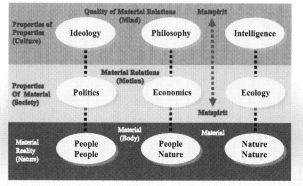

Brother Omowale

At the same time nature's intelligence is inside and surrounds ideology, philosophy and culture; ecology is inside and surrounds politics, economics and society. Ideology is inside philosophy, philosophy inside politics, politics inside economics and economics inside society. A people's society rests on their land which demarcates the area of nature they occupy. Politics and economics operate in society and form the base of culture. They also produce ideology and philosophy which operate at the cultural level. Culture is the sum total and container of all activities and ideas of people – it holds people activities (base) and ideas (contents) together.

People are the base of politics and politics the base of ideology. Nature is the base of economics and economics the base of philosophy. Nature is the base of ecology and ecology the base of nature's intelligence. Politics and economics infused with and surrounded by ecology make up society. Ideology and philosophy surrounded at their base by nature's intelligence make up culture. Society is the base of culture. Life belongs to nature, activities to society and ideas to culture. Culture is the outcome of history. As the cultural container - itself contained in nature - travels through time, history is left in its wake. History is the record of culture, the cultural mark of particular peoples in space-time.

3.1.4 Historical and dialectical materialism

At the heart of materialist methodology are the analytical tools historical and dialectical materialism. Predicated on science, historical materialism is the method of gathering relevant facts for analysis. The 3 material level dialectics provide the data/relevant facts, making the deployment of historical materialism possible. Predicated on philosophy, dialectical materialism is the process for correctly interpreting those facts. It utilises dialectics at the natural, societal and cultural levels to provide a framework allowing sense to be made of raw facts. The tools are scientific because they were developed as a result of observing the patterns of behaviour of matter, i.e. nature or the universe. This approach produces a number of materially based universal/natural laws, which further enhance the ability to contextualise and make sense of raw data i.e. historical material.

3.2 History: Masses contribution to time
3.2.1 History: a dimension of time

Nature and human beings are material, so too are the physical activities of human beings. Their activities produce *matspiritual* ideas and emotions, principles, parties, classes, societies etc. at one level and philosophy, ideology, politics, economics, culture etc. at another. All of this material and *matspiritual* activity stands together as one unified inseparable whole. That inseparable whole is matter (Material and *Matspiritual*).

Matter cannot and does not stand still. It is constantly on the move both internally at the atomic level and externally in nature. The measurement of that movement is what we call time. *Time is the measurement of movement of material*. It therefore depends on material for its existence and even though time and space (i.e. matter) are everywhere (i.e. eternal/infinite), time is inside matter (not separate from it) – in much the same way that wherever you find water, you also find its sub-components H_2O.

Time is multi-dimensional in the sense *we live in and are surrounded by time in - the present*. There was time before and we can be certain that there is more to come, even if we can't be certain of the details because it is a category of matter that: (i) never dies; and (ii) is always moving and changing. It is on this basis that we can look into the future and make projections, even though we lack the capacity or knowhow to make predictions with accuracy, on a consistent basis. *The certainty of time to come is what we call – the future*. Like nature/matter/space, time was before people and it contained people before present people. *Time which has already past, containing past activities of people is what we call history. History is a dimension of time*.

Human beings are therefore not only surrounded by time in the present, but by its past and future dimensions also. The relationship between the past, present and future can be variously summarised as:

Past	Present	Future
There and then	Here and now	Where and when
Yesterday	Today	Tomorrow
Has happened	Is happening	May happen
Were	Are	Will be
Ancestors	People	Descendants
Have lived	Alive	Yet to live
Elders	Adults	Children
Historical	Contemporary	Projected
Memory	Action	Purpose
Information	Analysis	Strategy
Reflect	Do	Plan
History	Culture	Vision

Time and its categories: past present and future are *matspiritual* categories of matter, containing information relevant to the lives and future existence of human beings. Also since time is relative, our experience of it varies according to our location in space/matter/nature i.e. our specific environment. Physical space i.e. nature/the universe is the material base of time, giving it its fundamental meaning.

The relationships of: (i) people with people; and (ii) people with nature together create society and culture, which as they travel through time, leave history in their wake. People, their history and environment are one organic whole. It is impossible to properly understand human beings unless they are considered together with their environment, history, culture and vision. No human activity falls outside nature, society, culture, history, vision and their contents. As human activities travel through time, people create ideas and emotions impacting their consciousness.

History: Dimension of Time

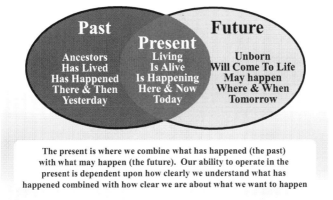

The present is where we combine what has happened (the past) with what may happen (the future). Our ability to operate in the present is dependent upon how clearly we understand what has happened combined with how clear we are about what we want to happen

Brother Omowale

Since activities that have already happened cannot be relived, it is material objects and activities plus ideas and emotions generated that live on. It is material clues, coupled with the activities, ideas and emotions of people amassed over time which constitute history. Social history is therefore a people's total material and **matspiritual** activities and experiences in whatever environments faced, from their origin to the present. It is made by all, not some of the people. The masses are the makers of history.

3.2.2 The masses are the makers of history

Capitalism focuses historical attention on particular individuals or small groups. 'Great' individuals are presented as icons and history is denoted by the reigns of 'kings', 'queens', 'presidents', 'prime ministers' whose identities become labels for particular eras. By ignoring those without 'superstar roles', the impression is given that:

- Individuals can make history by themselves;
- Others weren't involved; and

- Others don't matter.

No individual can make history by themselves since no individual is capable of making themselves. Everyone is dependent on others i.e. the collective for existence (parents/ancestors) - collectives create individuals. Nothing starts with individuals - at their beginning is a collective. Nor can individuals create collectives. Individuals cannot even create other individuals by themselves. There must be an appropriate partner to give life to another (their child). Individuals and collectives are both essential to each other's existence, but **the collective** (through its capacity to produce individuals) **is more powerful and superior to the individual**.

As individuals come together their collective power grows more rapidly than the number of individuals in the group. Collective power is greater than the sum of individuals within. Collectives are more powerful than collections of individuals and generate extra power from which individuals within can benefit. Collectives have greater duration than individuals. Individuals live for a lifetime, collective's progress towards infinity. Individuals' life spans are contained in the collective's experience, forming only a tiny part. **Collectives are infinitely wiser than individuals**.

Individuals are really a particular expression of the collective. Therefore, historical contributions made by individuals are really expressions of the collective. All individual expressions come from the collective - the masses are the makers of history. Each individual also has a collective history - collective activity of ancestors. Any activity of individuals automatically include the involvement of the collective that produced them and the further back in the individual's ancestral line, the greater the collective involvement – **the masses make history over time**.

Individuals are also influenced by others - non-relatives. Doctors save lives. Teachers share information. Social factors or collectively produced ideas contribute to the individual's understanding of and participation in the world and guide their behaviour. Those ideas are automatically part of the individual's actions, adding to the number of people involved. Furthermore, since each one of the individual's ancestors also learned from and were influenced and guided by multiple others, their contributions are also present in the individual's actions. All individual contributions to history have a history, inevitably involving masses through:

- Physical biological dependencies;
- Activities of people that kept them and their ancestors alive when we were not in a position to sustain themselves; and
- The body of ideas collectively developed through culture which increases the common reservoir of knowledge.

At time of writing, the fastest runner in the history of humanity is the genuinely talented Usain Bolt. There's no doubting his ability, but did he really do it by himself? No! His parents gave him life. His family added to his nurturing as did his schools. His coaches trained him, training partners ran with him, medics helped him heal when injured. Somebody cut the grass for him to train, cleaned the toilets for his convenience, made the spikes and kit he wore as child and adult. Others organised the events he participated in as a child, built the TV's he watched his heroes on, built the cars, buses, trains, boats and planes he travelled to events on. Each stadium he competed in, hotel slept in, home lived in was built and peopled by a multiplicity.

He lost to hundreds of people in races before beating hundreds in return, all of whom added to his experience. Each race he was in required scores of officials to measure, document and ratify performances. Media and publicity required thousands of people and millions watched. Each and every one on this incomplete list had thousands of ancestors who contributed and millions of ancestral influences. His achievement is unique and special, his ability exceptional, but without the collective it would never have occurred. The masses made that history and gave him a deserved key role in it. The masses are an inseparable part of nature which fortunately, didn't interrupt his progress with an earthquake or something less spectacular. *The masses are the makers of history*.

3.2.3 History develops in phases
History is made by people, not kings and queens, but by masses of people. People make history through interacting with other people and nature - through production. History develops in phases and those phases are determined by production relations. Put simply, the

relationship between people and land (where land is defined to include all that is on it and in it i.e. all means of production) forms a key part of the driving force of history.

Within this framework there are 6 known historical phases (Nkrumah, 1980a, p. 13). In chronological terms these are: communalism, slavery, feudalism, capitalism, socialism and communism. Communalism, slavery, feudalism and capitalism are absolute indisputable historical facts in the sense they have been or are currently in existence.

Phases of History Defined

Afrika	Europe	Philosophy	Ideology	State	Agriculture	Industry
Communalism	Communalism	Materialist	Humanist	No	Yes	No
	Slavery	Idealist	Exploitation	Yes	Yes	No
	Feudalism	Idealist	Exploitation	Yes	Yes	No
Slavery		Idealist	Exploitation	Yes	Yes	No
	Capitalism 1	Idealist	Exploitation	Yes	Yes	Yes
Colonialism		Idealist	Exploitation	Yes	Yes	No
	Capitalism 2	Idealist	Exploitation	Yes	Yes	Yes
Neo-colonialism		Idealist	Exploitation	Yes	Yes	No
Socialism	Socialism	Materialist	Humanist	No	Yes	Yes
Communism	Communism	Materialist	Humanist	No	Yes	Yes

Brother Omowale

The longest phase of history by far is communalism. It accounts for more than 90% of human existence. Communalism occupied the moral high ground, but because production was so low people were forced to live at subsistence level. It was a wretched existence. There was no advantage in starving in an environment of high morals which is what undermined it as a system.

In Europe humanity descended morally from communalism into the system and historical phase slavery. Though morally bankrupt, slavery created a new wealthy elite. That elite further entrenched its position by stealing land for themselves. When they controlled their own people's labour, together with the land, they created a new morally backward system and historical phase – feudalism.

The feudal lords amassed great wealth and used it to export their moral backwardness in search of even more wealth. They imposed the morally backward system and historical phase slavery on Afrika and her people. This brought them more wealth than they could possibly have imagined. They then used that massive wealth to industrialise giving birth to the current morally backward system and historical phase - capitalism. Industrial capitalists used their massively increased stolen wealth and power to colonise Afrika and 'repaid' by artificially disqualifying her from industrialising.

Imperialism's Second World War was a massive struggle between greedy capitalists for wealth they had stolen from Afrika and other parts of the world. In that process, finance capitalists defeated industrial capitalists and ushered in a second phase of capitalism in which they dominated.

They used their newly stolen wealth and power to impose neo-colonialism on Afrika and are currently stealing great fortunes from Afrikan people, at even greater human cost. As a result of having been artificially disqualified from industrialising, Afrika's historical route has followed the path communalism, slavery, colonialism and currently neo-colonialism.

For the last 100 years, socialism has been edging its way into existence, beaten back by its dominant foe capitalism. Communism has never operated anywhere on earth. It is an anticipated phase of history yet to come. The anticipated projection of history – socialism, will eventually overcome its foe capitalism.

At this point humanity will begin recovery of its lost moral ground and Afrika will successfully industrialise, thereby rejoining and recalibrating the global trajectory of human history. When socialism becomes the dominant phase of history and its system sufficiently matured, it is expected to create necessary conditions for its hand over to communism.

Communism is the phase of history expected to take over from socialism. It will retain the moral high ground recovered by socialism. That is the same moral high ground Afrika and the rest of humanity experienced for 90% of its existence under communalism. It will also retain and heighten the industrialisation process i.e. advanced technological development ushered in during capitalism and expanded/redirected during socialism. Finally, it will rid the world of oppressive state systems, restoring human freedom, liberty and dignity. Communism is the expected historical destiny of the whole of humanity, including Afrika.

3.3 History, consciousness and forward planning
3.3.1 Memory and History
Memory to the individual is equivalent to history of a people. When an individual loses memory, they become stupefied. A person with Alzheimer's for instance ceases to function as normal. They forget themselves and those around them including family, friends and enemies. They lose the ability to do for themselves including, feeding, bodily functions dressing etc. They lose all sense of principles, morals, pride, right from wrong, leading to an erosion of conscience as well as consciousness.

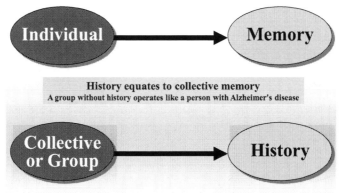

Brother Omowale

Having no sense of danger, they are as likely to self-harm as help themselves and no sense of enemy leaves them open to others intent on harming them. What becomes their total dependence on others further renders them, not only vulnerable, but impotent in the face of enemies, who can abuse them with impunity as they ultimately lose their understanding of the importance of survival and regress to death. In a sense they become useless to themselves and others.

All of the above are symptoms of a people who lose their collective memory i.e. their history. They increasingly cease to function effectively and under capitalism become prey to be abused i.e. exploited and oppressed. Capitalism takes their weakness a stage further and implants false history detrimental to their interests to reorientate and use them for its diabolical purposes. It teaches them to love it and its oppression and hate themselves and their kind, alienating them from their objective best interests. They become internally self-destructive and suicidal, attacking and killing themselves in support of their capitalist enemy. They are doomed to extinction unless they can change this pattern by remembering their true history and who and what they and their enemy are.

Alzheimer's is a disease for which there is currently no confirmed cure. Lack of historical knowledge is by contrast solvable through education. This confers a revolutionary duty on all Afrikan people to ensure that each of their number is educated to understand correct and truthful history of Afrikan people at home and in the Diaspora, together with tools and aptitude to correctly learn, analyse and interpret it.

3.3.2 Consciousness: space and time dimensions
The first noticeable thing about an unconscious person is they're motionless – *they lack action*. Secondly, they don't know who, what, when or where they are – *they lack knowledge*. Fast asleep, they have no idea why they are where they are or where they're going – *they lack purpose*. Lack of past knowledge and future purpose is matched by impotence in the present. Memory, action and purpose are essential components of the time dimension of consciousness. *Consciousness requires: (i) past knowledge; (ii) present action; and (iii) future purpose*.

Human consciousness in the space dimension must have a material base i.e. a body. If there is no body there can be no human consciousness. That body must also act. If it is inanimate, it is a sign of its unconsciousness. The animate body must also have a brain that thinks. If it exists and acts without thinking, it is instinctive but not conscious. Thinking must be positive/constructive. If it is negative/destructive, it works against progress and becomes the diametric opposite of consciousness, qualitatively worse that unconsciousness. In the time dimension consciousness requires knowledge of the past, action in the present and purpose in the future, giving human consciousness at least 9 dimensions.

Human consciousness (individual and collective) requires an animate body guided by thought. Those thoughts must be guided by comprehensive relevant accurate knowledge of the past and a clear constructive vision of the future provoking purposeful actions in the present through intelligent thinking. A conscious people are a united body with agreed processes to facilitate collective thinking and decision making that allows them jointly and consensually to move forward despite disagreements. Their united body is material i.e. at the level of nature, their thinking - politics and at even higher levels ideology and philosophy; their 'march forward' – action – is economic. They will have a thorough understanding of their history and destiny and act vigorously in the present to achieve destiny, whilst showing care for themselves, others and nature.

Consciousness Space & Time

	Past	Present	Future
Knowledge			
Action		Consciousness focused in the present through actions	
Purpose			

Brother Omowale

Our bodies and actions are in the present. They cannot be in the past or future. However, our thoughts are unrestrained and can draw from past ideas into the present, with ability to project into the future. To project is not to predict, but provoke the future. Physically we can't move between time dimensions, but mentally we can. Whilst we can't 'live in the past', we can remember. Memories can be assisted by historical material such as:

- Physical objects and relics, which at base level prove the existence of something from before;
- Recordings, books, photographs, statues etc, which give insight into past activities; and

- Procedures, processes and methodologies, which by repeating patterns from the past allow an understanding of things that went before.

We can project into the future and through visioning imagined desires. The clearer the vision, the greater is the likelihood of achieving it. Visions can be concretised and put into a measurable time frame by setting aims, objectives and targets which can be formed into strategies, tactics and operations constructed into plans. This must be founded on available material resources if the vision is to be realised.

3.3.3 History guides planning and planning guides action

Planning is the process of provoking history in an intended direction. It is an organised act of consciousness that helps codify ideas into a format allowing them to be practically put into action. There are a range of techniques to assist the process, none of which can be truly effective until the body i.e. the people, are unified into a functional collective. Its toolkit includes: strategy, tactics, operations, policy, aims, objectives, targets, monitoring and reviewing etc, organised and arranged to facilitate action towards an agreed purpose.

Planning Overview
Theory (Reflecting)

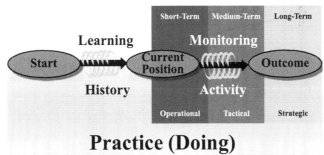

Practice (Doing)

Brother Omowale

Strategy includes an analysis of an organisation's grand strategic objectives in relation to its vision and the methods used to distribute and apply available resources to fulfil an organisation's overall purpose. **Tactics** complement an organisation's strategic objectives. They are concerned with the practical methods employed for achieving an organisation's vision. How organisations deploy resources in frontline activity are more specific, variable and flexible than strategy and should be continually adjusted to meet changes in frontline situations.

Policy advances strategy towards its vision. It is an internal force that creates vision, aims, objectives and targets and devises strategy, tactics and operations. It creates monitors and supports the implementation of the vision, within parameters of principles and values, ensuring resources are employed according to the plan. It determines what an organisation's management and staff can and cannot do and sets up protocols for operations.

Objective setting is the process of guiding or provoking shorter-term history in the envisioned direction. **Planning** is the process of noting which parts of history have and have not moved in the desired direction and adopting corrective or contingency processes to guide and revise actions to remain on or adjust course. **Activity** is the tangible and manifest making of history, ideally in the direction envisioned. **Monitoring** is the process of assessing what actually happened (historically) in order to decide which way to provoke or guide history to stay on or adjust course. Through it and the whole of this iterative process, ideas sharpen actions and actions sharpen ideas. It may also bring about practical even major alterations to the vision based on practicalities.

Planning is absolutely critical for making best use of history. It knits dimensions of time into a single format that can be collectively assessed and reviewed, positively impacting a people's consciousness. Sekou Toure expresses the connection as follows:

> "The past is the source which feeds conscience, and that conscience has a role in actualising in the present a portion of the past, in view of making it converge towards the future. This indicates that conscience is the sum experience (past) and knowledge (the present projected towards the future)." (Toure, No. 88, p. 56)

The present is where the past and future meet. We constantly live on the edge of both in the present. If we fail to take from the past and project into the future to achieve our desires, we neither understand history nor make good use of it. The present is where we combine what has happened (the past) with what may happen (the future). Our ability to operate in the present is dependent upon how clearly we understand what has happened combined with how clear we are about what we want to happen. History and plans can anchor actions the present.

Successful people do more than just act in the present. They bring their experience from the past into the present which grounds their actions. They bring their common vision from the future into the present to give direction to their actions. It is when actions are grounded by a correct interpretation of history and planning for collective vision that actions are purposefully advantageous.

Successful people draw into the present: (i) the labour of all of their people as an effectively organised co-operative collective force; (ii) all the resources of nature they have the power to direct and influence - ordering, prioritising and scheduling those resources as appropriate; (iii) all the relevant lessons they have learned from the past; (iv) the collectively agreed vision and outcomes they desire for an improved future and plan to make them happen. They act vigorously on them in the present, drawing in as many of the resources of time and space as they can and systematically apply their organised collective labour to them in a co-operative manner to make life better for themselves, others and to the benefit of nature.

Planning Cycle

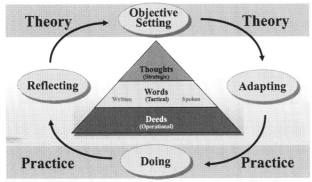

Brother Omowale

Understanding history is much more than recalling facts, incidents and stories from the past. It is important to understand the past, present and future in terms of historical phases to clarify where you came from, are currently and are going. Afrika is currently in the neo-colonial phase. This is the form the global capitalist phase takes in the continent. It is doing tremendous harm to Afrikan people and ecology, conferring on Afrikan people a duty to bring it to an urgent end by advancing to the next historical phase. Whilst the detailed operations are unknown at this point, it is known that the next historical phase is Scientific Socialism for Afrika and the world. In Afrika, it will manifest a Pan-Afrikanism. It will not occur by chance, the people must act to bring it into being.

Revolution is not achieved by leaders (individuals). People (the collective) are its vital ingredient. It requires the involvement of not some but all of the people, because only the force of the people united is capable of defeating the power of states and in Afrika's case the external forces backing them. The people will not take up their duty to themselves, their descendants and nature until or unless they understand their current situation with all its consequences and injustice. Where the people don't understand, the role of the revolutionary is to bring them to that understanding and organise them to act towards achieving the next phase of history.

3.3.4 Conscious Afrikan people
Conscious Afrikan people know who they are. They understand they are Afrikan people, are emphatically proud of it and are able to recognise and work with their kind. They know, understand and practice traditional Afrikan philosophy and ideology as custodians. They prioritise health, embrace learning as a lifelong continuous process and develop good relations between themselves, others and nature. They understand that as a collective they are more powerful than their sum as disparate individuals and unite as an organised force. They understand that as a united organised force, they are the masses that make history.

Conscious Afrikan people know their position and condition in nature, how they should be living and understand the difference. They know Afrika is the richest land in the world and by regaining control of it they become the richest and most powerful people. They know how to plan and interact with nature for their advancement, progressing from where they are to a better future. At the societal level they understand their politics and economics, at the cultural their ideology and philosophy and the history and trajectory of all four. They understand that political

90

unity drives economic prosperity, because over emphasis on economics fosters exposure to external divide and rule.

Conscious Afrikan people know where they come from. They know their history, as more than an assemblage of facts and stories. They understand history as process containing their cultural patterns, principles and phases from which they can learn and grow. They understand the meaning of consciousness in theory and practice; that they must absolutely master their history and draw lessons from it; they must use it to clarify exactly what they want and expect from the future and vigorously act in the present to achieve it. They know their success will create a better world for themselves and others.

They understand that history operates in phases; know how they reached their current phase; understand the current phase is capitalism, manifested as neo-colonialism in Afrika which is bad for them; they will not tolerate anything short of an exploitation free Afrika with an ever improving quality of life for themselves and their descendants; know the next phase Scientific Socialism will be good for them; know they can only get to Scientific Socialism when they consciously recognise themselves as the masses that make Afrikan history, organise and act on collectively agreed plans to make it happen; they know this next phase of Afrika's history will only come about when they unite and act to make it happen.

Drawing into Present Actions

	Past	Present	Future
Knowledge	History Culture Principles Methodologies Positives		
Action		Actions Operations Targets Reviews Monitoring	
Purpose			Vision Aims Objectives Strategy Planning

Brother Omowale

They understand that scientific socialism will bring them a step closer to recovering traditional Afrikan culture; that it comprises: (i) materialism - Afrika's nature respecting traditional philosophy; (ii) humanism –

Afrika's people respecting traditional ideology; (iii) a single centralised continental wide unified people's state for governance; and (iv) industrialisation aimed at meeting their needs. They understand that although states are alien to Afrikan culture, they will have to tolerate it for a period to prevent previous exploiters from recapturing Afrika and re-impoverishing them. It will provide political protection for other elements of traditional Afrikan culture – philosophical, ideological and economic, whilst Afrika recovers.

They understand that there are even greater benefits ahead of them than Scientific Socialism – good as it is. Their conscious mass action in the Scientific Socialism phase will see them progress to an even better phase of Afrikan and world history – Communism. Communism is the future embodiment of traditional Afrikan Communalism. They have identical methodologies and principles. Their political (i.e. no state), ideological (i.e. respect for people) and philosophical (i.e. respect for nature) approaches are exactly the same. They differ only in economics. Communism will have advanced industrialisation; communalism did not.

This will elevate Afrikan people from living respectfully with others in poverty, to being materially rich and still respectful. It will be traditional Afrika updated for the future. The only condition will be that we use our industrialisation in a manner that is in harmony with nature so as to enhance its rejuvenating capacity, rather than pollute or destroy it. If we look after nature, it will look after us. Communism is the cultural return of Afrika to a position of greatness in the world, greater than ever before achieved.

Culture
For Revolution

Chapter 4

4 Culture for revolution
4.1 Culture, life and levels
4.1.1 Culture: inseparable from life
The foundation of culture is life. Everything that lives produces culture and therefore has culture. It is life that gives culture its existence. Culture is a derivative and by-product of life. The fundamental purpose of culture is the preservation of life i.e. survival of the living. Culture preserves itself by preserving lives of the living. Culture depends on life.

Culture is the synthesis between space, time and living things, which can only be located in space and time. The higher purpose of culture is to solve problems of living things. Different categories of living things have different levels of success in solving their problems. In that sense, they have different levels of culture.

Unsuccessful cultures are, or on their way to extinction. Successful culture is therefore the culture that best utilises the resources of space and time in solving the problems of its living producers. The cultures of successful life forms do more than survive, they actively thrive. To our knowledge, the most successful cultures are those of human beings. One of the signs of this is they generally live longer than other animal life forms on earth.

4.1.2 Culture has four levels
It should by now be clear that from a philosophical materialist vantage point, nature and people form the base for developing and correctly understanding any social issue or concept. It follows that in order to

understand culture, so far as it relates to society, an understanding of the operations of people in their area of nature is required.

At the level of nature, culture is produced by living things in motion. At the level of society it is produced by people alive in motion. It is the sum total of people's experience. It incorporates the entirety of their ideas amassed over time: their economics, politics, ideology and philosophy, founded on the people themselves and the physical area of nature they inhabit. People and nature are material i.e. lower level ingredients of culture. Their respective ideas i.e. economics, politics, ideology, philosophy and histories are its *matspiritual* higher level ingredients. People and nature are the integral inseparable basis and source of their culture, with their ideas forming its centre.

Notice that culture does not begin with people. The first requirement of culture is life. Wherever there is life there is culture. Any and everything that is alive has culture. Culture thrives on the living. From this we can deduce that merely being alive represents the lowest level of culture. People on life support machines or foetuses are examples of this category. They have life, but are totally unable to self-protect. Instinct and senses are either completely lost or sufficiently depressed to be inoperative and life is completely dependent on powers external to the living thing.

The second level is instinct/survival which is largely taken for granted because it doesn't require conscious thinking. At its height it amounts to reactive level decision making, reliant on senses. This is where the cultured entity automatically (i.e. without having to think), seeks to protect and extend its life. There is an instinctive level to economics and politics; survival is an economic activity for all living things – it is instinctive.

Plants are alive with instinct. If we place plants in a darkened area with a pinhole of light, they will sense it and grow toward it. They realise that sunlight is essential and by moving towards it, they are preserving and extending their lives. Plants have culture. Animals are also alive with instinct. Breathing, heartbeat, blood flow are economic, all happening without conscious attention; yet survival depends on their correct operation.

The highest expression of politics and economics at this level comes in responses to sensed danger. There are three basic responses: fight, flight and freeze – the choice made may determine survival. Economics is the action to determine survival; politics is the choice of action taken to achieve the desired economic outcome – survival. Politics therefore determines economic outcomes i.e. just as thinking (at this level reactive) directs doing or thoughts direct actions, politics directs economics – politics is the thinking part of economics i.e. doing. Animals too have culture. Though not always successfully, at a basic level, both plants and animals can and will protect their lives.

Human beings distinguished themselves from other animals by the difference in their response to danger, manifested through their mastery of fire. Whilst all other animals literally run away, humans overcame their fear and learned to control it, putting it to use in their service. Fire is scientifically applied to run cars, heat homes, cook food and power energy plants etc. These are indicators of the third level which is marked by the ability to produce. Humans have a higher level of consciousness than other creatures and a correspondingly more sophisticated culture. They rose from four legs to two freeing their front limbs for handling. This assisted their ability to create tools, leading to an exponential increase in their ability to apply their labour to production.

As they produce things that nature would otherwise not, their economics becomes more overtly recognisable. No other animal on earth can interact with nature to produce sophisticated artistic and scientific creations as expressions of their economics. Their politics is similarly depressed through amongst other things, a lack of sophisticated language. Ideologically and philosophically they are not sophisticated enough to attempt the domination of nature and are therefore automatically in harmony with it.

There is no end or outer limit to time or space. Wherever there is time, there is space and wherever space, time. Space which is nature by another name is in perpetual motion and time, the measurement of its movement. Even though time and space are everywhere, *matspiritual* time is inside and dependent on material nature. Since they are everywhere and nothing can exist outside of time and nature, it follows that the infinity of dimensions must be within the first four i.e. within time and nature. Since time is inside nature, **matspirit** is inside nature. Nature, which is fundamentally material is inseparable from its inner **matspiritual** properties – it is everything.

Our senses are not designed to connect with **matspirit**; this is the domain of human conscience and corresponding consciousness. In Sekou Toure's words:

> "... multi-dimensional or polyvalent hyperspace is the produce of the conscience ..." (*Revolution,* No. 88, Toure, p. 110)

Human senses i.e. sight, hearing, smell, taste and touch allow engagement with aspects of nature. Sight and hearing engage its wave aspects; taste and smell, particles; and touch both. Conscience and consciousness facilitate a deeper level of engagement with **matspiritual** elements embedded in nature. In much the same way humans devised clocks to scientifically engage **matspiritual** time, the potential to utilize material objects (i.e. tools) as means of engaging other **matspiritual** dimensions is real.

Books for instance, allow engagement with economics, politics, ideology, philosophy and a whole range of **matspiritual** dimensions. Similarly, equations facilitate an engagement with pure mathematics. One such tool specifically designed to assist the recovery of Afrikan culture is Kwame Nkrumah's *Consciencism: Philosophy and Ideology of De-Colonization and Development with particular reference to the African Revolution.*

Human beings are an inseparable part of nature. They interact with each other through the communication of thoughts, words and deeds. Furthermore, human beings interact with nature in everything they do. They must breathe, drink and eat. As they interact, nature interacts with nature. Rain falls to the earth; flora and fauna draw water from the soil; the excess flows from the rivers to the sea; water vaporises, rising up to make clouds. This is interaction. Plants and animals reproduce as another form of interaction. Nature interacts with nature with or without people. People have consciousness and are a part of nature, meaning it must have at least the level of consciousness of the people it contains. Nature interacts with itself and its living parts, which contain a level of consciousness.

Nature is interacting with itself all the time as a plethora of changes in the universe. Whilst people may dominate some aspects of these changes, have a peripheral influence on others, they are not even aware of all of them and are not their cause. Their most potent tool in the vastness of nature is the discovery of its natural laws. People are surrounded by nature's changes and laws and in many cases rely on them for their survival and existence. They are essentially limited to existing within the parameters that nature and its universal laws permit.

Nature is the producer i.e. the giver of life to all that there is: bio-organisms, plants, animals etc. It is the context within which all life exists, marking the fourth level of 'culture'. It does not however follow that nature is alive, life can come out of death. Nature is neither dead nor alive, it simply exists as the arena of the living and dead. Operating at a level lower than impotent life, the continuous movement inherent in nature's non-living parts is an outcome of nature's intelligence.

Nature surrounds, is bigger and more powerful than people. It also entirely fills people (i.e. atomic level) and is therefore inside them. It gave birth to people and provides all they need for their survival. Nature is infinite; it is so vast that humanity can never know it in its entirety. They cannot even survive in the majority of what they know of it. They cannot even look at the sun, and though they can harness aspects of it, cannot control it. Human domination of nature is therefore impossible.

Furthermore, people depend on nature for their life sustaining environment, but nature doesn't depend on people. If the activities of people alter their part of nature beyond certain limits, they make themselves extinct. Though not alive, nature's intelligence impacts all living cultures.

The culture of people is therefore subject to nature's intelligence. Nature is a greater power on earth and in the universe than human beings who are little more than a spec in comparison. Human beings cannot just do as they like. They are bound by their need to survive, to live in a way that is compatible with nature and her requirements. Ultimately, whilst they can manipulate nature, they must live in harmony with nature as there is no possibility that they can dominate it.

Levels of Consciousness

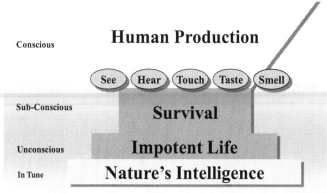

Brother Omowale

Many points flow from the above analysis, but the essential one for our current purpose is to highlight the fact that culture operates at four levels:

- Nature's intelligence;
- Impotent life;
- Survival; and
- Human production.

The focus in this paper will be on the fourth level – human production.

4.2 Ideas: Essence of culture
4.2.1 Ideas come from nature

If we examine the relationship between ideas and actions by observing a human being, we notice every action is preceded by an idea. The person must, at some level, think before they act. The idea or thought will be present even if they are not conscious it. It is therefore tempting to conclude that ideas are the source of people's actions. However, if we drew such a conclusion we would be wrong because although they precede, they are not source.

Our error would result from looking at the person in isolation from environment i.e. nature or the universe. Nature exited long before humans who are part of nature. They are conceived, born, live and die in it. They cannot be separated from or outside it. Indeed, nothing is outside of it; it has no outer limit, no end. There is one reality i.e. nature or the universe and humans (and everything else) are part of it. Therefore in order to properly understand the relationship between ideas and actions the person must be viewed as part of her/his environment i.e. nature or the universe.

Nature: Source of Ideas

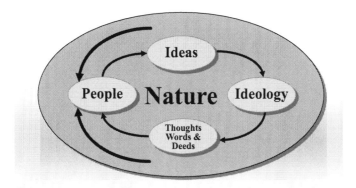

Brother Omowale

Ideas are formed by circumstances of people's lives as perceived through senses. For instance, they do not suddenly have the idea to drink. That idea has a history. Nature is constantly impacting people in many ways including by extracting water; they go to the toilet, sweat etc. Eventually they reach a point when they do not have enough water in their bodies. As their brain realises it triggers thirst. Thirst gives the idea that they want to drink and they quench it.

The idea of drinking, which came from within as thirst, was preceded by the material process of nature extracting water. Nature's forces act on people who respond by producing ideas – it is source. This confirms material aspects precede *matspiritual* ones; from material comes *matspiritual*; *matspiritual* is built on material reality and nature is source of both ideas and actions. In this example, material – nature's extraction of water, was source for the *matspiritual* – the person's idea of drinking. Also the idea could not have come into being without the aid of the person's brain – a material entity. Sekou Toure sums up the process as follows:

"Therefore nature acts on man, space acts on man, time acts

on man, society things animals act on man, man acts on himself. All these actions that man undergoes and that he perceives through his senses are transformed in him into idea. To man, idea is the continuation and the result of action engendered upon his social environment and of the action exercised by his physical, human and upon his social environment." (Toure, No. 88, p. 133).

We must view all human actions in the context of nature (not isolated from it) if we are to properly understand. It is impossible to understand humans unless considered together with environment. The material base of culture i.e. people and environment (nature) are one organic whole; society and its primary contents (people and nature) are one organic whole. Ideas come from interactions in the material base.

4.2.2 Ideas are the centre of culture
Kwame Nkrumah breaks matter into 3 constituent categories which he calls logical types. He explains there is matter in the physical sense, with properties beyond the solely physical and those properties also have properties, making the third. Matter is another label for nature, or a microcosmic reflection of it, meaning there is: (i) nature at the material level; (ii) properties of material nature; and (iii) properties of properties of material nature.

People and nature constitute the material category. As they interact they produce politics and economics which in turn produces their society in nature. Society is not completely material, being made real by interactions between people and nature. Society and its interactions are therefore properties of material nature at **Matspiritual** level.

Whilst it is technically possible for a person to act without thinking i.e. reflex, it is not possible to act without ideas. Thoughts are processed ideas consciously engaging the brain. The brain can however, process ideas unconsciously or subconsciously such as breathing, heartbeat etc. This means ideas are present in all actions.

Whilst people interact in nature producing politics, economics and society, they are simultaneously producing ideology and philosophy thereby producing culture at the level of ideas in their society. Culture though based on it, is not overtly material. It is made real by the ideas of people produced in their society in nature. Ideas – and their sum total, culture - are therefore properties of properties of material nature.

Cultural Layers

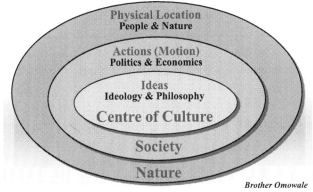

Brother Omowale

Society is based on nature and culture on society. The content of nature is living and dying things including people. Where organisms are composed of a multiplicity of elements, life is dominance of active over decaying elements at the microscopic level and death vice versa; nature is the arena of life and death. The content of society is specifically the activities of people; society is the arena of people activities. The content of a people's culture is their ideas; culture is the arena of ideas. In the logical type sense, people are the centre of nature, their actions (politics and economics) the centre of society and their ideas (ideology and philosophy) the centre of culture.

4.2.3 Ideology the centre of people's ideas
Viewed from another angle, people operate in nature at the level of society. As part of their operation they interact with other people and nature, producing political and economic actions. The manner in which they treat other people and nature produces ideological and philosophical ideas respectively.

Philosophical and ideological ideas are the core i.e. the centre of people's conscious ideas, but have to be wrapped in political and economic actions because there is no way to them other than through people and nature in the first instance and politics and economics in the second. At this level, ideology which is inside philosophy is the centre of human ideas and culture. However, without its political and economic clothing, no human culture can be complete and without people and nature, culture cannot be produced.

Another way to interpret this is if your culture's outer layers i.e. politics and economics are not up to standard, your cultural core i.e. ideology and philosophy cannot function properly. Antiquated politics and economics in the form of jigsaw puzzle pretend states and pre-industrial production methods are preventing core ideological and philosophical aspects of Afrikan culture from operating properly. This dysfunction invites better politically and economically organised external cultures to come and do with Afrikan people as they choose as their cultural core remains unprotected.

By way of analogy if ideology is likened to the inner self; philosophy the body; politics under garments; and economics clothes, the change from neo-colonialism to Scientific Socialism equates to keeping the inner-self and body intact, whilst changing both the under garments and clothes. If our clothes fail to protect us in the operational environment, we must improve them. Our politics and economics are not fit for the current phase of history - we are therefore bound to bring them up to date. Only then will our culture be intact and sufficiently protected to allow Afrikan people to flourish and take our true position in the world.

4.2.4 Nature's intelligence surrounds culture

At the level of nature, culture has an environment. The interaction of nature and nature produces ecology, on a level equivalent to society. Nature's intelligence is produced at a level equivalent to culture. It can be thought of as the culture of all living things and intelligence in all non-living movement - in that sense vaster than human life. The manner of nature's interaction with itself can be either life giving or taking (good or evil/"God" or "Devil"), producing what some might refer to as "spirituality", but to distinguish it from other interpretations, it will here be referred to as *nature's intelligence*, with its non-living aspects located outside culture and living aspects in it[8].

People cannot ordinarily make a connection with *nature's intelligence*,

---

[8] Non-human living things are another dimension of *nature's intelligence*, accessible via interaction with animals and plants.

because its basis is nature's interaction with nature and as soon as people enter the interaction they transform it into economics i.e. people interacting with nature. People are therefore superficially excluded from *nature's intelligence*. However humans are nature, which opens the possibility of their connecting with it as nature, as distinct people in nature.

This implies shutting down the element within them that distinguishes them from other known life forms – their consciousness. If they can achieve this, they can potentially tune in with nature in the sense that other creatures do. This would make their interaction ecological in character, mimicking nature's interaction with nature. In a conscious less i.e. meditative state, people may have the potential to connect or tune-in with *nature's intelligence*. If this is so, it potentially offers a scientific basis for explaining meditation and the human capacity to connect with nature's non-living intelligence.

From this perspective meditation can be viewed as a process whereby humans connect with the collective consciousness of all living things, even possibly all things that have and have not yet lived, through *nature's intelligence*. Such connection may help them better synchronise, understand and function within their environment i.e. nature. At this stage of human development, this hypothesis remains unproven.

4.2.5 Some general characteristics of culture
At the human level culture is the total material and *matspiritual* way of life of an entire people and their society. A people's culture incorporates the entire physical and moral wellbeing of their society developed over time. It underlies all of their society's experiences incorporating the totality of their thoughts, words and deeds. It is driven by the collective consciousness of that people, based on their interaction, among themselves, with others and nature. It acts on them, shaping and impacting the duration, quantity and quality of their lives as well as relationships between them and their capacity for production. It manifests as an emergent set of rules, mores and patterns of behaviour that unite and regulate their activities for the attainment of the aims of those who control their society.

People are the producers of culture and the culture created by a particular people is their development, which makes all cultures unique. Cultures vary according to factors such as location, historical development, conscience and power and also contain sub-cultures, sometimes with divergent interests. However, no culture is a perfect finished whole, like history it is always evolving, developing, unfolding and expanding.

A people's collective consciousness is the prime mover of their culture, which in turn guides their conscience, consciousness and activities. Collectives create individuals, but individuals cannot create collectives, making the production of culture a group phenomenon. Individuals receive their culture from the collective and receive more from culture than they can give to it. Culture is collective and has mass character. Individuals merely inherit, live in, contribute to and pass it on.

This tells us that culture is transferable. People transmit culture through language (verbal and physical). Language is the container of transmitted ideas and ideas the centre of culture. Transmission of language is enhanced through media. People consume culture through education, which must develop both actions and ideas to be effective. As they consume culture they are transformed as people and develop their capacity to contribute more effectively to culture. Education is therefore a necessity for any society seeking progress. Nothing can be done without cultural consumption and fundamentally culture is manifested by patterns of people's activities. Culture's physical operation is experienced through their senses in society.

In this historical phase, two opposed and antagonistic sub-cultures typically develop in societies, one which sees human beings as an end in and of themselves representing positive progressive revolutionary culture and another which sees them as tools - negative regressive and reactionary. These opposing cultures of the masses and oppressors, fight within each individual as well as within society and the world.

The masses conflict with the oppressors to achieve their freedom and this clash (class struggle) drives the history of humanity forward. *Class struggle is the principle factor driving the history of any human group*; it is expressed in all societies and nobody exists outside a certain class. The economic interests of social classes condition their member's approaches and attitudes to culture. On the world stage at the level of society (i.e. essence), this is the clash between socialism and capitalism. In Afrika in the current phase, the antagonistic sub-cultures are Pan-Afrikanism and neo-colonialism; they represent the form and their conflict drives Afrika forward/backward.

The oppressor's capitalist culture realises that it is not strong enough to hold back the united workers of the world resolutely struggling for freedom. It cannot even hold back the united Afrikan agricultural and industrial workers. It therefore implicitly operates through a system of divide and rule in all external engagements – its neo-colonial expression. Internally, it internationalises its operations, which it now manages through corporate capitalist culture. At the base of all of this activity is land.

4.2.6 Traditional Afrikan Culture and Scientific Socialism
At the centre of culture are ideas, philosophical and ideological. Our philosophy is manifested in how we treat nature. If we treat nature as an end in its own right worthy of the upmost respect, we are materialists. If we treat it as a tool, a means to our end, we are idealists. Socialism is materialist, capitalism idealist. Afrikan philosophy is manifested through its traditional Afrikan spirituality. Afrikan spirituality posits 'spirits' as inculcated and inseparable from nature. It treats nature and its contents as its highest priority. Its 'Gods' are particular manifestations to be found and accessed in nature.

Traditional Afrikan spirituality is materialist because it connects with 'spirit' via nature rather than treating 'spirits' as abstract entities. Practitioners must engage with 'spirits' via natural objects. This calibre of engagement gives Afrikan spirituality a materialist foundation ripe for scientific methodology. Afrikan spirituality therefore inculcates within its practice an uncompromising respect for nature and its primacy. It accepts ideas as coming from nature and treats nature as source.

Our ideology is manifested in how we treat people. If we treat people as ends in their own right worthy of the upmost respect, we are humanists. If we treat them as tools, a means to our end, we are exploiting them. Humanism is the core principle of socialism, exploitation that of capitalism. The ideology of traditional Afrikan culture treats human beings as the highest priority within nature. Humanism is the natural outcome of this pattern of behaviour.

109

In traditional Afrikan culture, nature and its contents are the highest priority and people, the highest priority in nature. These materialist and humanist approaches are requirements of both traditional Afrikan culture and Scientific Socialism, making them consistent and compatible at philosophical and ideological levels. They concur at the levels of universal laws (philosophical) and core principles (ideological). At the highest levels traditional Afrikan culture and Scientific Socialism are one.

Afrika's Natural Systems

	Materialism (Philosophy) Respect for Nature	Humanism (Ideology) Respect for People	State (Politics) People's State	Industry (Economics) People's Industry
Traditional Afrika	Materialism	Humanism	No State	No Industry
Pan-Afrikanism	Materialism	Humanism	State	Industry
Scientific Socialism	Materialism	Humanism	State	Industry
Communism	Materialism	Humanism	No State	Industry

Brother Omowale

Differences between them are political and economic. There was never a time when Afrika was politically united. Nor was there a time when Afrika's production was industrially driven i.e. mass producing factories. Traditional Afrikan culture has never had a unified state structure or industrial production. A politically unified state and industry are requirements for Scientific Socialism. Introduction of a continental wide state and industrialisation under the sovereign control of Afrikan people transforms Afrikan communalism to Scientific Socialism. This means the essence i.e. centre of traditional Afrikan culture remains, whilst its form (political and economic societal layers) is updated for modern living. This is the mission of Pan-Afrikanism.

4.3 Culture from its material base
4.3.1 Three logical types in nature
All material has motion, but not all material is alive. Only living material can produce ideas, since ideas fundamentally exist for the preservation of life. There are three logical types inherent in nature and matter:

material; *movement* inherent in material; and *ideas* inherent in movement inside material. Movement and ideas cannot exit unless there is material to move. They are wholly dependent upon material for existence. They are internal to material in much the same way that muscles and the brain are internal to the live human body. Without a live body, there cannot be functioning muscle or brain.

There is no separation between material and *matspiritual* – they are really one. The first category of the *matspiritual* is really material – without which it cannot exist; the second motion; and third ideas. The way in which the terms are used here, material is made explicit and discrete to describe the first logical type and *matspiritual* used specifically to describe the second and third – the intangibles. Nature i.e. matter is composed of all 3, with time being a derivative of motion – time is inside nature i.e. inside space.

4.3.2 Nature moves everywhere all the time
At the atomic level material (the first logical type) is composed of particles. It is impossible for particles to remain still. They are in constant motion. Part of that motion is the source of atomic level waves – essential proof of material's continuous motion (the second logical type). Waves are a symptom of movement which is the source of this *matspiritual* category located inside material. The inseparability of the particle and wave functions of the atom has caused scientists to relabel them 'wavicles' rather than 'particles'.

Human beings have eyes and ears to see and hear waves, but these are restricted. They developed tools to gain glimpses of wave spectrums from which their senses are normally excluded, but even with such assistance cannot see or hear atomic waves. Nature allows them to see atomic particles and their external movements, but not their internal and atomic waves. They can prove the existence of atomic waves circumstantially, but are prevented from seeing their operation (Pert-em-Hru, 2017c, p. 274)[9].

---

[9] The double split experiment in quantum physics provides circumstantial proof of atomic waves

4.3.3 Movement plus survival produce ideas

A stone for instance is inanimate looking completely still, but inside its plethora of atomic waves are one proof of its internal movement. However, no matter how hard people look and experiment nature refuses to let them see this aspect of the stone's movement. That refusal is one proof of *nature's intelligence*.

In the case of *living* material objects, there is the deeper level of ideas. Life requires material and wherever there is life there is also motion and ideas. At their lowest, ideas equate to survival – survival is a symptom of ideas (the third logical type) and also the *matspiritual* category, on the face of it, exclusive to the living. Nature acts on living objects which respond by producing ideas and actions.

Ideas are not produced by stones as they do not have life and are not trying to survive. Therefore inside living material objects there is motion, but that motion is endowed with ideas giving it direction and purpose. In the living, ideas are inside of and drive motion and motion is inside of and drives material. One difference between the living and dead is presence/absence of ideas. Integral to life, ideas are also central to culture.

4.3.4 Nature's movement produces intelligence

Some parts of nature are alive and produce ideas others are not but nonetheless moving. This betrays a level of intelligence lower than instinct/ideas. It is derived from movement inherent in matter/nature, devoid of thought. It implies aspects of nature happen without purpose, planning or reason i.e. containing intelligence unprocessed by thought. Some parts of nature (the majority of the environment) are 'just being' – in a sense operating mechanically as a platform for life. Life is totally dependent in that it cannot exist without it. That said quantum physics experiments prove nature:

- Has self-motion (Pert-em-Hru, 2017c, p. 274/5)[10]; and
- Is intelligent[11].

---

[10] Superposition principle; Schrödinger's Cat experiment; and Spontaneous emission.

[11] Matter refuses observation of its wave functions & does not allow nuclear explosions of its plethora of atoms.

Nature is infinite i.e. everywhere all the time. It is not capable of dying, meaning its intelligence cannot be an act of survival. Nor is there sufficient evidence to claim nature (here distinguished from its contents) is alive. The implication is nature (more precisely the non-living parts of it) does the 'impossible' as standard, putting one foot in both camps i.e. operating intelligently whilst not being alive. Alternatively, if production of intelligence is a sign of 'life', then nature could in a sense be simultaneously dead and alive. This dialectical conundrum is consistent with the results of the Schrodinger's cat experiment. Could it be the live part is overriding the dead part's inability allowing production of intelligence to continue from nature's live parts even in the midst of death?

Consider a dead body – it is a part of nature. Despite being dead movement within it continues, proven by decay. From 'decaying' material i.e. the dead body springs life in the form of maggots. Even though the body is not alive, life springs from it. This process is scientifically explainable and has no reliance on spirits – its basis is material. This analogy may go some way towards illustrating a condition inherent in nature (the arena within which life and death occurs) and if correct implies an instinct like level of culture inherent in nature 'equal to' or 'below' the threshold of life, instinct and survival.

At the logical level nature includes animate and inanimate objects. Animate objects try to survive and to that extent at least, must influence society its practices and ideas. However, inanimate objects are not really inanimate. They are all the time moving:
- As part of nature's rotations – Change of place;
- Internally at the atomic level – Property change.

Regardless of whether or not they are alive i.e. trying to survive, their movement means they are not neutral. They too influence the direction of society its practices and ideas.

The stone is not alive and cannot produce ideas. Yet the fact that none of its atoms explode is proof of the presence of intelligence. Intelligence is in the stone, but not ideas. This means that not only is there a level of intelligence containing ideas, but one devoid of them also. Furthermore, not only does nature's innate movement operate at a level equivalent to society as ecology, but so too does its intelligence at: (i) the base boarder of culture for inanimate objects; and (II) at the instinct level for animals and plants. **Nature's intelligence** means, at some level, everything in the universe influences everything else:

- People's ideas act on people (and vice versa);
- People's ideas act on **nature's intelligence** (and vice versa); and
- **Nature's intelligence** acts on nature (and vice versa).

4.3.5 Volume/'first logical type' contains everything

Mimicking physical dimensions, the relationship of the three logical types can be represented as material being equivalent to three dimensional volume; composed of motion – equivalent of two dimensional area; in turn composed of ideas - equivalent of one dimensional lines. Having volume, material is three dimensional with the fourth dimension time contained within. However the first and second dimensions are also within as areas and lines respectively. Volume is composed of layered areas and areas of sequential lines. This implies movement as second and ideas as third **matspiritual** categories, residing inside material – the true first. It also implies all other dimensions higher and lower are inside the third.

The first logical type (3rd dimension) is material, comprising nature and its living things. Living things are busy merely surviving. Many avoid being killed, whilst killing other life forms to preserve their lives. Nature is the arena of life and death. Only people move beyond survival to development, which is an indication of their consciousness. This makes people a special category of nature.

The second logical type (2nd dimension) is motion, from which no material thing is exempt. The movement of planets, solar systems, galaxy's etc. is confirmation that wherever a thing is located in nature, it is in motion and cannot be still. Furthermore, all material is composed of atoms, with protons, neutrons and electrons in constant internal motion. Every aspect of material is moving from within and that internal motion is the source of both movement and change. Motion and its measurement – time - are inside material, meaning the second logical type is inside the first.

Movement is inside of and drives relationships. It produces ecology (nature to nature relationships); economics (people to nature relationships); politics (people to people relationships); and society (the container of all people related relationships). Society is the arena of people activity.

The third logical type (1st dimension) is ideas which cannot exist without the first two and intelligence. Anything that is alive produces ideas, meaning survival is a fundamental idea. Ideas give direction to motion imbibing it with qualities. They determine qualitative aspects of relationships i.e. how living things treat each other and their environment. The pattern of these behaviours produces methodologies and principles which can be fundamentally helpful or harmful to life.

4.3.6 Intelligence ideas and qualitative aspects of culture
Everything in nature is a manifestation of *nature's intelligence*, every idea in nature influenced by it. Where nature helps and preserves life, it is the purveyor of good, where it harms and takes life it is a representation of evil.

Nature's intelligence more precisely refers to the treatment of nature by nature with no human element. How living things treat themselves, others and their environment produces *nature's intelligence* at a higher level in the form of cultures. For people, it produces ideology, philosophy and culture. Culture is the arena of ideas and emotions. Culture and society are internal to nature; ideas, emotions and motion are internal to society, similar in operation to the way the brain and muscles are internal to the live body. Material is infinite and everywhere, so too is the motion contained within it and intelligence is in movement everywhere.

People's higher level of consciousness causes their treatment of nature and its contents to be of a different calibre. The manner in which nature is treated by people determines their philosophy. If it is treated as the source of all else, their engagement with it is fundamentally scientific since they will look to and examine nature to understand the unknown. If abstract spirits are treated as source, engagement with nature is 'unnecessary' for new knowledge and inquiry takes on a mystical character. In Afrikan culture spirits are in nature thereby grounding them and making them scientifically explainable.

The manner in which people treat people determines their ideology. If they treat people as ends worthy of respect in and of themselves for no reason other than the fact that they are people, their ideology is founded on humanist principles. If they treat people as a means to their own ends i.e. as tools, it is founded on exploitative principles.

Ideas of survival and killing to survive where necessary are inside all living things. They are inside and inform motion and direction of life forms. It follows that in living things ideas are inside and driving motion and motion is inside and driving material. This implies *nature's intelligence* is inside and driving ecology; philosophy is inside and driving economics and ideology is inside and driving politics; ecology is inside and driving nature; and politics and economics are inside and driving society. Also, philosophy and ideology are inside and driving culture.

One part of *nature's intelligence* relates to the ideas of non-human living things with no human involvement. Another relates to aspects of nature beyond human senses assisted by tools. Furthermore, there are aspects of nature unknown to people, where they know they don't know. There are others where they don't even know that they don't know. Areas of such complete ignorance are part of *nature's intelligence*.

The fact of human ignorance does not deprive *nature's intelligence* of its material base. It simply means that human knowledge has not yet reached the point of locating it in relation to material. Nature is infinite which means it will never be possible to know it all. There will always be parts unknown to humanity. *Nature's intelligence* is therefore also infinite and ultimately scientifically unexplainable. It will always exist, providing philosophical idealists with an eternal playground.

4.3.7 Consciousness and conscience - oppression or resistance

There are limits to human senses. They are our means for engaging material reality, but are incapable of exploring the entirety of nature's material aspects, as the majority is out of range. Our senses smell and taste are receptacles for atomic scale particles. However, they do not allow us to experience all particles. If we smell certain of nature's particles we die through gas inhalation. Similarly with taste we die through poisoning. Nature excludes humanity from directly experiencing certain particles.

Our sense of touch responds to both particles and waves. We feel rain, snow and wind on our skin; we also feel the sun. We feel certain waves as temperature which penetrates our skin, going right through us. Waves go beyond our simple sense of touch. Nature places limits here too – put us in microwaves for instance we die.

Our eyes and ears are receptacles for our wave senses seeing and hearing. They allow us limited access to wave spectrums light and sound respectively. Many animals see and hear more of nature than humans. Through observation and experimentation we know that there are other aspects of nature's wave spectrums beyond direct human experience. Our senses therefore allow us only limited access to nature, the vast majority is qualitatively and quantitatively beyond them.

Quantum physicists discovered nature actively hides its wave capacities from human observation. Its prevention method, detectable at the atomic level, is to behave as particles when being observed and waves when not. However hard long and "scientifically" we consciously look, nature only permits us to observe its atomic particle functions, but when we're not looking/observing it leaves signs that its particles were behaving as waves. Nature's wave capacity operates independently of humanity. Some of them actively prevent human consciousness from seeing or hearing them.

There is much more going on in the wave category than our eyes and ears are able to detect. We can observe atomic particles and through scientific experimentation uncover aspects of them hitherto unknown. However, scientific methodology has so far shown itself incapable of even observing atomic waves. We cannot even see certain waves let alone experiment with them. This poses a conundrum for scientific methodology, which on the face of it, we cannot solve. Furthermore, it is unscientific to merely believe that science will solve this problem.

The inadequacy of our senses for exploring nature's material aspects is by far surpassed by their impotence in helping us understand what is going on in nature's *matspiritual* sphere. For this we need a different calibre of engagement. Our senses need the assistance of conscience and consciousness. Conscience is our innate philosophical tool, our inner barometer of right and wrong. Consciousness which is learnt operates at the ideological level and is triggered by our objective understanding, clarity and compliance with our principles.

Characterised by mastery over fire, use of tools and writing, conscience and consciousness give humans a special capacity beyond other creatures on earth. However inadequately, they are our connectors with **matspiritual** elements of nature. They connect to politics, economics, society, ideology philosophy, culture and are underpinned by principles, morals, values and ethics etc. As with our senses the majority of nature is out of physical range, leaving us with no primary notion of the goings on in **nature's intelligence** realms – an area of nature from which human consciousness is ordinarily excluded. We only have the possibility of engaging through use and manipulation of tools.

Consciousness is generated by human beings in motion. Conscious ideas require experience and are best served by mastery of relevant factually correct history. They must also have purpose, ideally with crystal clear vision for future direction. Their third and perhaps most critical ingredient is action, precisely aimed at making the desired vision happen.

Consciousness & Conscience

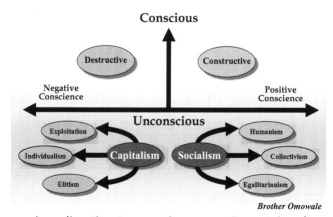

Brother Omowale

Conscience gives direction to consciousness. It contains the principles that drive consciousness in particular moral/ethical directions. Where conscience is inculcated with the exploitative cluster of principles, people and nature are used as tools doing harm to both – it is destructive. This calibre of conscience is the motivating force behind slavery, feudalism, colonialism, settler-colonialism, zionism, racism, sexism, neo-colonialism and imperialism.

Peoples ill-treated under a culture with an exploitative conscience instinctively know they are being wronged and resist. However, their instincts are insufficient to overcome it. Only a revolutionary combination of conscience and consciousness can defeat it. In the consciousness of exploited and oppressed people, ideas of resistance, revolution and liberation take shape – their conscience imbibed humanist principles, pictures a better future. Their raised consciousness prohibits tolerance of exploitation and prompts liberation. A conscious people have no choice but to sweep aside unjust hindrances to their humanism, freedom and liberty.

They typically exhibit a great blossoming of culture prior to acting to releasing themselves from their bondage, their conscience treating the welfare of people and nature as paramount, thereby utilizing consciousness to their benefit. This is the combination that genuinely drives humanity forward and is found in communal, socialist and communist social systems. A people's consciousness determines the level of their culture's rational operation and their conscience, its qualitative character and direction.

4.4 Culture and liberation
4.4.1 Land: foundation of culture, society and power
All living things produce culture - the result of life. All life on earth is based on land. Some creatures live on the land; others live in it; even sea creatures are fundamentally based on land, because at the bottom of the sea there is land. Land is the basis upon which human society is built. Even when human beings venture into different environments, they create their own artificial land and take it with them. Examples include ships and submarines for water navigation and aeroplanes and space craft for travelling through air and beyond the earth's atmosphere. In all cases, they took off from land and materials used extracted from or connected to land. Humans have never created independent societies or nations on sea, in air or space. On earth, land is the fundamental base for societies, nations and cultures.

Furthermore, Afrikan land is the richest in the world, not just marginally richer than the other continents, but massively. Whosoever controls Afrika become the richest and most powerful people. Currently European imperialism (including its modern leader US Satan imperialism) controls Afrika through its system of **neo-colonialism**. They use their **capitalist corporations**, supported by their other capitalist killer institutions the **IMF**, **World Bank** and **WTO** to effectively invade and subdue Afrikan people so that they can illegitimately extract massive volumes of Afrikan resources. This is what makes **capitalist corporations** the richest and most powerful entities in the world. Control of Afrikan resources is therefore of critical strategic importance to the maintenance and survival of the worldwide **neo-colonial** system.

The problem Europeans, Chinese and Indians have in common is none of them have legitimate claim to controlling Afrika. The only people with a legitimate claim to Afrikan land and resources are dispossessed people of Afrika. When Afrikan people around the world truly realise they are Afrikans and assume their legitimate control of Afrika, they will become the most powerful people in the world. When an Afrikan people's government takes control of Afrika, **Capitalist corporations** will: (i) cease to be the most powerful entities in the world; (ii) cease to have the power to dominate Afrikan people and our resources; and become dependent upon Afrikan people for vital resources.

All other nations will then have to trade fairly with an Afrikan people's government. The corrupt anti-Afrikan **neo-colonial** mechanisms i.e. the **capitalist corporations**, the **World Trade Organisation (WTO)**, the **International Monetary Fund (IMF)** and **the International Bank for Reconstruction and Development (IBRD)** colloquially referred to as the **World Bank** will all become redundant. This means **capitalist corporations** and their allies have a vested interest in preventing an Afrikan people's government from taking control of Afrika.

If we are to survive and ultimately thrive as a people, we must prevent all foreign entities from taking control of Afrika. We must organise ourselves to take and exercise our complete legitimate right to the control of our land and resources. If we do not know we are Afrikan people disconnected from our land, culture and history, we become alienated from and impervious to the most important mission in our lives i.e. the recovery of our riches and with it, Afrikan liberation. It is realisation that we are Afrikan people that makes us conscious of our

120

responsibility to restore justice for Afrika and her people and through that, contribute to restoring justice to the world. It is therefore a benefit to the whole of humanity that Afrikan people connect proudly with our Afrikaness and fully embrace our history and culture as a prelude to liberating Afrika and bringing justice to the world.

Some brands of nationalism in the Afrikan Diaspora suffer from the fundamental problem that they are landless, in some cases without even an intention to have a land base. Nationalism without land is a contradiction. Any nationalism that does not have sovereignty over land or at least the aim of achieving it is not true nationalism. This is what Malcolm X was alluding to when he said land is the basis of all independence, freedom, justice and equality (Beitman, 2002, p. 21). The glaring weakness of landless nationalism contributed to Malcolm X reconsidering his position on the issue.

By 18th January 1965 it became clear that Malcolm, triggered by an earlier meeting with the Algerian ambassador to Ghana Franz Fanon, developed serious concerns about whether 'Black nationalism' he previously advocated could solve Afrikan people's problems. Openly reflecting he said:

> "So, I had to do a lot of thinking and reappraising of my definition of Black Nationalism. Can we sum up the solution to the problems confronting our people as Black Nationalism? And if you notice, I haven't been using the expression for several months. But I still would be hard pressed to give a specific definition of the over-all philosophy which I think is necessary for the liberation of black people in this country." (Beitman, 2002, p. 234; Beitman, 2003, p. 181)

His earlier notion of 'black nationalism' focused on Afrikan people taking control of their communities - it was strictly local in its scope lacking national and international dimensions. It did not recognise the importance of state power – i.e. the most powerful entity within a nation. In US Satan the state is controlled by capitalist corporations and acts in their interests. Those corporations operate on an international basis – their oppressive interests are not bound by US Satan national boarders or government. Part of the capitalist corporations' power comes from their control of an international network of capitalist states, not just the US Satan state. Their culture is on a scale bigger than nations.

The corporate-state partnership ultimately means no matter how many politicians and shops etc. Afrikan people control in their local communities, they will not be able to control their destiny inside US Satan, or anywhere else without displacing the capitalist corporations controlling those states. If those Afrikan communities really want to be self-determining, they have to control state power. This means defeating the culture that facilitates corporate capitalism's control of state power.

Afrikan people in US Satan are a minority, just 10% of the population. They cannot take control of that state. Furthermore, that land belongs to American Indians. Afrikan people worldwide have a deep problem predicated on the fact that they do not fully own and control their own land. Afrikan people's only legitimate claim to land is Afrika. Their solution is to be part of the process of establishing an Afrikan continental-wide state in the hands of Afrikan agricultural and industrial workers worldwide in order to control a stake in their legitimate land – the richest in the world.

Afrikan people must continue to fight for their rights wherever they are. However, by actively engaging in the process of bringing that about, Afrikan people whether at home or in the Diaspora are contributing to the primary and at this stage fundamentally most critical action for the recovery of Afrikan culture – reclaiming and controlling our land. Sovereign control of Afrikan land will bring a united society and culture, the first essential base for Afrikan culture to develop and flourish at home and abroad.

The practical defence of Afrikan culture in the Diaspora is therefore double pronged where Afrikan people need to balance their citizenship in foreign nations with their duties as Afrikan people to their motherland – Afrika. The working guide is Afrika is primary. They must always put the interests of Afrika first, never engaging in actions on behalf of foreign agencies that will disadvantage Afrika.

4.4.2 When cultures meet

All cultures are uniquely founded on:

- Distinct people's
  o Historical development/maturity;
  o Location in nature;
  o Qualitative combination of consciousness and conscience; and
  o Level of power.

Cultures borrow from other cultures, or more precisely learn or steal depending on conscience and level of power. Live culture continually grows and changes unless some parts are forgotten or history lost. Where two cultures meet, each with a humanist conscience, they can live happily side by side sharing borrowing and learning from each other. Disparities in their relative level of power and technological development will not be used in a hostile manner, meaning the less powerful culture has nothing to fear from its more powerful neighbour.

The history of imperialism has been expansion of culture with exploitative conscience. One manifestation of this has been its subjugation of people through external *domination*, which required:

- Organised suppression of other people's culture denying them their proper historical development;
- Liquidation of essential elements of the *dominated* people's cultures; and
- Cultural alienation from their own culture through *dominated* elites.

It is easier to *dominate* people whose culture is similar to the *dominators'*, because *domination* does not have to change them greatly to achieve conformity. However, even this closer knit *domination* is a mighty and difficult task as illustrated in the relationship between England and Ireland.

In some instances, imperialist culture went beyond domination and *annihilated* innocent unsuspecting peoples, almost wiping them from the face of the earth. It learnt that without *dominated* people and their labour, the conquest loses its essence as experienced in the case of Amerindians and Aborigines. It is both inefficient and ineffective and in these cases led to imperialism putting out calls for emigration to replace those murdered to make those stolen lands economically viable. In the case of the Americas, Afrikan people were subjected to an additional genocide. They were kidnapped and forcibly extradited to bring viability to imperialist culture's anti-human theft and genocide in the Americas.

When Cultures Meet

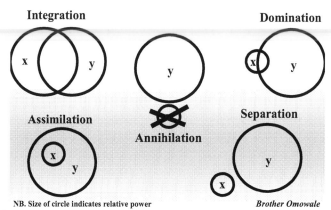

NB. Size of circle indicates relative power   *Brother Omowale*

Imperialist culture also has the 'problem' that within its metropolitan centres it imprisons the Diasporas of externally subjugated peoples. It attempts to turn them against their own people through *assimilation*. It seeks to impose its culture onto its internal captives and sets up indoctrination programmes aimed at turning them against their culture. This level of *assimilation* can never be fully achieved and captives sit like time bombs in its centres waiting to explode. They are imperialism's enemy within – its most potent and dangerous foe – with the power to bring imperialism down. The revival of captive's culture can spell the death of imperialism. Afrikan people are potentially the greatest internal foe, which explains why imperialist culture adopts its systematic anti-Afrikan culling programme.

4.4.3 Culture and Struggle

"The aim of Afrikan culture and Afrikan Peoples should be nothing else but the struggle for liberation, unification and rehabilitation of the Continent." (Toure, No. 88, p.18)

In this period of history the part of our culture in need of urgent attention is the liberation part. The political part is fragmented and in disarray. The initial cultural battle is to correct this problem. We need first to liberate ourselves politically by recovering firm control of our land governed through a single unified state controlled by Afrikan agricultural and industrial workers. We then need to stabilize economically, through a centrally organised industrialisation programme. This will provide the platform from which central aspects of our culture (ideology and philosophy) can flourish.

To kick start this process we must get our ideas about liberation right through developing a thorough knowledge of the history of our liberation struggle. This must be guided by a common plan putting those ideas into action, using our liberation ideas to sharpen our liberation actions, and actions to further sharpen ideas. Nkrumah exemplified this in his *Handbook of Revolutionary Warfare*.

Since cultures grow and borrow from other cultures, it makes sense to also look for successful liberation models outside our culture, with a view to adapting and applying them to our liberation programme of action. This implies forming tactical alliances with other cultures fighting the same imperialist enemy. Alliances with other oppressed people are necessary for the defeat of imperialism, but only Afrikan culture can liberate Afrika and Afrikan people. This implies structuring and developing national liberation movements which become the *organised political expression* of our people's *culture.* Their likelihood of success is increased if the movement is based on our popular culture.

Cultural Analysis

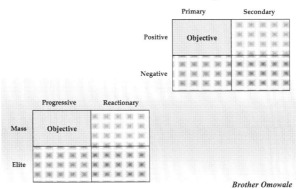

Brother Omowale

The Leadership of Afrika's liberation movement must know and value their culture, setting this as the standard for all participants. They must ensure that our culture is based on history and achievements in struggle. They must be on guard for opportunists who join for their own aggrandisement, placing their own class interests above the interests of our people. They must also be discerning, recognising some parts of our culture are good, propelling us towards liberation and others bad. Their cultural analysis must honestly distinguish between:

- Primary and secondary;
- Positive and negative;
- Progressive and reactionary;
- Mass and elite elements.

Through a process of analysis and selection *the national liberation movement must develop and work with primary, positive, progressive and mass elements of national culture* whilst eliminating the unhelpful parts. This process will become a catalyst for driving liberation forward to victory (Cabral, 1979, p. 147). Having gone through these processes, Cabral advises National liberation movements to foster unity by:

- Bringing diverse interests into harmony;
- Resolving contradictions within and amongst its constituent elements;
- Defining common objectives;
- Remaining determined in the face of difficulties and sacrifices; and
- Preparing for the necessity of armed struggle to achieve liberation.

Cabral agrees with Nkrumah that liberation can only be achieved via armed struggle (Nkrumah, 1980b, p. 80; Nkrumah, 1981, p. 41; Milne, 2001, p. 41, 44, 71, 170, 294, 302, 322, 335 & 404). Armed liberation struggle is a special act of culture, it liberates other aspects – in Afrika's case its politics and economics. It requires:

- Mobilisation and organisation of a substantial majority of the population;
- Political and moral unity of the nation's various social classes;
- Efficient use of modern arms and other means of war;
- The liquidation of tribal, parochial or myopic mentality; and
- Rejection of social and religious taboos and restrictions which inhibit the struggle's development to the point of successfully liberating the people.

Despite emphasising necessity of armed struggle, Nkrumah and Cabral offer the following advice:

> "Imperialism constantly infiltrates revolutionary opposition groups with agents, 'special police', and others, compelling such groups to arm even before they have attained the organisational stage of armed struggle." (Nkrumah, 1980b, p. 54) ... [and] ... "Between one man carrying a gun and another carrying a tool, the more important of the two is the man with the tool." (Amilcar Cabral quoted in Hay, 1984, p. 165)

4.4.4 Measuring cultural advancement

Imperialism's hostile culture focuses on property and profits, treating people as inferior to material wealth. It is driven by exploitative principles. In it, enslaved and oppressed people producing material wealth are considered less important than their produce. Afrika's friendly culture is driven by humanism and focuses on quality of relationships, recognising people and nature as priorities. Material produce is important but it is recognised as the fruit of human genius and therefore dependant on people. The purpose of wealth is to assist people fully develop their faculties so they can make more effective contributions to the full development of culture.

The level of productive forces indicates the stage of development of the society and culture. The highest level of productive forces requires:
- The best treatment of human beings and nature; plus
- The highest level of technology.

Imperialism's centres have the technological advantage through their possession of industrialisation. It used industrial power to disqualify Afrika from industrialising thereby holding Afrika and humanity in general back. It maintains its advantage by exploiting the majority of human beings and by doing so disqualifies itself from full and proper development.

The philosophy and ideology of Afrikan culture, already based on proper treatment of people and nature is perfectly placed to take humanity forward to the next stage of history and with it a better standard of living for all. However, its externally imposed technological retardation makes fighting off imperialism's war machine's invasion and theft of its resources an ultra difficult, though achievable task.

The purpose of culture is to solve the problems of living things. The purpose of Afrikan culture therefore is to solve our people's problems. Our biggest problem is our wealth is being stolen with relentless vigour by corporate capitalist culture and this evil continues unabated. It follows that the current priority for Afrikan culture is to stop the theft and get everything back (in the first instance). In the longer term the objective is completely freeing our capacity to produce the things we need which will require:

- A halt to the theft of Afrika's resources;
- A political shift from the Berlin constructed jigsaw puzzle state structure to a continental wide unified state controlled by the masses of Afrikan people leading to:
  o Afrikan people collectively deciding how to allocate Afrika's resources in theirs and humanity's best interests;
- A comprehensively planned industrialisation programme leading to:
  o The elimination of poverty and associated ills such as hunger and disease;
  o Substantial sustainable improvements in the quality of life of Afrikan people.

Afrikan culture is shackled politically and its resources stolen economically, which stifles it philosophically and ideologically. Throwing off the shackles means taking political control of Afrika's land - the richest in the world. An immediate end must be put to resource theft and those resources redirected into servicing the needs of Afrikan people. This will trigger economic development, releasing the shackles constraining Afrika's philosophy and ideology i.e. the higher levels of Afrikan culture, bringing it back on balance. Successfully releasing the shackles and redirecting the resources catapults Afrika into its Scientific Socialist historical phase, which is the necessary condition for its culture to recover, survive and thrive.

Identity
For Revolution

Chapter 5

5 Identity for revolution

5.1 Locating identity in matter

5.1.1 A Materialist approach to Identity

It should by now be established that Pan-Afrikanists operating from their materialist philosophy must begin by scientifically identifying the material base of any problem they seek to solve. In general terms that will be nature (the foundation of which is land) and people (that special part of nature endowed with relatively higher consciousness). People are at the heart of the identity question since particular peoples have particular identities.

Human beings have a range of biologically based physical characteristics. A fundamental element distinguishing relative appearance of various sections of humanity is the volume/quota of melanin contained in their bodies. Another (crucial to survival) is reproduction i.e. the continuous ongoing reproduction of new people, happening all over the world - reproduction is not randomly distributed.

Where in nature we are located is another fundamental component. Sekou Toure states human beings are inseparable from their environment (Toure, No. 88, p. 126). They are products/extensions of environments which vary from time to time and place to place creating difference. Differences have a corresponding impact upon people's identities.

Specific locations are centres for reproduction of differing categories or types of human being. A person's/people's reproduction centre is often the geographical point of origin for their group/type/category. It marks the core of the relationship between a particular people with a particular biological make up and their particular land/location/environment. Since biological make up and land/nature are material, that combination forms the material base upon which a person's identity is founded. All other aspects rest on them.

Relating this to levels of the **4 Dialectic Analytic Tool**, elements of nature together with biology and reproductive capacity of people form the economic base for identity. The next level is political i.e. how people relate to each other i.e. which groups we are associated with and which are primary. The ideological element is next highest and is determined by dominant principles, both for us as individuals and our primary group. It speaks to the level of consistency between the two.

The highest level is philosophical which determines our methodology/approach to identity. Is it scientific or mystical, rational or emotional, objective or subjective, accepted or denied, a source of pride or shame? This is the arena in which identity confusion operates – a condition that causes similar people to identify differently. It can mark the difference between what we are and what we don't/want to be.

At the material level nature acts on people and people act on people. This causes people to produce **matspiritual** ideas and emotions which amongst other things, help them subjectively decide who and what they are. This is an ongoing process for all people. Those ideas and emotions impact their thinking on a whole range of issues relating to how they interpret their identity.

Differing vantage points and perceptions of identity complicate matters evoking the realm of reality v perceptions. Subjectivity is based on perceptions which can be right or wrong, correct or incorrect. Therefore one of the central questions for correct identification is: what is material reality? This is important because there is only one reality which we are all in. Once perceptions are in accordance with material reality, we can make objective/correct assessments, choices, decisions and affiliations.

5.2 Some implications of Identity
5.2.1 Identity contradictions, group affiliations and consequences
The central contradiction in identity is human beings are all the same, whilst simultaneously different/unique. This is compounded by all things changing all the time, meaning we are not the same as we were even a second ago, nor the groups we form a part of, nor the environment within which we operate. Modes of identifying and their boundaries are in a continuous state of flux. Cabral emphasizes this with the following observations:

> "The dialectical character of identity lies in the fact that an individual (or a group) is only similar to certain individuals (or groups) if it is also different to other individuals (or groups) ... The definition of identity, individual or collective, is at the same time the affirmation and denial of a certain number of characteristics which define the individuals or groups, through *historical* (biological and sociological) factors at a moment in their development. In fact, identity is not a constant, precisely because the biological and sociological factors which define it are in constant change. Biologically and sociologically, there are no two beings (individual or collective) completely the same or completely different, for it is always possible to find in them common or distinguishing characteristics. (Afrika Information Service, 1973, p. 64/65)

Identity helps guide us through the complex maze that is matter, by helping us understand which group/section of humanity we have most in common with, are fundamentally linked to and from. Common identity differs from 'sameness' and 'identical' and changes over time. By contrast, our uniqueness is our individuality, not our group identity. Group identity requires sharing common features. There are many changing aspects, characteristics or features that potentially affect identity but the starting point for correct classification is the determination of which common features are primary and why.

At the political level, individuals are simultaneously linked to many different groups. Their identity is therefore distinguished by linkages to their most fundamental grouping thereby identifying who and what they are. It also helps classify from whom, what and where they come as well as providing a basis for locating their people's collective point of origin in time and space. The importance of identity, in a changing world full of complexity, is it helps orientate us. It:

1. Links us to a biological grouping;
2. Locates us in time and space;
3. Gives us the vantage point from which to view the world;
4. Links us to particular peoples and their causes;
5. Links us to a purpose greater than ourselves;
6. Links us to principles, values & beliefs that guide our behaviour; and
7. Gives us a base from which to organise in our best interests.

Identity & Purpose

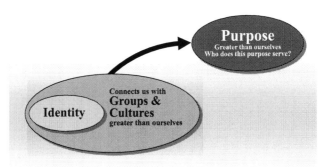

Brother Omowale

When we choose an identity, we simultaneously choose, associate and bind ourselves to a group, making it more powerful. We then work towards the interests of that group, often putting its collective interests above our own. The more individuals that identify with a group, the more powerful it becomes. There is also a multiplier effect making group power greater than the sum of individual members'. This raises deeper level issues such as who gets or doesn't get our power.

If we make the wrong identity association, we link ourselves and give power to a group whose purpose is not in our fundamental best interests. In worse case scenarios this leads to self-harm through serving interests of our enemy. At the same time the wrong association deprives our fundamental and genuine identity grouping of power, thereby weakening ourselves and our capacity to achieve our aims. Identity must genuinely serve *our purpose*, not my individual purpose, or other people's purpose but *our purpose* – we must be absolutely clear as to what is the real 'our'.

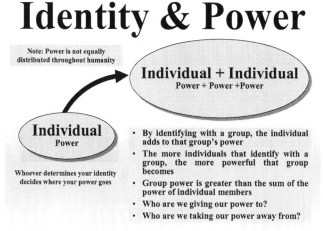

Identity & Power

Note: Power is not equally distributed throughout humanity

Individual + Individual
Power + Power +Power

Individual
Power

Whoever determines your identity decides where your power goes

- By identifying with a group, the individual adds to that group's power
- The more individuals that identify with a group, the more powerful that group becomes
- Group power is greater than the sum of the power of individual members
- Who are we giving our power to?
- Who are we taking our power away from?

Brother Omowale

If we get 'our' identity classification right, the foundation is laid for unity based on fundamental common interests. If we get it wrong, internal division is sown, coupled with either active or passive assistance to those keeping us divided, exploited and oppressed. The latter is a foreseeable consequence of identity confusion or rejection.

5.2.2 Attack on Afrikan identity

Since Afrikan culture has collectivism as one of its base principles, it required an almighty shift to force Afrikan people away from their natural tendency towards collectivising and uniting. That shift came in the form of an imperialist invasion organised by Europe's elite. European invasions, according to Eric Williams (1997), led to the birth of capitalism as a social, political and economic system. Capitalism has individualism as one of its base principles and this automatically operates to undermine Afrikan culture.

For the last 500 years there has been an unrelenting savage attack on all things Afrikan. One of the main tactics used was divide and rule. It took many different forms including slavery, colonialism and neo-colonialism, marked by: (i) the arrival of Columbus to steal the Americas and commit double genocide; (ii) the 1884/5 Berlin Conference to counter Afrikan people's defeat of slavery by stealing Afrikan land instead; and (iii) 1944 Bretton Woods Conference to maintain the stolen resources by other means. The attack on Afrikan identity was initiated during the first two phases and is maintained in the third.

When European imperialism came to Afrika it engaged in a massive programme of theft. When it was confronted with the natural resistance of a people seeing their wealth stolen, it engaged in the most horrendous genocide in history. To disguise the full sadistic horror of its evil conduct, it spun the most shameless web of lies known to humanity, audaciously labelling them 'history', 'education' and 'news'. That process - *theft followed by genocide followed by lies - is the logic of imperialism.*

Logic of Imperialism

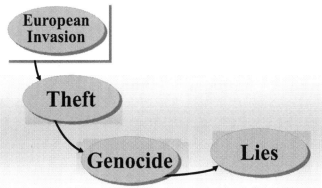

Brother Omowale

European imperialism succeeded in stealing virtually every Afrikan thing it could get its hands on. It stole Afrikan land, Afrikan people, Afrikan gold, Afrikan diamonds, Afrikan chocolate and a whole range of Afrikan valuables too numerous to mention. The fact that in some cases nominal payments may have been paid does not excuse or disguise the massive scale of theft.

The ultimate material objective of imperialism is theft of the whole of Afrika – the richest continent in the world. To achieve this it must exterminate, or at least substantially cull Afrikan people to pave its way to a settler colony. The template has already been set out in North America and Australia where American Indians and Aborigines respectively have been all but wiped from the face of the earth and their lands stolen by Europeans.

European imperialism may try to wipe Afrikan people out also, but to do so would present it with serious strategic problems. Firstly, it does not have enough population to fully and exclusively occupy stolen lands in North America and Oceania – peopling Afrika is therefore beyond its demographic capacity[12]. Secondly, its scientists have been unable to solve the malaria problem. Afrikan people and Asians developed a level of immunity naturally through sickle cell – Europeans simply die. Attempts to populate certain parts of Afrika are for them, tantamount to suicide. This is why they've limited their settler colonisation to the edges of Afrika.

Their anti-Afrikan annihilation programme is stalled until they find solutions to these problems. In the meantime they continue genocidal activity short of complete annihilation via proxy wars, invasions, coups, biological warfare in the form of contraception programmes, Aids and Ebola attacks in Afrika and Cholera in the Afrikan outpost Haiti. Despite the scale of veiled anti-Afrikan genocide programmes, Afrikan people continue to successfully reproduce and grow. There are approximately 1.6 billion Afrikan people in the world, 1.2 billion of whom are in Afrika and the continent has the youngest population of any. Our reproduction success against this massive calculated genocidal onslaught means at the fundamental demographic level, we're winning the physical war.

European imperialism also set about stealing many *matspiritual* aspects of Afrikan culture which it was unable to get its hands on in any literal sense. Whether by force or persuasion one of the first acts of wicked enslavers and colonisers was to get us to change our names; to give up Afrikan names given to us by our fore parents for their Christian names. This was a specific and calculated attack on Afrikan identity, the first stage in its process of *matspiritual* theft.

From there it proceeded to steal Afrikan ideas, Afrikan languages, Afrikan religions, Afrikan customs, Afrikan rituals, Afrikan practices, Afrikan memory i.e. history and Afrikan culture in its entirety. The process of theft of the *matspiritual* was cunningly wicked. It simply prevented Afrikan people, by methods of force or dissuasion from using those things that were from Afrikan culture and supplanted them with

---

[12] China and India have sufficient people to at least begin such a process

its equivalents.

Over a period of time, many Afrikan people lost use of a range of **matspiritual** aspects of our culture because we simply forgot. The problem was compounded by Afrikan people being taught to resent anything Afrikan, based on the lying premise that Afrikan people and our culture are inferior. European imperialism created an illusion in which to be Afrikan is not only inferior, but sub-human. Since no one in their right mind wants to be sub-human, the automatic response for anyone captured by this false belief is to reject all things Afrikan, including Afrikan identity. This calibre of psychological torture completed the alienation of Afrikan people from things Afrikan.

The ultimate **matspiritual** objective is theft of Afrikan humanity - Afrikan principles i.e. our humanism, to be replaced with European imperialism's exploitative cluster of principles. If achieved, it will not be necessary to annihilate Afrikan people, since the replacement of our humanity and principles transforms us into 'slave' fodder to be used to extract wealth from our land on imperialism's behalf – enslaving us in our own land is more cost effective. Afrikan principles have responded by retreating into the villages (Cabral, 1979, p. 148), with imperialism's NGO's in pursuit. It is within this context that the attack on Afrikan identity should be viewed – it is part of imperialism's anti-Afrikan theft programme, requiring the weakening of its victims through divide and rule.

5.3 Some complexities in choosing identity
5.3.1 Identity and Similar Concepts
The attack on Afrikan identity devastated Afrikan people triggering mass schizophrenia. The theft and supplanting of our Afrikan identity left us completely disorientated; dehumanisation, vilification and character assassination of Afrikan identity caused even us to hold it in contempt and reject it. Stripped and contemptuous of our true Afrikan identity, we've been reduced to scratching around in a vein quest for a replacement. How disorientated Afrikan people self-define varies, but erroneous criteria such as: place of residence, citizenship, birth place etc often feature. In trying to bring us back on course, Marcus Garvey made a number of interventions helping to clarify these misconceptions. Though shrouded in the language of his time, his core message is clear:

"... the UNIA embraces [Afrikan people] everywhere; that the UNIA has no national bar, no colour bar, where [Afrikan people] are concerned. The UNIA is not insular; not parochial, is not national, is not Barbadian, is not Jamaican, is not Trinidadian, is not American; it is purely an [Afrikan] institution. When you join the UNIA, you will not join it as a Barbadian, Jamaican, Trinidadian, American, you join it as an [Afrikan]. And we recognise anyone as [an Afrikan] who has one 16th drop of [Afrikan] blood in his veins. If he does not claim to be [an Afrikan] he may stay to himself and we welcome him to stay there; hence you realise, I am here representing not an insular institution, not a parochial institution, not a national institution, but a universal movement for [Afrikan people], that is Universal Afrika for [Afrikan people], by [Afrikan people], a government of our own. Barbadians can work for it, Jamaicans can work for it, Americans can work for it; just as you worked for the Panama Canal." (Hill, 1984, p. 384).

Others may define by the equally erroneous notion of profession and yet others speak of identity being based on unspecified 'influences'. Our profession is what we do, not who and what we are and the idea that our identity is founded on things that influence us is an obvious misnomer. So many things influence us that if we took each of them as our identity we would have an endless list. Furthermore, the most fundamentally/critical influences on us are: air; water; sleep; and food, yet it would be an absurdity to claim these as our identities.

Another area of potential confusion is in the difference between the *matspiritual* name/label and the material entity/Afrikan person which it describes and categorises. The name ought to help recognition of the entity, facilitating our agreement that we are referring to the same thing. It should help identify the entity, giving it meaning. It can even symbolically merge with the entity, mixing the two – a source for another element of potential confusion.

In our current schizophrenic state, Afrikan people can and sometimes do label themselves in ways designed to hide their true identity. In a determined effort to reject and deny their Afrikaness, they seek 'comfort' through dissociation, clasping at inaccurate labels as a vein form of disguise. Unaware of the depth of the anti-Afrikan propaganda attack and as a consequence gripped by a deep sense of 'shame', they grab at any straw or crumb of an argument that appears to facilitate their claim to non-Afrikan status. In the most severely affected cases, otherwise intelligent people will publicly chirp total and utter nonsense in attempting to defend the most ridiculous, patently and obviously false identities – such is their determination to be anything other than Afrikan.

The following is a case study brining out some identity confusion/rejection issues typically found amongst Afrikan people. It is by no means the most chronic example of identity confusion/rejection, but gives an indication of some of the false lines of reasoning. The correspondence between the author and a highly able and intelligent Afrikan third party is genuine. However, as the object is specifically to assist learning, that third party and others on the circulation list are left anonymous. One internet link and the words supporting it have been removed from the anonymous contributor's email to protect his identity. Minor alterations have been made, purely for the purpose of removing 'typos'. The included diagrams were not part of the original email. Identity confusion/rejection is not limited to the examples covered in the case study below.

5.3.2 Case Study in Identity Confusion – Rejection of Afrikan identity
From: Anon
To: 6 people
Sent: Sunday, 4 October, 2009 17:32:43

Hey everyone!

Since joining the Pan-African Society Community Forum, in early September, I have learned additional things about the continent of Africa, the former leader of Ghana, Kwame Nkrumah and Jamaican-born Marcus Garvey. Therefore, I have enjoyed the meetings however, I did not agree with some issues and the other night, I was not able to disclose my views! Now, I will do so!

.

First of all, I'm NOT an African but I'm an African DESCENT (ethnicity)! Period! There is a difference between the two. Descent means.......a group of individuals, through the passage of time, passing genetic, national and cultural traits to its offspring (from parents or ancestors). Personally, I fall into that category! In other words, I'm an African descent simply because my ancestors **(not me)** were born and raised in Africa.

Now, if Africa was really my homeland, why didn't I have a passport or citizenship (still don't) from any country in Africa???????????? Yes, I know there are immigration laws in every country. But, "home" means.......a place where individuals can reside on a permanent basis and I cannot reside anywhere in Africa. Therefore, I'm not an African but only an African descent. I can only visit a country in Africa for a short period of time (cannot work nor live there). At work, one of my fellow workers, a white male, was born in South Africa and therefore, he can live in the southern part of Africa at anytime. Anyway, as a British citizen, I'm glad I have the luxury to live anywhere in Britain and Europe (European Union citizen) like any person who was born in the UK and Europe.

In terms of Jamaica, I'm not a Jamaican either but I'm a Jamaican DESCENT. I'm a Jamaican descent simply because my parents **(not me)** were born and raised in Jamaica. Last year, I met a Chinese lady who was born in Jamaica and she spoke like a real Jamaican. I don't have a Jamaican accent.

Furthermore, I'm a Canadian! Yes, I was born and raised in Toronto, Canada (Central Canada). The fact my color is black, I can be considered a Black Canadian or an African descent Canadian as well. I grew up in a Canadian society, experienced the country's environment, had a Canadian education at the University of Windsor in Windsor, Canada (history degree) and adopted Canadian norms and values on CANADIAN SOIL (not African nor Jamaican soil). In Canada, I grew up playing Canada's national sport of ice hockey but my ancestors and parents did not. Different individuals! You see! Anyway, ice hockey was invented in Canada.

... [Link removed] ...

Speaking about Nova Scotia, in the meetings, I'm surprised I never heard anything about the Jamaican Maroons' connections with Nova

Scotia, Canada.
http://www.guysboroughacademy..ednet.ns.ca/ANS/History/jamacan
marons.htm

Well, I'm sorry that I have to connect ethnicity with nationality. After all, I'm not living in the 5th or 11th century, I'm living in the 21st century and ethnicity and nationality go hand in hand. Therefore, I cannot eliminate nationality all together. Although, nationality was invented by man but nationality is part of my identity in terms of the way I speak, dress and the way I carry myself.

Although African-American history is very popular throughout the world and famous people such as King, Malcolm X, Washington were born in the U.S. but American history has NO CONNECTIONS with me at all. My ancestors, parents, and myself were not born nor raised in America. Therefore, I really don't get much into African-American history.

Moreover, Canada is NOT the 51st state of the U.S. and the two countries are totally different in many areas such as politics, history and domestic policies. As a matter of fact, we Canadians have a lot more in common with Britain simply because of the Commonwealth connections. The Queen is still Canada's Head of State and our leader Steven Harper (not Barack Obama) is the prime minister (not the president) of Canada. After all, Canada was colonised by Britain for over 400 years.

Finally, I do NOT speak for Africans, Caribbeans, Black people, British nor Canadians, I only speak for myself.

From: Brother Omowale
To: 7 people
Sent: Wednesday, 7 October, 2009 12:16 AM

Warmest greetings to you Anon my brother.

Many thanks for taking the time to express your views in writing on the issue of identity. It is clear to me that this is a very important area of learning for you, as indeed it is for all of us. For some reason I did not receive my copy even though my email address is included in the circulation, but thankfully it was forwarded to me. This is my initial response to your observations.

5.3.3 The appropriateness of your intervention
We were all participants in a workshop entitled *Nkrumah and his early years including the Struggle to achieve state power in Ghana*. It is not immediately obvious to me why you felt that it was appropriate for the issue under discussion should be overridden or sidelined in favour of a discussion on identity. What motivated you to take the discussion in that direction? What were you hoping to achieve by focusing the meeting's attention or the issue of identity?

These questions are also relevant to your statement: *'I'm surprised I never heard anything about the Jamaican Maroons' connections with Nova Scotia, Canada.'* My brother, when we discuss the undefeated Jamaican Maroons we do mention the fact that the Trelawny Maroons went to Nova Scotia. In the time since you have joined us, we have been discussing other subjects and it is unrealistic that we should automatically mention this particular subject out of context.

5.3.4 Identity confusion was deliberately injected into the Afrikan world
I am happy to learn that you have a history degree. My hope is that your studies will mean you understand that all things have a history (including identity and identity confusion). History can also help us to explain happenings in the present. For instance, one of the main tactics used by the invaders to destabilise Afrika and the people of the Afrikan continent was the method of divide and rule. It took many different forms including the:
- ⬜ Encouragement of wars and antagonisms between different tribes which led to tribalism;
- ⬜ Separation of enslaved Afrikans from other Afrikans and their Afrikan homeland;
- ⬜ Separation of enslaved Afrikans into Jamaicans, Dominicans, St Lucians, Bagians, Americans and even Canadians etc;
- ⬜ Creation of an 'assimilados' elite class to rule their fellow Afrikans on the European imperialists' behalf;
- ⬜ Creation of antagonisms between different 'assimilados' elite class sub-groups;

- Partitioning of the Afrikan land into separate micro-nations. This had the dual effect of separating Afrikans from Afrika psychologically whilst, at the same time, cutting one set of Afrikans off from their fellow Afrikans even though they share the same continent;
- Separation of Afrikans from the wealth of their land;
- Separation of Afrikans from the product of their labour.

Identity & Unity

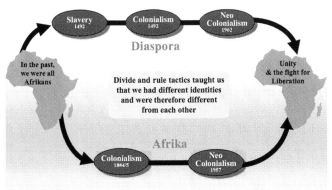

Brother Omowale

An additional range of divisive methods are identified in the William Lynch speech (Morrow, 2003) purportedly given on the banks of the James river, USA in 1714. Even though this speech has now been demonstrated to have failed the test of historical authenticity, it still retains some scope for use as a tool to help assist our analysis. In this alleged speech Lynch outlined a number of differences between Afrikans which he proposed should be used as tools to generate fear and envy amongst enslaved Afrikans for control purposes. He recommends that the enslavers of Afrikan people actively encourage and perpetuate divisions among Afrikans based on a range of apparently trivial criteria including:

- Age;
- Colour or shade;
- Sex;
- Height;
- Size;
- Hair texture;
- Intelligence;
- Attitude of owners;

- ☐ Status on the plantation;
- ☐ Size of plantation;
- ☐ Whether Afrikans are located on hills or in valleys;
- ☐ Whether Afrikans are located in the north, south, east or west.

He also recognised that enslaved Afrikans and European indentured servants had a common interest in overturning the enslavement system that exploited both of them. He therefore deemed it absolutely essential that European indentured servants and enslaved Afrikans be thoroughly divided.

At an even deeper level, not touched upon by the alleged Lynch speech, Afrikans were divided and separated from the **matspiritual** aspects of their culture. This included the forced deprivation of their:

- ☐ Names;
- ☐ Languages;
- ☐ Ideas and culture;
- ☐ Spiritual practices and rituals;
- ☐ Principles (including collectivism).

5.3.5 Some results of the divisions systematically imposed on Afrikans

Hundreds of years of this scale of calculated inhumanity perpetuated against Afrikans, has taken a devastating toll on them. The idea of dividing and separating themselves from fellow Afrikans and denying their Afrikan identity has been deeply inculcated into the psyche of Afrikans. They have also been forcibly trained to carry out and practice these self-destructive behaviours for centuries. These behaviours have therefore been thoroughly imbedded through generations of practice coupled with parental reinforcement.

All of this places formidable historical, cultural, psychological and practical barriers in front of any group of Afrikans seeking to unite. Afrikan liberation organisations are no exception to this and will need to take all of these factors into account in order to overcome the many problems that they are likely to face in the process of developing united frameworks of operation.

5.3.6 Locating your analysis in this context

You have emphatically stated that: *'I'm NOT an African but I'm an African DESCENT (ethnicity)! Period! There is a difference between the two.'* There is a difference between the two, but it does not follow that they are mutually exclusive. Has it occurred to you that all Afrikan people are of Afrikan DESCENT? Do you know any Afrikan who is not of Afrikan DESCENT? DESCENT links your chosen categories into a common history and a common biology, both of which are essential components of a person's identity.

There are a number of examples of you expressing your belief that your identity is determined by where you are born. For instance you say: *'my ancestors (not me) were born and raised in Africa.'* With respect this is an error. Our identity is not determined by where we are born. The confusion comes about partly because there is usually a high level of coincidence or correlation between our identity and the land where we are born. Then some of us, because we have not been trained to, are unable to distinguish between the two. Answer the following questions and it will help you to clarify: If a person was born on an Air Lingus aero plane (Irish airline) does that make them an 'Air Ligusian'? Why? If somebody was born on the QEII ship (British), does that make them a 'QEIlian'? Now that the British have sold the QEII to the Saudi Arabians, does that person's identity change? Why?

You say: *'"home" means........a place where individuals can reside on a permanent basis and I cannot reside anywhere in Africa.'* Again my brother this is a misconception. The Palestinians have not ceased to be Palestinians because the Zionists have thrown them off of their homeland - Palestine. Aborigines have not ceased to be Aborigines because the invaders calling themselves Australians have thrown them off of their lands on to reserves. The American Indians have not ceased to be American Indians because invaders calling themselves Americans and Canadians have thrown them off their land on to so called reserves. It is not automatic that an individual or people have the right to reside in their home.

At one point you describe yourself as: *'a British citizen'* and later you say: *'I'm a Canadian! Yes, I was born and raised in Toronto, Canada (Central Canada).'* You appear to be recognizing that there is a difference between citizenship and nationality. In your line of reasoning is your identity British, Canadian or some permutation of the two and why?

You also state: *'ethnicity and nationality go hand in hand. Therefore, I cannot eliminate nationality all together. Although, nationality was invented by man but nationality is part of my identity'*. This is a misconception my brother. Ethnicity and nationality do not go hand in hand, they simply often coincide. When they do not coincide, it is incorrect to confuse them with each other. Nationality is not part of yours or anyone else's identity, but it can have a big impact upon how we interpret our identity. From what you have written, you appear to hold dual nationality: does that mean that your identity is Canadian/British? You appear to be in a position to apply for Jamaican nationality also does that make your identity British/Canadian/Jamaican? Citizenship is one of the symbols of nationality. Birth certificates, passports and naturalizations papers are some of the symbols of citizenship. In essence they amount to a contract between the citizen and the nation-state. They are in essence legal agreements between nation-states and individuals. They are not your identity which deals with the questions: Who am I? What am I? With whom do I belong? Which land do I belong to?

Approaches to Identity

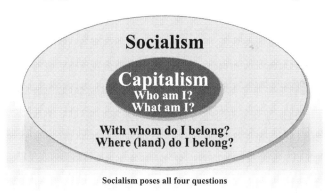

Socialism poses all four questions

Brother Omowale

The nationality/citizenship question also speaks to the other issues that you have raised. Namely: *'if Africa was really my homeland, why didn't I have a passport or citizenship (still don't) from any country in Africa????????????'* Our legal, human and moral rights were taken away from us when we were kidnapped and stolen from Afrika. Our nationality and citizenship were therefore unceremoniously and unjustly revoked. On top of that, we were deliberately and wicked deceived and confused into believing that we were not Afrikans. Our sisters and brothers who managed to avoid being kidnapped, stolen and sent away, had our Afrikan land stolen from under their feet. They too were wickedly deceived and confused into believing that their kidnapped sisters and brothers were not Afrikans.

We do not have our nationality and citizenship rights in our homeland Afrika because they were stolen from us and Afrikans at home and abroad have been so confused that the majority of those abroad do not know that they are Afrikans and will not fight for their citizenship rights, whilst the majority of Afrikans at home do not know that those abroad are Afrikans and therefore will not fight for their appropriate citizenship rights. One of the key tasks before us is to raise the collective consciousness of All Afrikans on the issue of Afrikan identity so that Afrikans at home and abroad can join together in correcting this injustice.

Look again at the way that you treat the identity of non-Afrikans. For instance you state: *'I met a Chinese lady who was born in Jamaica and she spoke like a real Jamaican. I don't have a Jamaican accent.'* This proves that at a deeper level, when you are identifying people other than Afrikans you understand the issue of identity. Notice you did not say that she was 'a Jamaican lady who was born in Jamaica' or 'a Chinese DESCENT lady who was born in Jamaica', you said *'a Chinese lady who was born in Jamaica'*. This confirms that you understand that she is Chinese regardless of where she was born or how she speaks. When you apply this same criterion to yourself, it means that you are an Afrikan regardless of where you were born, what your nationality is or how you speak.

Similarly notice what you said: *'one of my fellow workers, a white male, was born in South Africa and therefore, he can live in the southern part of Africa at anytime.'* Notice that you have not made the error of identifying your colleague as an Afrikan. You described him as a 'white male'. It is precisely because he is not an Afrikan that, in this context, you are forced to identify the fact that he is a 'white male'. The fact that he is a 'white male' is your expression of his identity regardless of where he was born.

5.4 Challenging false identities
5.4.1 Prompting identity questions

In a desire to extricate from being Afrikan, some have embraced one or more of a plethora of bogus labels contending and posturing to supplant Afrikan identity. The purpose of the following is to examine a cross section and dismiss them, helping our people see through imperialism's fog so that they can comfortably embrace their correct identity and become an active part of the process of making Afrikan unity and liberation a reality.

The fundamental test of their claim to representing Afrikan identity rests on whether or not they fulfil the land and biological (i.e. material) criteria. If they can't do that, they're excluded from serious consideration and further examination is only to more fully demonstrate their lack of credibility.

A more thorough examination would involve systematically testing each label against the series of questions below, which add to the robustness of the enquiry. Anyone wishing to take the analysis further is welcome to do so, since the full testing of each is beyond what is necessary for this essay:

- What is your chosen Identity?
  - What does the name mean?
- Who created it and for what purpose?
  - What cause/purpose does the name/entity serve?
  - Whose cause/purpose does the name/entity serve?
    - Who really decides it?
  - Is it founded on land and if so which?
    - What type of new people are dominant there?
    - What type of people originated there?
- What is the origin of the name/entity?
  - Why was it chosen?
  - Where does it come from?
  - Which entity does it support?
- Who/What benefits from your chosen identity and who loses out?
  - You personally?
  - Your genuine identity grouping?

- o Others?
- o Does it unite or divide Afrikan people?

The fundamental issue underlying these questions is whether the 'label' disempowers/divides or empowers/unites Afrikan people. If it disempowers/divides us or puts us into the service of entities that do not have Afrika's best interests at heart, it should be dismissed. If it unites us, we ought to be clear on what its power base is and whether the direction in which it takes us is in Afrika's and our best interest.

5.4.2 Some Illustrations

The following is a list of labels under which Afrikan people are sometimes grouped for identity purposes. To a lesser or greater extent, they are all misrepresentations of Afrikan identity. By generating/supplementing existing distortions, they assist capitalism's undeclared agenda of creating, stimulating and sustaining identity confusion amongst Afrikan people. This list is by no means exhaustive:

- Citizenship
  - o British (5.4.3)
  - o Partitions i.e. Ghanaians/Nigerians/Gambians/South Afrikans (5.4.4)
  - o West Indian/Afro Caribbean/Jamaican/Dominican/Barbadian etc. (5.4.5)
- Sub-national
  - o Tribes i.e. Yorubas/Nubians/Ashanti/Zulu (5.4.6)
  - o Urban/ghetto (5.4.7)
- Descriptive
  - o The 'N' words (5.4.8)
  - o Coloured/Of Colour (4.4.9)
  - o Multi-Racial/Multi-Cultural/Multi-Ethnic (5.4.10)
  - o Black (5.4.11)
- Undialectical
  - o Human being/all the same/does not matter (5.4.12)
  - o I'm an individual/it's a personal thing/I am me (5.4.13)

5.4.3 British

We originate from Afrika not Britain. Amongst other things our identity links us to a land, locating our group's collective origin in time and space; not to the land of our individual birth or residence which may equate to citizenship. Garvey repeatedly exposed the bankruptcy of citizenship as an indicator of Afrikan identity. He said:

> "Now, let us go back to the natur[al] existence of the individual. I had a Black mother and a Black father. Can you imagine that you could have conceived me as a British first before I was conceived as an offspring? Just argue that out for yourselves. How impossible it is for a man to be first a nationality before he was completely born. He was part of a man and part of God's own image before he was brought to see the light of day, therefore he must first be of his race before he could be of his nation." (Hill, 1995, p. 188) ... [and] ..."I am not an Englishman by race, I am a Britisher by nationality. Just as you are true to your Anglo-Saxon race and type – and you would be unworthy if you were not – so am I true to my Afrikan race and Afrikan type ... Before a man is born to a nation he is conceived to a race; so his nationality is only accident whilst his race is positive ... God intended us to have different outlooks from the social and political points of view; that is why geographically he suited you for Europe and me for Afrika." (Mackie, 2008, p. 155) ... [and] ... "... you have made me by compulsion a British subject, when by election I would be an Afrikan citizen ...." (Mackie, 2008, p. 151)

Furthermore, the shameless British imperial track record equates to genocide - the worse in the history of humanity. The adjacent table provides a sample of the mayhem, remorselessly heaped on the world through British imperialism's invasions conquests and occupations. Britain currently disguises its sadistic anti-human global assault under the title 'British Commonwealth'.

Ireland Gibraltar	Iraq Palestine	US Satan Canada	Australia New Zealand	Zimbabwe Nigeria
	India China	Caribbean		South Afrika Sierra Leone
Europe	**Asia**	**America**	**Oceania**	**Afrika**

Each and every conquered nation/region provides conclusive proof of the systematic bloody carnage perpetrated by the British through war against innocent unsuspecting fellow human beings in their own lands. If you are British, your ancestors were responsible for this. Afrikan people should not disgrace our ancestors by claiming to be British. They are totally innocent, never having committed genocide. The evil was done *to them*, not *by them*.

The British elite are the scum of the earth - the worse (most evil) set of people in history of humanity. They stole, killed, lied on a massive scale and are still doing it today. In fact, British imperialism gave birth to its settler-colony US Satan. This label goes further than merely dividing Afrikan people. It associates unsuspecting Afrikan people with our objective enemy. By identifying as British, we enter the slippery road of giving our loyalty to our oppressor. The natural outcome of this course is self-oppression. It is difficult to conceive a worse possible identity choice for Afrikan people.

Total dissociation from 'Britishness' is not an absolute requirement if we recognise the difference between citizenship and identity. Afrikan people born or resident in Britain may be British citizens. Citizenship is basically a contract between an individual and a state conferring rights and responsibilities. There is no reason for Afrikan people to give up their citizenship rights for no gain. The essential point is that it must not override Afrikan identity – their primary loyalty must remain uncompromisingly to Afrika.

5.4.4 Partitions i.e. Ghana/Nigeria/Kenya/South Afrika
All modern Afrikan micro/jigsaw puzzle pretend states are derivatives of entities created by European imperialists at the anti-Afrikan Berlin Conference of 1884/5. Its purpose was to invade and where feasible occupy our motherland as a basis for stealing our wealth. These militarily enforced divisions were to advance imperialism's interests, not Afrika's.

In a flurry of 'independence' in the 1960's we renamed many of them. As we put our names to our enemy's artificial entities imposed on our soil, at a deeper level we made ourselves loyal to false constructions, designed to be against our best interests. It is an objective error to be loyal to artificially constructed enemy entities. We must not lose sight of the fact that they were imposed on us as an act of war to dispossess us of our land.

The partitioning of Afrika was designed to separate and divide us from fellow Afrikan people. Its continuation keeps us divided as opposed to united, making us politically, economically and militarily weak and unable to protect ourselves. This is consistent with the intentions of our imperialist enemy. Furthermore, these enemy constructed entities seduce us into giving up Afrika as a whole for just a part of it and limit our horizons and national viability. The political objective of Afrikan people is continental unity for our worldwide governance. The enemy constructed jigsaw puzzle pretend states stand in open opposition, undermining our common identity.

5.4.5 Jamaican/West Indian/(Afro)Caribbean

According to European mythology, the Caribbean was discovered by Christopher Columbus in 1492. There was no Caribbean before 1492 i.e. the term 'Caribbean' as applied to the region has no history before that date. It follows that 'Caribbean people', if they exist at all, are nothing more than babies in history. Worse still, their only history is slavery, colonialism and neo-colonialism. They are disconnected from Afrika's great history – the longest and richest in humanity.

They are separated from their status as the original human being i.e. the mother and father of humanity to which all other branches owe their existence. Furthermore, Afrikan people did not arrive in the Caribbean by choice they were stolen from Afrika and left stranded. Added to this is the absurdity of giving up the richest continent in the world for a tiny speck of land. This is objectively unwise because, regardless of how beautiful those specs are, they are no match for our motherland Afrika.

The historic truth is, when Columbus (a European, not an Afrikan person) stumbled across the Americas he was lost. It wasn't as though he was at the Houses of Parliament looking for Trafalgar Square or London's Wembley stadium looking for its Olympic stadium or in London (England) looking for Manchester (England) or in England looking for Germany. The region is called West Indies because he thought he was in India when he was actually the other side of the world in the Americas. This disorientated being was arguably the most intelligent European of his era, his peers thought the world was flat and feared falling off.

His arrival was symbolic of the arrival of genocidal maniac murderers, who practiced their evil against American Indians and Afrikan people as well as some of their own. He paved the way for an ongoing 500+ year anti-Afrikan holocaust in the form of Slavery, Colonialism and Neo-Colonialism. His 'discovery' is symbolic of a double genocide (American Indian and Afrikan people).

Current names in that region have the impact of dividing and segmenting Afrikan people, separating them by island or region. They encourage Afrikan people at home and abroad to believe that those abroad are something other than Afrikan people. By blocking us from uniting, these terms operate in active service of the imperialist enemy agenda. This problem was recognised by Garvey who emphasised Afrikan unity through identity in the following words:

> "All [Afrikans], whether in [US Satan], the West Indies, South and Central America or Afrika, have but one common parentage ..." (Hill, 1984, p. 160) ... [and] ... "Everybody knows that there is absolutely no difference between the native Afrikan and the American and West Indian [Afrikans], in that we are descendants from one common family stock. It is only a matter of accident that we have been divided and kept apart for over three hundred years, but it is felt that when the time has come for us to get back together, we shall do so in the spirit of brotherly love, and any [Afrikan] who expects that he will be assisted here, there or anywhere by the UNIA to exercise a haughty superiority over the fellows of his own race, makes a tremendous mistake. Such men had better remain where they are and not attempt to become in any way interested in the higher development of Afrika." (Garvey, 1986, p. 70)

In addition there is the problem that whoever defines your land decides where your power goes. Also whoever defines your land decides which purpose you serve and in truth those lands belong to the Arawaks and Caribs. We may have legitimate tenancy rights, but fundamentally ownership belongs to American Indians. The same basic arguments apply to each and every Caribbean island and their labels given by

Europeans.

It is also true for terms such as West Indian and to cap it all the literal interpretation of 'Afro-Caribbean' is a hairstyle that eats people. Yes, Caribbean means cannibal! This derogatory title for the region and its people is additional confirmation that Columbus was a seriously disorientated being and certainly not worthy of naming us. It is folly to allow our enemy to name us.

5.4.6 Tribes i.e. Yorubas/Nubians/Ashantis/Zulu

The tribe is the largest family grouping known to humanity. It is biologically based in that all of its members claim descent from a single human being. In sequence, there is family, extended family, clan and tribe. Since a tribe is a family unit, there is no need for oppression of its members. All modern nations without exception deploy state mechanisms to oppress sections of their populations. The tribe does not have a state mechanism, which is a critical feature distinguishing it from a nation.

Tribes come with nepotism in-built and if this is not kept in check, the seeds are sown for tribalism – the antagonistic confrontation between tribes, which is both destructive and counter-productive. Furthermore, the historical phase of tribal governance is effectively over as industrialisation disperses people around nations and the world on a non-tribal basis. In this era, tribes are unable to provide their members with an adequate support base/infrastructure. Increasingly, their members leave to seek work. Industrialisation in this phase of history requires the nation state and overpowers tribes/monarchies everywhere, which are retained in some instances as historical/emotional relics.

Our tribes are deeply rooted in our identity. They are an intimate part of who and what we are. They are natural and are objectively and scientifically sound as a basis for identity at the biological and geographical levels. However, in addition to their inappropriateness as a mode of governance in an industrial setting, tribal level identity limits our ability to unite on a continental and global scale, if we are not prepared to make it secondary to our allegiance to Afrika. It can keep us separated and divided, limiting our horizons to outdated non-viable sub-nations that cause us to give up our collective right to the whole of the richest continent in the world, for just a section of it. Imperialism has specifically fostered tribalism to keep itself in a position of power.

The term 'Nubian' has attracted some attention in recent years, being wrongly used as a description for all Afrikan people. There was never a time when the term 'Nubian' depicted the whole Afrikan continent. It refers to a mountainous region of what is today Sudan. Perhaps it was chosen because it is the region of the continent to which origin of the Pyramids of Kemet/Egypt can be traced (Diop, 1974, p. 156).

It is also a section of the continent where Afrikan Christians successfully warded off invasions from the north (at least for a period) and is possibly remembered favourably by some for that act of resistance. However, the fact remains that it is the name of a tribe and therefore suffers from all of the inherent weaknesses of any and all of the tribal labels as markers of Afrikan identity.

5.4.7 Urban/Ghetto/Post Codes
The terms 'urban' and 'ghetto' have in common the fact that they refer to localised living conditions/environments. They are not identities at all. Urban is a by-product of capitalism, associated only with cities. At the heart of capitalism is industrialisation and its mass producing factories. Those factories require workers living in close proximity. In order to fulfil this need, capitalism condensed low cost concrete housing close to its factories.

It is the replacement of soil through concretisation that characterises the term urban. Urbanisation separates people from their land through concrete infrastructure. It is in a sense the skeleton of the city. One of the major trends of capitalism during the twentieth century was drawing people from the soil of countryside to concrete of cities (sometimes across national boarders) and through that process urbanising them.

Similarly the term ghetto describes a section of the city. It was originally used in Venice, Italy to describe a part of that city to which Jews were restricted/segregated. It is now more generally applied to impoverished areas containing slums occupied by socially disadvantaged/segregated 'minority groups'.

Both 'urban' and 'ghetto' are deliberately misapplied to Afrikan people in order to promote identity confusion. They foster disunity by linking and limiting identity to whosoever happens to be in a particular neighbourhoods. This distorts our bio-geographical allegiances and because the catchment area is so small, is an obvious means of dispersing Afrikan people to foster disunity.

They are the domain of gangs and a basis for small scale group violence, particularly among young people fighting over territories owned by others. The beneficiary of the splintering and disunity is our capitalist/imperialist enemy, since these entities are too small/powerless to pose substantive threat to state power. Post codes in this context are merely a variation of the others with essentially the same drawbacks.

These labels fail as a basis for unity on at least two counts: Firstly, they encourage Afrikan people to group with non-Afrikans as their primary allegiance. It is unreasonable to expect non-Afrikans to have the unification and liberation of Afrika as their primary or even prioritised concern. By linking in this way, Afrikan people are diverted into other agendas, not necessarily supportive of Afrikan people's critical issue – our liberation.

Secondly, the localised nature of these groupings, coupled with antagonistic relations with others in their vicinity, create scenarios where Afrikan people in one locality can find themselves in pitch battles with their local fellows. Groups can actively encourage Afrikan members to fight each other even to the death, rather than unite for common liberation. Created by non-Afrikans for their purposes, the labels 'urban', 'ghetto' and 'post codes', are false identities throwing Afrikan people off course, enticing them away from the Afrikan liberation agenda.

5.4.8 The 'N' words
The various versions of the 'N' word can be traced to the term 'Negro', which comes from the Portuguese language meaning Black. At one level, it is an attempt to describe what Afrikan people look like. There are those who claim it to have its etymological root in the Latin term 'Nerco' meaning dead. This version of its origin implies a negative connotation, which does not automatically flow from the word Black.

Regardless of the original meaning, the various versions of the 'N' word, through their association with slavery, became negative, derogatory and destructive, used to demean Afrikan people. The 'Negro' was by enemy design, a specimen less than human. By accepting and adopting these labels we unite, not for our purpose of liberation, but to languish in a cesspool of inferiority. They are to a greater or lesser extent insults, unworthy of recognition as an identity.

There has been a recent trend amongst a sub-section of young Afrikan people to reuse the 'N' word as an apparent term of endearment. This is counter-productive because by using these terms, Afrikan people empower others including enemies to do likewise. They claim to be turning/transforming it into something positive; something to be proud of in an apparent 'reclaiming' of the word. This calibre of argument amounts to nothing more than unmitigated nonsense. It is not possible to reclaim something which was not yours in the first place. These labels have always been owned by their creators – Europeans. If there is any reclaiming being done, it is our European imperialist enemy that is doing it, through us.

5.4.9 Coloured/Of colour
In truth the terms 'coloured' and 'of colour' are not identity labels at all. They are used to project Europeans as 'centre' of humanity against which all else should be excluded and measured as inferior. They are specifically designed to reduce the collective 'other' to the position of 'object' in relation to Europeans, who are treated as 'subject' and therefore superior. In short they are biased, used as terms to misleadingly group together 'non-Europeans', simultaneously denying them their particular identities.

If they were relative or neutral, to Afrikan people they would mean Asians, American Indians, Aborigines and Europeans etc. To the Asian, Afrikan people, American Indians, Aborigines and Europeans etc. To the American Indian, Afrikan people, Aborigines, Asians and Europeans etc. To the Aborigines, Afrikan people, American Indians, Asians and Europeans etc.

By separating Europeans from the rest of humanity, they can have the unintended helpful impact of encouraging broad alliances between oppressed people worldwide. However, this should not be confused with ascribing identities, nor do we have to pretend to be the same to make them. Each group needs to be clear on its own identity as a basis for determining its particular interests. It is common interests that provide basis for alliances not shared identity. For Afrikan people specifically they are another dilution, grouping Afrikan people with non-Afrikans to divert them from focused concentration on Afrikan liberation.

Equalised Relationships

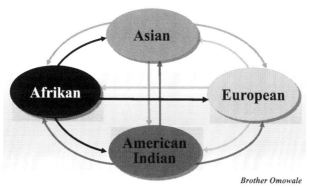

Brother Omowale

The main exception to the above usage of 'coloured' is in South Afrika where steeped in the abhorrent racism of the apartheid system introduced by Afrikaaners in 1948, the term 'coloured' is used as a derogatory reference for people of mixed Afrikan and European heritage. It is treated as a badge of superiority over Afrikan people and inferiority under Europeans. Imbibed with elitism and hatred, it has no role to play in ascribing Afrikan people's identity.

5.4.10 Multi-Racial/Multi-Cultural/Multi-Ethnic/Multi-National

The shameless anti-human racism of the Afrikaners in South Afrika raises its head in this area, through its use of 'multi-national':

> "For Apartheid, drawing on organic notions of 'national' communities derived from German romanticism, has created and given popular credence – through legislative structures – to the view that South Afrika is a multi-national country comprised of discrete ethnic groups, such as Zulu's an Xhosas, each having a sense of common unity stemming from common origin, each possessing immutable cultural

and psychological attributes." (Taylor, 1991, p. 6)

This abstract usage of the term is completely arbitrary, having no scientific basis. Its purpose was to create and stimulate violent conflict between sub-groupings of Afrikan people as a means of assisting minority European racists maintain power and control.

This usage turns on its head the manner in which other European racists use similar terms. 'Multi' is used as a catch all allowing disparate groups to be lumped together as one. In this scenario, these terms lose Afrikan identity in a loose nebulous grouping of any and everything that might be broadly categorised as an identity. They therefore treat very different peoples, each with their distinct histories and cultures as though they are all the same. As with terms like 'coloured' and 'political Black', their impact is to dilute Afrikan people's liberation efforts. Terms such as 'ethnic minorities' and 'diversity', have been added to the mix to achieve the same purpose.

This heads imperialism wins, tails Afrikan people lose scenario sees on the one hand Afrikan people battling each other to the death to indirectly keep their oppressor in power, whilst the other parcels them off into non-descript groupings that cannot have Afrikan liberation as their main concern since they are also composed of non-Afrikans with different agendas. Created by Europeans for their own purpose, neither usage is of advantage to Afrikan people.

5.4.11 Black

The term 'Black' is a scientifically inaccurate attempt to describe what Afrikan people look like. It is an approximation for appearance, mimicking the biological component of identity, but it does not say who we are or where we're from and in truth is not a valid name of a people. Whilst there are some ancient names (some still used in areas) meaning black, there is no land called Black. No land base implies no point of origin and means having no secure base for resources, power, history and culture.

Used as a metaphor in the context of identity, the word Black is descriptive with no actual meaning. In Britain, the word has been stripped even of its descriptive character and reshaped into a metaphor with a different meaning. The term 'Political Black' has been adopted by Europeans and others in a bid to take it over and use it for their own purposes. Used on an as and when needed basis, non-Afrikans adopt it at discretion.

For instance when government grants are issued to 'Black' groups, non-Afrikan groupings rush to the front of the queue, take the money and having successfully achieved their objective revert to their true identity. When poor housing, police brutality, shorter life expectancy etc is issued to Afrikan people, these 'politically black' groups are nowhere to be seen. This is not an option available to Afrikan people, who cannot remove that label at will.

Another issue with the term is its negative connotations. Simply pick up a dictionary and compare the terms 'Black' and 'white'. 'Black' will describe bad or negative attributes, whilst 'white' is associated with good. The only situation which goes against this trend is banking – here 'black' means to have a surplus in your bank account. However, even this has its origin in the enslavement of Afrikan people, where money and gold was measured in Guineas i.e. enslaved Afrikan people from Guinea.

Despite these setbacks, 'Black' was to an extent successfully adopted by Afrikan people and deployed as a source of pride in the 1960's. It represented an advance from more derogatory labels to a source of pride during the period in question. We moved from 'Negro' to 'Coloured' to 'Black Power'. The older terms were chosen by European elite for their purposes, but we chose 'Black' for ourselves. In that sense, it represented an advance. It also represented a qualitative leap towards unity amongst Afrikan people.

'Political Black' has the impact of undermining the unifying successes gained under Black Power. Capitalism's invitation to any and everyone to use it, supported by money to encourage its adoption, has reduced 'Black' to the status of words such as 'coloured', 'multi-racial', 'ethnic minority' and the like. These are melting pot terms which encourage Afrikan people to link primarily with non-Afrikans. It distorts their ability to organise as Afrikan people for liberation by incorporating non-Afrikans with different agendas. Furthermore, it should not escape our notice that 'Black Power' has (as Kwame Ture – the person who popularised the term - reminded us) moved on to Pan-Afrikanism.

5.4.12 Human Being/All the same/Part of the world

Not all people are the same and not all people are Afrikan. Some people are good whilst others are bad; some are poor and oppressed whilst others are their rich oppressors; some fight for just causes whilst others for unjust ones. There are people that are actually harming us and joining with them is tantamount to self destruction.

The argument that we are all the same misses the central and dialectical point of identity i.e. that we are all the same and at the same time different. Its concentration is on sameness, not identity. In failing to recognise that humanity has sub-groupings with different, sometimes competing/antagonistic interests, it is less than unhelpful and actually misleading. It is obvious that all individuals and groups have their distinct point of origin – it simply is not possible to originate from everywhere at the same time.

A distorted interpretation of Nkrumah's definition of Afrikan may appear to give credence to the false notion that everyone on earth is an Afrikan person with the same origin and are therefore the same. He writes:

> "All peoples of Afrikan descent, whether they live in North or South America, the Caribbean, or in any other part of the world are Afrikans and belong to the Afrikan nation." (Nkrumah, 1980, p. 87)

On the face of it, it might appear all inclusive in the sense that everyone in the world could claim Afrikan descent. There are some non-Afrikans who mischievously advance this falsehood as a basis for staking bogus claim to the riches of Afrika. It is only when the quote is put into context that its correct meaning becomes clear. Nkrumah provides an endnote further explaining his definition:

> "The Afrikan revolutionary struggle is not an isolated one. It not only forms part of the world socialist revolution, but must be seen in the context of the Black Revolution as a whole. In [US Satan], the Caribbean, and wherever Afrikans are oppressed, liberation struggles are being fought. In these areas, the Black man is in a condition of domestic

colonialism and suffers both on the grounds of class and colour." (Nkrumah, 1980, p. 87)

He clearly identifies areas of the world where the Afrikan Diaspora resides and struggles against oppression. The initial quote is therefore underpinned by a biological requirement for Afrikan identity. It is not open to everyone.

It is true that everyone can trace their origin to Afrika, but for the purpose of identity further clarification is needed. Two things happened simultaneously with the birth of humanity. Firstly there was the birth of the human race and secondly there was the birth of the Afrikan segment of the human race. Archaeologists trace this birth to between 100,000 and 200,000 years ago.

Between 20,000 and 40,000 years ago the European segment of humanity was born under the conditions of the ice age. Around 15,000 years ago Asians were born as an admixture between Afrikan people and Europeans (Diop, 1991, p. 11-23; Van Sertima, 1996, p. 288-307). These are the three main branches of humanity with their respective reproduction centres in different parts of the world. These categories of humanity are in all likelihood the root of the others.

Afrikan Origin of Humanity

Brother Omowale

These geo-biological changes are significant at the level of identity. They provide obvious distinguishing features between categories of people although at the boarders it is not necessarily possible to determine where one category ends and the other begins. The borderline is to that extent arbitrary, but that doesn't alter the material fact that the groups are distinct.

These differences have nothing to do with superiority or inferiority. When Europeans emerged, whilst they ceased to be Afrikan they were no less human and the same is true for Asians and the other branches of humanity. They have all ceased to be Afrikans, but the changes were not significant enough to impact their humanity - their humanity remains intact. The point is Afrikan people are the original human beings and the other branches are neither Afrikan nor original, not that they are not human. Afrikan people are the prototype of humanity to which all others owe their existence – no other group can claim this. Though we have many significant things in common, we are not the same.

5.4.13 I'm an individual/it's a personal thing/I am me

Even though it is true that we are all unique and have individuality, the essential point of identity is to link us with our fundamental grouping - a grouping which came into existence at a point in time and space. Focusing on the individual separates us from our parents, ancestors and groupings from which we are derived. It therefore disconnects us from our history and culture and stands in open opposition to the fact that matter is one unified inseparable whole. It therefore separates us from and defies reality. By failing to recognise the connections and similarities between people, this set of labels is useless for ascribing identity.

4.4.14 Summary of imposter Afrikan identity labels

The following is a breakdown of the pretenders to Afrikan identity, broken down into 4 categories:

- Citizenship:
  - British
  - Partitions i.e. Ghanaians/Nigerians/Gambians/South Afrikans
  - West Indian/Afro Caribbean/Jamaican/Dominica/Barbados etc.
- Sub-national:
  - Tribes i.e. Yorubas/Nubians/Ashanti/Zulu
  - Urban/ghetto

- Descriptive:
  - The 'N' words
  - Coloured/Of Colour
  - Multi-Racial/Multi-Cultural/Multi-Ethnic
  - Black
- Undialectical:-
  - Human being/all the same/does not matter
  - I'm an individual/it's a personal thing/I am me

The undialectical contenders can be summarily dismissed for failing to take proper account of the fact that all humans are the same and simultaneously different. Engaging this contradiction is at the heart of identity and for opposite reasons they miss this central point.

Descriptive labels are just that 'labels', much like sweet packaging. The packaging is somebody's invention. Designed for their purpose, it eventually becomes associated with the sweet in our minds – as does the label with the entity/identity. Objectively, they have nothing to do with each other outside the association we're trained to make and in describing Afrikan people, they are always inaccurate.

Furthermore, since they are inventions they can be reinvented/reformatted. Whatever was the intention when invented, capitalism uses its dominance to recalibrate them to mean all groupings that are not European. They then become a basis for including non-Afrikans in our primary group, who divert us because Afrikan liberation is not their main concern.

Sub-national labels are actively encouraged by capitalism as they are ideal for ensuring that oppressed people remain divided. Whether it is tribes in Afrika or gangs in ghettos, they operate below the level of state power. Gangs cannot achieve state power and tribes achieve it against the resentment of others. They entrench permanent divisions, whilst posing no threat to the state which has the power to dispense with them at will. They divert Afrikan people's attention away from liberation to relatively petty emotionally charged localised antagonistic issues.

At the heart of capitalism's agenda is theft of other people's resources. It created conquered nations, giving citizenship to its hostages.

Highlighting citizenship as a badge of honour directed conquered people's attention away from their identities and corresponding interests. If they know their identity, they will better understand their relations with their oppressive enemy and the need to overthrow it. Its role therefore is to defuse the revolutionary threat by supplanting their identity with an alternative making them loyal to their enemy, confused and impotent.

Capitalism uses citizenship to deceive and draw loyalty from its victims, to turn them into its active willing servants. If they can be persuaded they're British or of an Afrikan or Caribbean neo-colony, they are more likely to wound their own people on capitalism's behalf and capitalism can rest assured that it has them firmly under its control. The object of capitalism's trickery, is to diffuse the threat of revolution from its root.

5.5 Classification of Afrikan identity
5.5.1 Material components of Afrikan identity
Out of an estimated 1.6 billion Afrikan people in the world, approximately 1.2 are to be found in Afrika. Furthermore, no other category of humanity comes even remotely close to that number in Afrika. The geographical centre of gravity for Afrikan people unsurprisingly is Afrika. Whilst there are 400 million Afrikan people outside Afrika, that doesn't move the centre of gravity from the continent. The presence of 120 or so million Arabs, other Asians and Europeans in Afrika also has a negligible impact on Afrikan people's geo-biological centre of gravity.

Biologically, the Afrikan person is typically characterised by high melanin content, producing darker hued people. There will be variations around this central theme, but it nonetheless remains correct. There will be and are Afrikan people with lower levels of melanin and correspondingly lighter hues, but their number is not significant enough to alter the central theme. There will be non-Afrikans born, living or otherwise resident in Afrika, but again too few in number to significantly impact the central theme.

Similarly, there will be Afrikan people born with one non-Afrikan parent, with a corresponding impact on their biological make up. In addition to their number being too small to change the central theme, group identities are best categorised, not by their extremities where the lines

168

between them are blurred and there may be overlap, but by their cores where the differences between what is typical of each are pronounced and clear. Identity is underpinned biologically/scientifically/materially by melanin.

Afrikan people also have satellite reproduction centres around the world including the Caribbean, parts of South and Central America, zones in metropolitan centres etc., but their numbers are nowhere near a match for the reproduction rates in our centre of gravity. The continuous ongoing reproduction of new people in the Afrikan centre i.e. the Afrikan continent typically brings forth human beings high in melanin content in volumes far in excess of any other part of the world. This biological point has no connection whatsoever with notions of superiority and inferiority. Being composed of the same matter makes all human beings equal in essence.

Taking account of all of the geographical and biological variations and inconsistencies, *the core material elements of* what it is to be *an Afrikan person* remain intact i.e. *your people's central reproduction and point of origin is Afrika where the new people being produced are typically dark hued with high melanin content – Afrika is the location of your people's collective origin about 200k years ago*. There is no getting away from the scientifically verifiable material reality of the core geographical and biological elements of Afrikan identity. We can think of it as the prototype of Afrikan identity, a yardstick against which to measure, rather than an absolute. It can be expected to operate a bit like Standard English. There are many variations, but that is the version around which they vary to a greater or lesser extent. In relation to Afrikan identity, if you fit the criteria, you are materially an Afrikan person. How broadly the material element of Afrikan identity is interpreted was addressed by Garvey. He explained:

"The programme of the UNIA is the drawing together, into one universal whole, all the [Afrikan] peoples of the world, with prejudice towards none. We desire to have every shade of our colour, even those with one drop of Afrikan blood, in our fold; because we believe that none of us, as we are, is responsible for our birth; in a word, we have no prejudice against ourselves in race. We believe that every [Afrikan person] racially is just alike, and, therefore we have no distinction to make, hence wherever you see the UNIA you will find us giving every member of our race an equal chance and opportunity to make good." (Mackie, 2008, p. 130)

5.5.2 A 4 Dialectic framework for Afrikan identity

Cabral and Garvey point to the error of relying too heavily on the essential, but potentially misleading biological component of identity. If we treat it literally it becomes unscientific, unable to accommodate variation and leads to false conclusions such as – the darker you are the more Afrikan – an obvious absurdity. By utilising the 'one drop' criterion, space is left for Afrikan people indistinguishable from Europeans in appearance, to nonetheless retain and claim their Afrikan identity – Afrikaness is not rigidly about colour.

The material base for identity is land of central reproduction and origin coupled with the biological group from which the individual comes. Its *matspiritual* categories simultaneously sit on top of and lay within its material elements. As Afrikan people interact with nature in their natural environment i.e. their reproduction centre, they produce their unique history and culture, comprising: economics, politics, ideology and philosophy – the *4 Dialectic categories*. We can say history and culture are expressed in the *4 Dialectic categories* or the *4 Dialectic categories* come out of history and culture.

More precisely, culture comes out of history and the *4 Dialectic categories* are contained in culture. This means history and culture are implicit in the *4 Dialectic categories* and are therefore incorporated within it. The *4 Dialectic categories* is shorthand i.e. a reference point for a people's history and culture. Its economic, political, ideological and philosophical categories relate to culture, as production, governance, principles and methodology relate to society. Afrikan identity has expressions at all four of these levels, with material reality as their base.

5.5.3 Economic and political components of Afrikan identity

The economic element of our identity is indelibly linked to what we produce. In Afrika this is hampered by: (i) outside interference; and (ii) outdated internal production methods devoid of industrialisation. Our disrupted relationship with our land through slavery, colonialism and now neo-colonialism, undermines Afrikan identity at this level. We are nonetheless still winning economically because of our reproduction successes. Despite imperialism's induced proxy wars, famines, Aids/Ebola attacks etc., our population has risen fourfold from 400 million to 1,600 million in the 100 years since Garvey and the UNIA was at its height.

However, reproduction success by itself is not enough. To have people is one thing, what those people are capable of is another. Afrika must industrialise to look after the interests of its people effectively, overcome poverty and become self-sustaining. Afrikan people must have the technical ability to drive an industrialisation programme. This will bring the economic element of Afrikan identity up to date and end our dependency. It will positively impact Afrikan pride and wealth, restoring and bolstering our identity at the economic level.

At the political level it is here assumed that the basis of our grouping is as Afrikan people. The main identity issue here is our lack of unity, which betrays a lack of political organisation and education. So long as we remain disoriented, allowing our identity to be directed by outsiders, it will not be possible to solve our identity problem at any level. The Afrikan Union (AU) currently operates as an obstacle, but cannot fully contain our ground level movement towards Afrikan political unity. Despite it, the continent and Diaspora edge ever so slowly in that direction.

To speed up the process, Afrikan people must join genuine liberation organisations and undergo political education *en masse*. This will be a prelude to taking, controlling and effectively managing state level political power. This will be a catalyst for our political unity, providing the basis for restoring the full character of Afrikan identity. The overthrow of the outdated externally controlled Afrikan Union (AU) and its replacement with a unified modern people controlled continental super state responsible for Afrikan people worldwide is the political antidote for bringing us up to date and restoring Afrikan identity at this level.

5.5.4 Ideological component of Afrikan identity
Ideology in the cultural plane is expressed as a principle or cluster of principles in the social. Nkrumah's Afrikan Personality (Nkrumah, 2009,

p. 79) is the summary of the ideology of the Afrikan group. The principles underlying the Afrikan Personality are: (i) Humanism – people before property; Egalitarianism – we're all equal; and Collectivism – we before me. The Afrikan Personality is the codification of what it is to objectively be an Afrikan person at the ideological level i.e. a critical part of the *matspiritual* expression of Afrikan identity.

It should also be noted that the cluster of humanist principles inculcated in the Afrikan Personality are precisely the same as those of: (i) Afrikan culture; (ii) Communalism; (iii) Socialism; and (iv) Communism – they are all part of the same ideological family. It follows that hysterical anti-socialism and anti-communism, in addition to being anti-Afrikan and counter revolutionary, are signs of identity confusion in Afrikan people at the level of political economy.

Afrikan purveyors of these sentiments are confused. The ideological element of their identity has been corrupted to the point where they neither understand Afrikan culture, nor know what they are ideologically. They hysterically condemn the very outcome that is their freedom i.e. socialism, mistakenly believing the fabrication that it is a 'white man's system' and no amount of rational explanation seems able to surpass their subjective misunderstanding.

Where the individual's ideology is out of sync with their geo-biological group, there is identity confusion; where it is consistent, there is identity congruence. One objective for Afrikan people is to achieve identity congruence. This forms one of the bases for unity and common purpose. Purveyors may genuinely desire freedom, but their ideological confusion is blocking their path to it.

The Afrikan Personality is the medicine for identity confusion amongst Afrikan people. The remedy is the development of structured mass education programmes aimed at helping our people thoroughly understand and live by the principles/ideology underlying the Afrikan Personality. The organisation that can bring together the mass fanatical desire to be abundantly proud Afrikan people with the mass fanatical desire to practice socialism scientifically in the modern era, is the one that will plot the path to Afrika's true liberation.

5.5.5 Philosophical component of Afrikan identity

At an even higher/deeper *matspiritual* level there is the person, their emotions and subjectivity. In this realm it is possible for somebody to objectively fit the geographical, biological and ideological criteria for Afrikan identity, be aware that they fit, but nonetheless subjectively deny their Afrikan status. This calibre of behaviour moves beyond identity confusion to identity rejection. Their rejection is more than a refusal to embrace what they objectively are, it is a deeper level emotional refusal to associate with the 'bad', 'wrong', 'lesser' or 'losing' side.

If a European man Tarzan can swing through Afrika single-handedly 'beating up' any and all Afrikan people he chooses with consummate ease; If naked Afrikan children with bloated bellies are dying of starvation on camera, unaided by Afrikan adults; If Afrikan people can be shown to be killing fellow Afrikan people at a rate higher than any other identity grouping as recent and current wars in the Congo, Sudan, Sierra Leone, Rwanda etc. demonstrate; if it is a source of shame, why should anyone want to associate with Afrika and her people?

What matters at this level of identity is not whether the picture presented is true, but whether: (a) it is believable; (b) the subject chooses to believe it; and (c) the subject acts on their belief. Cabral reminds us of the importance of the *matspiritual* ingredients of identity, when he says:

> "One must point out that in the fundamental binomial the definition of identity, the sociological factors are more determining than the biological ... the need not to confuse, the *original identity*, of which the biological element is the main determinant, with the *actual identity*, of which the main determinant is the sociological element." (Afrika Information Service, 1973, p. 65)

At the philosophical level, the subjective mind has such an impact that it exercises a kind of 'power of veto,' even over objective material reality. This is why capitalism invests so much time and energy dehumanising and denigrating Afrika and her people – it must make Afrikan people appear sub-human. If it can imbibe disdain for Afrika and self-hatred into Afrikan people, causing them to dissociate from Afrika, they won't protect it; the path is then left clear for its theft of Afrikan resources with little or no resistance.

The remedy for this was pointed out by Marcus Garvey about 100 years ago. The first step is the objective acceptance of Afrikan identity. The second is pride; pride in being an Afrikan member of humanity; and if necessary, the unrelenting exhibition of Afrikan pride in abundance, coupled with the unremitting desire to be Afrikan regardless of whatever negatives, reality or myth might throw forward.

Garvey gave scientific expression to confronting this deeply embedded subjective problem in the form of Afrikan Fundamentalism, in which he emphasised our unassailable reason for being proud Afrikan people, despite our objectively wretched state:

> "The world today is indebted to us for the benefits of civilization. They stole our arts and sciences from Afrika. Then why should we be ashamed of ourselves? Their modern improvements are but duplicates of a grander civilization that we as [Afrikan people] reflected thousands of years ago." (Garvey, 1986, p. 145)

Garvey countered imperialism's dehumanisation/demonization project, not by merely stating the obvious truth that we are human, but by identifying Afrikan people as the pinnacle of humanity, not in the sense of superiority, but in the sense that Afrikan people and their provable ancestors are the source of absolutely everything that we call civilisation today. The whole of humanity is indebted to Afrikan people biologically, ideologically and every other way. For this they should all be grateful and we should be abundantly proud.

The restoration of Afrikan pride will be based on more than historical greatness. There must be contemporary sources, such as the land under the feet of 1.2 billion of us – the richest in the world. Afrikan people must work tirelessly to regain collective sovereignty over it. Success here will ignite Afrikan pride in abundance.

5.5.6 Afrikan identity summarised
To summarise, the ingredients of Afrikan identity are:
1. At the material/primary level:

      a. Your biological type's centre of reproduction and point of origin is Afrika; and

      b. Your biological type is typically high in melanin content;

2.   At the *matspiritual*/secondary level:

      a. You work tirelessly towards Afrikan people's unification and recovery of the richest land in the world - Afrika.

      b. You embody the Afrikan Personality i.e. the principles of humanism, egalitarianism and collectivism in your interactions with others and nature;

      c. You exhibit abundant pride in being Afrikan, even in the face of the most demeaning portrayals of Afrikan people; and

When everything else is stripped away (i.e. the false/misleading pretenders to being its base), what we are left with is the material essence i.e. the primary base of our Afrikan identity. 'Primary' is not an indicator of relative importance, but rather the starting point or foundation. Leaving aside the mental illness implied in the act, if we were to go to Tiananmen Square, strip naked and ask in Mandarin, what am I?, they wouldn't define us by our country of abode, citizenship, birth place, profession, religion or 'influences'. With no other point of reference, they would state what they see – an Afrikan person – perhaps a mad one, but an Afrikan person nonetheless. Their conclusion would be founded on our inescapable materially based geo-biological make up. Even if we didn't know or blatantly denied our Afrikan identity, the result would be the same.

Being Afrikan does not prevent us from being other things (plumbers, Christians, Moslems, citizens or residents of other nations etc.), but if the other thing is held primary over being Afrikan, where it conflicts with the interests of Afrikan people, it will cause us to act in ways that are to the disadvantage of Afrika and our people. Where the other thing is secondary, the contradiction is harmless.

5.5.7 The term 'Afrikan'

The term 'Afrika' has come under attack as an identity label in some quarters. Without going into them in detail, they all rest on the notion that the *matspiritual* label is incorrect. Afrika is not a *matspiritual* name, it is material land – the richest continent and second largest in the world. Whatever name we give to that territory, both the land and the darker hued people populating it are the objectively real basis for its classification. If we want to change the name to one which we can prove to be better, that's our right. However there are tactical issues to consider such as, when and by what process.

Our problem is a substantial proportion of our people neither know that they're Afrikan, nor understand the importance of knowing. Our task is to bring our people home to their Afrikan identity. If we change the name mid-process, when they don't yet know they're Afrikan people, we take away their sign post, add to their confusion and make the situation even worse. If the 'problem' of the name is real, the correct process for solving it is to continue to use the recognised name for the time being, to bring our people back home to their Afrikaness and when we all understand we are Afrikan people in need of a 'better' label, discuss prove vote on and if agreed change it.

5.6 Afrikan identity and orientation for liberation
5.6.1 Imperialism's identity agenda
Nkrumah opens his *Handbook of Revolutionary Warfare* by warning we must know our enemy (Nkrumah, 1980, p. 1). One critical part of knowing the enemy is deciphering and understanding its agenda. In the area of identity the enemy's higher objective is to dehumanise us thereby eliminating from within us pride, self-esteem and notions of subjective worth. It seeks to replace objective material reality that Afrikan people are human beings, with the subjective lie that we are beneath human status. It seeks to alienate us from being proud Afrikan people ready, willing and able to defend our space on earth. This is critical to dividing us so that it can continue to rule over us.

The enemy wants divisions to be intensely antagonistic leaving us at each others' throats. It aims to foster battles which undermine us from within, destroying our internal development. If it cannot get us to engage in internal acrimony, the next best thing is to get us to dissociate from fellow Afrikan people, physically and emotionally separating from them. This promotes individualism with its objective of 'doing what's best for me' and 'to hell with my brothers and sisters'. It is a more subtle method of divide and rule. This stands in stark contrast to our objective which is to unite and rule ourselves together.

5.6.2 Identity and the Afrikan liberation objective

Our task is to bring our scattered and disorientated Afrikan people back to who and what they really are. This requires something that objectively marks us as both special and successful whilst raising a desire within us to be associated with and recognised as Afrikan people.

One such thing is recognition that Afrikan people are the original human beings – the prototype of humanity from which all other branches of humanity flow. This means all of the other branches of humanity owe their very existence to Afrikan people. In other words, had Afrikan people not existed, no other section of humanity could have. To that extent all other branches are indebted to Afrikan people in much the same way that a child is indebted to its mother.

Another consideration is the fact that Afrikan people built great civilisations, some aspects of which, such as the great pyramids remain unequalled to the present. The fact that modern science is unable to reproduce what Afrikan people are known to have produced is objective evidence that no section of humanity can claim superiority to Afrikan people.

Yet another is under the feet of 1.2 billion of us – it is our land, by far the richest in the world. Regaining political and economic control of it through unified state power and industrialisation controlled by the Afrikan masses will turn Afrikan people into the richest and most powerful in the world. This will bring with it an obvious boost to our esteem and identity.

The fundamental operational dialectic of Afrikan identity is whether it divides Afrikan people so others can rule over us or unites us so that we can rule and govern ourselves in freedom, justice, peace and happiness. Amilcar Cabral summarises the positive impact of correctly classifying a people's identity and the imperialist agenda behind promoting their confusion:

> " ... to attribute, recognise or declare the identity of an individual or group is above all to place that individual or group in the framework of a culture." (Afrika Information Service, 1973, p. 66) ... [and] ... "to try to keep the permanency of its domination, it needs to destroy the social

structure, culture and by implication identity, of these groups." (Afrika Information Service, 1973, p. 67)

Afrika's imperial enemy is very clear on this issue. Not only does it realise that it must divide Afrikan people to rule over us as a prelude to stealing our wealth, it has been carrying out anti-Afrikan divide and rule for the last 500 years. Its unremitting attack against Afrikan identity, where it used its power and influence to actively block us from assuming our Afrikan identities whilst inventing and implanting false dehumanising ones, is an important element in its wider divide and rule strategy.

By contrast the masses of Afrikan people are not yet clear on the fundamental necessity of Afrikan unity and the critical need for our common and correct understanding of Afrikan identity in that process. Our identity confusion is partly because of imperialism's savage attacks, but fundamentally because we have never historically achieved Afrikan unity and common identity and therefore don't really know what we're missing.

Afrika was organically developing on its historical path towards continental unity. Certainly in the initial phases there were no outsiders, meaning it was free from external domination. Its principles and social systems were broadly just in that they were not based on exploitation. Communalism, the longstanding dominant social system was developing into the early phases of feudalism in some parts.

As part of that process, Afrika was developing larger and larger political, economic and social aggregates. It developed from family to clan to tribe to nation and even 'empires'. Examples include: (i) Ghana; (ii) Mali; (iii) Songhay; (iv) Zimbabwe; and (v) Monomatapa. These were all signs of its organic progression towards a kind of continental unity.

Before Afrikan people achieved organic unity, our progress was interrupted by imperialism's savagery. Through enslavement and colonisation it ravaged our identity in a calculated programme of divide and rule. In the modern day, its sinister tactic is to get us to:
1. Join it in destroying Afrikan people; or
2. Join anything that is against Afrika; or

3. Join anything so long as it is not Afrikan or not bothered with Afrika's best interests to keep us distracted from Afrika whilst it steals our resources.

Its reason for behaving in this way is to promote identity confusion. It is imperialism's desire to maintain control of Afrika and resources. People who are confused about their identity in addition to not knowing who and what they are do not know what their best interests are and don't protect them. Their ignorance presents a barrier to them uniting to fight imperialism which is the evil that stands against their collective interests.

In our case Afrika is the richest land on earth. Whoever controls Afrika are the most powerful people on the earth. The imperialist enemy currently control Afrika (European imperialists), making them the most powerful people on earth at this point in time. Imperialists don't want us to control Afrika. At the level of identity, they keep us from controlling Afrika by making us think we're not Afrikan people, actively hate Afrika (our identity, history, culture) and dissuading us from even thinking about Afrika in positive terms.

Pan-Africanism Overview

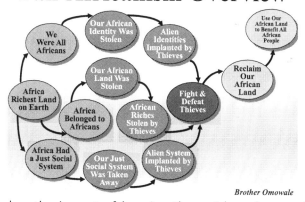

Brother Omowale

This tactic has the impact of keeping them rich and powerful and us poor and weak. When we take control of Afrika, we will become the most powerful people on earth. Aware of this they know their job is to prevent us from controlling Afrika. Our job is to take control, to re-establish ourselves and our power in the world. The first step is, not only knowing we are Afrikan people, but being abundantly proud of that honour i.e. recognising that it is an honour to be Afrikan. Garvey understood this and built it into the centre of his strategy for Afrikan people's redemption. In his words:

> "God almighty gave you a country – the richest and most prolific among all the continents. He gave you the great continent of Afrika. It is for you to repossess yourselves of it. Remember, men, the Afrikan is in each and every one of us coloured men. We cannot get away from it if we tried. One sixteenth of the bloo[d] makes you an Afrikan and we cannot get away from it. Therefore do not play the fool and talk about your not being an Afrikan. All of us are Afrikans. But the only difference is: some are Afrikans at home and others are Afrikans abroad. We are the Afrikans abroad, unfortunately. Why, I am so sorry I was born abroad! I wish I was born at home; there could be some trouble here today. I was born in an alien country ..." (Hill, 1983b, p. 414)

5.6.3 Afrikan identity: Towards solution

The whole point of clarifying Afrikan identity is the achievement of Afrikan unity - a point repeatedly emphasised by Garvey:

> "We of the UNIA are determined to unite 400,000,000 [Afrikans] for their own industrial, political, social and religious emancipation ... we are determined to unite the 400,000,000 [Afrikans] of the world for the purpose of building a civilization of their own. And in that effort we desire to bring together the 15,000,000 of the United States, the 180,000,000 in Asia, the West Indies and Central and South America, and the 200,000,000 in Afrika. We are looking toward political freedom on the continent of Afrika, the land of our fathers." (Garvey, 1986, p. 95)

If we don't know that we're dispossessed Afrikan people and that is fundamentally what we have in common, we are likely to make the error of uniting with wrong or even enemy groups in our quest for liberation. In short we will never be able to achieve unity if we don't even know what the base is for achieving it. Identity as dispossessed Afrikan people is the orientator of the Afrikan liberation movement. It clarifies for us who we should join with in the first instance and who we should avoid. It is the starting point for becoming an effective unit in the Afrikan liberation process.

One of the methods of helping confused Afrikan people come to terms with and accept their Afrikaness is reconnecting them with those things that are great in Afrikan history and culture. By recognising themselves as the mothers and fathers of humanity and creating a positive association with great Afrikan achievements, the image of Afrika is raised. This helps create an environment in which Afrikan people can be proud to be associated with Afrika and recognised as Afrikans. Another is to clarify the collective benefits of recovering the richest continent in the world.

Clarifying our Afrikan identity is part of the larger process of liberation. Understanding and loving our Afrikan identity is the gateway to understanding our *collective interests* – including our need for total unmitigated control of our land. *Collective interests* is the gateway to understanding *collective purpose*; *collective purpose* sets objectives to build successful *organisation;* practice of *organisation* brings *unity*; *unity* is linchpin of *liberation*; *liberation* gateway to *justice*; *justice* to *peace*; *peace* to *prosperity*; and *prosperity* to *happiness*.

Identity & Purpose

Brother Omowale

Put another way, a correct understanding of our identity i.e. we are dispossessed Afrikan people, helps us organise and unite as a basis for ruling ourselves; this in turn helps us clarify our interests which are objectively to fight oppression and redeem our land; fighting for our interests will bring us ever closer to our intentions i.e. our objects of

Pan-Afrikanism, peace, prosperity, liberty and happiness.

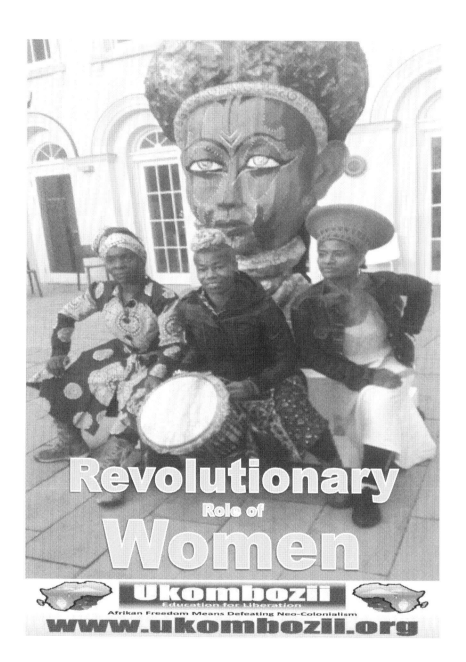

Chapter 6

6 Revolutionary role of women
6.1 Nature and the feminine principle
6.1.1 Feminine philosophical and ideological principles

As philosophical materialists our analysis must begin in the material. In order to speak of women we must first place women and their kind in their material context. From there it becomes possible to make more accurate assessments of Afrikan women, their condition and theirs and Afrikan men's roles in correcting their condition.

At the philosophical level principles are expressed in nature as masculine and feminine. Philosophers usually refer to them as idealist (masculine) and materialist (feminine) and through those labels, sex and gender become anonymous. It is only through the scientific examination of nature that it becomes possible to prove their sex and gender manifestations and their relationship to universal laws.

Land operates on the feminine principle which has similar characteristics to women's wombs. The land is fertilised by rain, in a manner similar to the way in which the sperm of a man fertilises the egg in a woman's womb. Trees, fruits and vegetables come out of the ground in a manner similar to the way in which human beings come out of the woman's womb. When human beings live in a manner that complements the principles of land, their behaviours generate *feminine principles*. When they run counter they generate *masculine principles*.

Philosophical principles relate to our treatment of nature and ideological to the treatment of people. At the ideological level feminine principles are represented by the humanist cluster of principles i.e. Humanism (people before property); Collectivism (we before me); and Egalitarianism (we're all equal in essence). The ultimate expression of:

- Humanism is the recognition that each human being is an end in and of themselves for no reason other than the fact they are human beings. According to this principle, both women and men are intrinsically valuable and must be respected on that basis.
- Collectivism is unanimous acceptance of each and every member of the human family, coupled with unanimous loyalty to that family. According to this principle, women and men are inseparable complementary parts of the whole – humanity.
- Egalitarianism is the recognition that each and every person, being made of the same matter is equal in essence. There are no exceptions. According to this principle women and men are equal in essence.

The feminine principle emanates from nature manifested as one of the sexes. Humanist principles found in societies, are generated by people's treatment of one another. Nature was before people and therefore feminine principles were before humanist ones. The feminine principle is the mother of humanist principles. Humanism is born from the feminine as a child is born from its mother. The essence of feminine and humanist principles is the requirement that nature and all human beings are intrinsically valuable and treated with respect. Women fall naturally within this realm and humanity lived by these principles for the better part of 200,000 years before deviating.

6.1.2 Women – foundation of humanity

Becoming pregnant, giving birth and breast feeding are exclusive domains of women biologically - if not politically (Davis, 1983, p. 202-221). The universal law is not that all women have these capabilities, but that no man can – it is a grave error to ignore universal law. The process of recreating human life takes place almost entirely inside woman – she is therefore the source of new life. Whilst women and men are both essential, women occupy a superior position in the cycle, creation and reproduction of life. They produce new people to replace the old thereby facilitating the continuation of humanity. Reproduction is directly linked to survival and women are the *natural* masters of this element of it.

The woman's sacrifice in reproducing life is much greater than the man's. Whilst the man can have only minimal involvement, the woman sometimes loses her life. As givers of life who sometimes lose their lives, women generally develop a greater understanding of life's real value. They are therefore much more likely to be careful in preserving theirs and their family's lives.

Women give their very being to their unborn children. In order to experience life, we all (i.e. women and men) are compelled to live like parasites in our mothers' wombs sucking essential nutrients from her body. During pregnancy, we drain our mother's natural resources. Nobody can ever repay this debt; it is eternal. In the nine months following conception, the death of a child's father is a great tragedy: the child loses the benefits of both parents' influence. If the mother dies, the child usually loses the chance even to exist.

Women Superior
in the Cycle of Life

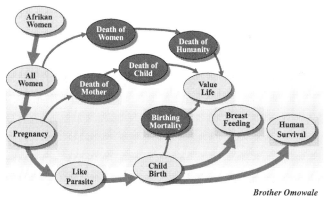

Brother Omowale

If a great tragedy struck the earth and killed all women that would mean the end of humanity, but if a similar tragedy killed all men, humanity would survive. Some of the women would be pregnant with boys who would eventually resume their role in the cycle of life. Women are the carriers of life which means their collective lives are more important to survival than men's. (Toure, Undated, p. 35)

The whole of humanity (i.e. women and men) must pass through the woman in order to live. The Afrikan woman is the original woman; the inheritor of the longest track record of bringing new life into the world. She has been bringing forth new life for 200,000 years (i.e. the emergence of homo sapien sapien) or 3 to 5 million years depending on starting point. This means all other peoples passed through the womb of Afrikan women. The Afrikan woman is therefore the mother and giver of life to all humanity.

Extolling the virtues of Afrikan woman is not an attempt to patronize. It is recognition of the debt universally owed; which non-Afrikan male dominated societies play down or ignore.

> "Placing the emphasis deliberately on woman's qualities in no way means we have an idealistic view of her. We simply aim to single out her qualities and capacities that men and society have always hidden in order to justify her exploitation and subjugation." (Sankara, 2004, p. 280)

In societies where women's superior contribution to the reproductive cycle is valued, they are held in high esteem. Where it is thought of as a handicap, sexism reigns supreme. In matriarchal societies, women retain their natural control of the reproduction process. In patriarchal nations, systems are developed to take control away. Regardless of how particular societies respond, their superior reproduction role makes women the foundation of humanity.

6.1.3 Feminine: Land, society and women
Soil is internal to land in a manner similar to the way wombs are internal to women and people to society. Soil is one of four elements internal to nature – along with air, water and fire; wombs one of two internal elements of people's reproduction, the other being sperm; and people one of two material components of culture, along with nature.

Land is foundation, the base of nature. Birds come down to land. Sea and rivers are based on land. Gravity pulls everything in the earth's atmosphere down towards land. Land is the material base from which all life on earth springs. Land is also the base of people. As people interact with other people and nature, they create society and culture in the area of nature they occupy.

Society is based on land, but has no meaning without people. Women are the material base of human life. Since life comes out of them, they are part the material base of society, producing its human ingredient. People come out of and are based on women and their wombs, making them the people base of society and culture. Land is the fundamental base of people, society and culture, with women the base of their people ingredient. Nature rests fundamentally on land, culture rests on society and people rest on women.

People rest on **Women**

Nature	People	Culture		People	Society	Culture
Land	Women	Society		Womb	Women	People
Soil	Womb	People		Soil	Land	Nature

When the womb (our source) is free – we're all free

Brother Omowale

To enslave women is to claim ownership of her womb. This is in essence the same as claiming ownership of land and generates *patriarchy*. When women are held in high esteem, their wombs are free. We recognise that we all came from woman and we were once a part her, living like a parasite in her womb relying on her for our every need and our very survival. When the womb our source is free, we are all free.

The womb is to woman what soil is to land. Land provides us with what we need. We are like parasites on the land, depending on it for our needs and survival. To claim private ownership of land is a bit like two fleas arguing about which one owns the dog. If anything the dog owns the fleas, but the fleas could never truly own the dog. People belong to land, when the land is free, we are all free. When land and wombs are free, our foundations are free and *matriarchy* generated.

As the base of nature, land is also the base of society and women and the fundamental base of culture and people. Land, tribe, society and women operate on the feminine principle. Their masculine counterparts are rain, state, nation and men.

6.1.4 Women, societies and masculine nations

Societies were originally built on families, extended families, clans and tribes. These units have no need to oppress their family members and therefore have no need for a state mechanism. They contained no class contradiction as everyone was in one class - the family class. Societies are the base for communal and communist social systems in which there is no facility for nations (which must have states).

The state which is implicit in all nations, cuts across family ties and is used by one section of the population (the dominant class) to bring to submission another (dominated class(es)). It allows the dominant class to do with the nation as it chooses. The dominated class' resistance to the above is the basis of class struggle and conflict.

This is the difference between nations and societies. All nations must have a state. It is not possible to have a nation without one. Some societies are nations since they have states, but others are not precisely because they don't have a state. When a society or nation has a state, they are the same thing – a nation. When a society doesn't have a state, it is precisely a society and not a nation.

Tribes exist where there is no class contradiction, where everyone is in one class, producing a society of equals. The existence of the state effects class contradiction and produces dominant and dominated classes which in turn leads to an unequal mutation of society called a nation. Feminine societies are united by tribe, masculine nations divided by state.

The state is violence. It is the greatest organised vehicle for violence in a nation. Its violent capacity can only be defeated by the people organised in unison internally, or a more violent foreign state. That organized violence operates on the masculine principle. It is imposed by patriarchy on land, society and women to control them in the interest of the oppressor class. Through this they control the bases of:
- The area of nature controlled by that nation; and
- The people reproduced in that area of nature.

Nations are masculine. The introduction of the state is the masculine principle brought in to arrest feminine land, tribes, societies and women. Women will not be free until the state is gone. This is true for land and society also. Communism is therefore the freedom of land, tribe, society and women as was its less developed ancestor communalism.

6.2 Gender inequality - Nature or nurture?
6.2.1 Muscle mass argument
On average men have greater muscle mass than women, creating a discernible physical difference which might be argued is the reason for inequality between women and men. However, muscle mass differences are insufficient for imposition of a system of inequality. In the Olympics, Afrikan people consistently win almost all running races. This might indicate a slight muscle mass advantage over Europeans. However, Afrikan people do not dominate Europeans in any nation in the world. Europeans are able to exert greater force through superior organisation and industrialisation which overrides muscle mass. The relationship between organised groups of women and men has more of a bearing on inequality between the sexes than individual or collective muscle mass.

6.2.2 Women's reproductive capacity
The reproduction of people is fundamentally the most important activity of human beings because it produces new people and ensures continuation. People's labour interacts with nature to produce wealth. Whoever controls reproduction and education, potentially have supreme control by controlling who is born and what they know. This gives them the potential to be immensely powerful.

Nature gave women a type of control over reproduction, since the major part takes place inside them (their wombs). In a sense this grants the natural capacity to be more powerful than men. However the education process has a profound impact upon people's attitudes, beliefs and behaviours. The relative power of women and men depends upon whether the education process supports the natural advantage of women or undermines it, because once the reproduction process happens it is soon overridden by the education process i.e. the power of ideas.

The process of education is conditioned and controlled by the dominant ideas and principles in a society. The relative power of organised groups is determined by those dominant ideas and principles – not muscle mass or reproductive capacity. The dominant ideas and principles of a society are derived from the type of relationship that exists between people and land. In other words, on who owns and doesn't own property.

Neither muscle mass nor reproduction, demonstrate nature to be the source of inequality between sexes. Furthermore, given all human beings are made of the same matter and therefore naturally equal in essence, we can dismiss the notion that inequality between women and men is caused by nature. The source is nurture founded on private property.

6.3 Initial subjugation of women
6.3.1 Women were the first slaves
In communal society where feminine and humanist principles were dominant, women controlled both their labour and reproductive capacity – they were equal. In some Afrikan societies they wielded considerable political power (Hay, 1984, p. ix). However, from the moment people began to produce more than they consumed the problem of what to do with the excess existed (Machel, 1973, p. 26/7). Exploitation - the anti-thesis of humanism - began when a sub-group claimed 'ownership' of the collectively produced excess. They were in effect 'stealing' from others. This subtle form of exploitation which happened in varying degrees in all parts of the world marked the beginning of slavery.

When the exploiting sub-group made its move, women hardly participated. It is not that women were not interested, but given their basic needs were met, women were much too busy caring for their families to fight budding thieves. As a result of their love, kindness and dedication, women were not oppressed into serving others, which later turned out to be to their social disadvantage. Women willingly made concessions for the benefit of their families and community. Their generosity was then taken advantage of and used against them by men. This led to their subjugation with little rebellion (Sankara, 2004, p. 260).

Brought into existence by theft, private property became the basis of power. Men who were now oppressed by the privileged class usurped the position of 'head of household' and whatever property the family had became the father's. This ushered in a subtle form of sexism making women the 'first slaves', now relabelled 'housewives'. Once women fell into the trap, it became necessary for men to oppress them to keep them there. More oppression was then exerted and further concessions forced by men and the enslavement of women intensified. Enslavement at this level meant the male family 'head':

- Controlled women's labour in the household and potentially beyond, by sending them out to work;
- Had sex on demand;
- Controlled women's reproductive capacity and importantly the new labour produced.

Enslavement of Women

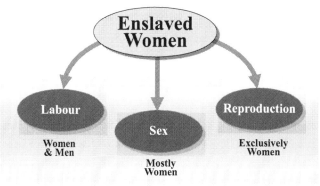

Brother Omowale

The European concept of 'race', a term used as a base for European racism was unconnected with slavery's origin - sexism is older than racism.

6.4 Patterns of pre-colonial gender relations
6.4.1 Wealth exchanges and pre-colonial Afrikan women
Squashed underneath *neo-colonial* state structures, tribes and their traditional practices exist to the current day. Examining the processes by which tribes exchange/transfer people, wealth and property provides a reference for understanding pre-colonial gender relations. There are at least 4 areas which provide clues on the condition of women in pre-colonial Afrika:

- Matriarchal/Patriarchal systems of societal operation;
- Matrilineal/patrilineal systems of passing wealth between generations;
- Dowry systems of passing wealth between tribes; and
- Polygamy and the distribution of wealth within families.

Afrika is the second largest continent with many tribes and practices. Despite the rich diversity of traditions, there are three important broadly common pre-colonial themes:

- The dominant social order in Afrika was communalism, with its key feature of non-ownership of land or people. Under this system nobody could own another, which meant no notion of slavery in the ownership sense;
- The absence of state structures made family/tribe and their feminine principles dominant; and
- The tendency towards 'women friendly' matriarchal systems.

Though not prevented, sexism was undermined by those cultural tendencies and therefore Afrikan women did not suffer the intensity found in feudal Europe. That said, where people and property exchange/transfer occurred, the calibre is an important indicator. If wealth was payment it would generally have been indicative of sexism, if it was a gift, the opposite. Similarly, where women were perceived as burden there was likely to be sexism. Where they and their reproductive capacity were valued, it was less likely.

6.4.2 Matriarchy and Patriarchy

Matriarchy exists where people are of primary importance and property secondary. Women's capacity to produce people is held in high esteem. They are seen as the centre of the family and society because they produce its most vital ingredient - people. The reproduction capacity of women raises her to a position of importance. To hate or abuse women is seen as hating or abusing self, because we all come from women.

Patriarchy originated with private property and gives property priority over people. Under patriarchy, the father became the sole owner of all the family's wealth. Others needed the father for access to food, clothing and shelter etc, to which he was able to block access even though they created it together. This gave him power over 'his' family, upsetting him could lead to destitution. The father controlled 'the person' (including the women's womb) and labour of everyone in 'his' family. 'His' wife and children were reduced to 'beasts of burden'. Nobody could be disobedient for fear of his power.

Exploited females are more valuable than males. To control man is to control his labour. However, to control woman is to control her labour, sexual pleasures derived from her and her children's labour. Patriarchy does this by keeping the wife in a state of absolute dependence on her husband to keep her in 'order'. Her husband owns everything and if he leaves, she is left with nothing – not even her children. She is in effect relegated to third place after men and children.

Because she has nothing, she is reduced to being 'kept' by her husband as a burden he maintains. He is only putting up with her because of love for which she should be grateful. This false notion prevails despite the reality that the father's wealth increases as a result of her labours.

6.4.3 Patrilineal and Matrilineal systems [Passing wealth between generations]

The Patrilineal system derives from the need of man to pass 'his' property to his heir, usually his eldest son. Even though his exploited wife's labour is the basis of his wealth she is not worthy to receive it, though the heir she produced is. Cut off from her wealth, her husband's death leaves her destitute and penniless and in some cases compelled to marry her brother-in-law. The image portrayed is of him reluctantly taking her in to protect her, although in reality her labour is his bonus.

The truth is the son cannot accept that particular part of the 'property' (i.e. his mother). 'Owning' his mother and the womb that brought him into existence has connotations of incest, catastrophically undermining the patrilineal system. Therefore, that element of the husband's 'property' (i.e. the wife) is passed to the brother. The rest of the property then goes to the son – his heir.

If her husband divorces her things get even worse. Her husband takes everything and she genuinely finds herself in a condition of total destitution. The situation worsens in some Asian societies where women are considered to be less than property, a burden that nobody wants. She is put to death – cremated alive and if bereaved, alongside her husband's dead body.

Under the matrilineal system people are more important than property. Property is made to follow the route that people pass through. People pass through the female into life. Property is made to pass through the female line. Mothers typically nurture and serve all of their children without favour or exception. The wealth goes to benefit all of her children, not exclusively her eldest son.

This approach mimics nature where life passes through the woman's line. Children come from the woman. Everybody can be certain that the child is the woman's. Wealth following this route definitely stays in the family, which cannot otherwise be guaranteed given the uncertainties of fatherhood.

6.4.4 The dowry [Exchanging wealth between clans]
There are 4 theoretical dowry permutations with potentially varying degrees of good/bad treatment of women:
1. Man goes to woman's clan, dowry to man's (Dowry crosses with the man)
2. Woman goes to man's clan, dowry to woman's (Dowry crosses with the woman)
3. Woman goes to man's clan, dowry to man's (Dowry follows the woman)
4. Man goes to woman's clan, dowry to woman's (Dowry follows the man)

Whether matriarchy or patriarchy operates is an important factor. Under matriarchy, notions of private property tend not to exist, meaning dowries of any sort are more likely to be gifts than payments. Under patriarchy it is the extent to which private property is coveted that determines the calibre of transaction. If it is highly coveted, the tendency is towards payments. If not, towards gifts.

Patriarchy values property over people. It does not permit women to own property making women property less. If she is unable to own property she is in effect available to be property, a 'beast of burden' or in any event less valuable than a man. Here, the man's clan compensates the woman's for her labour (and the labour of her children). The transaction can operate on a similar basis to the sale of an animal. Women are devalued in this process indicating the presence of sexism.

Overview of Dowries

	Matriarchy	Patriarchy
Female Price	Gift of thanks	**Payment or Release from burden**
Male Price		**Gift of thanks**

Brother Omowale

Under matriarchal systems, people are more important than property. Women are people with the bonus that they produce new people. Whilst all people are priceless, the ability to reproduce makes women ultra valuable. Here, the dowry could never be a payment for woman or man – no amount of whatever currency could ever reach human value. Therefore the dowry operates as a gift of thanks for the clan that has lost the labour of their daughter and producer of valuable new people who are an extra source of wealth to her new clan. In some matriarchal societies the children, too valuable to give away, continue to belong to the mother's clan. The mother's clan insists on retaining their wealth i.e. future generations of their people. Sexism is not overtly present in this process.

6.4.5 Polygamy [Multiple wives to one husband]
Polygamy can exist under matriarchy, the essential condition being too few men relative to women. This occurred in Afrika during the enslavement era where more men were kidnapped and extradited than women. This was also the case in times of war, where men were killed disproportionately. Polygamy is also considered a necessity upon the death of a husband in some traditions, where his brother is expected to take over his matrimonial duties. This latter example is not necessarily a trait of matriarchal systems.

In addition to multiple wives to one man, the essential condition for polygamy under matriarchy is women have the final say on marriage. Whilst husbands can marry others, it is based on women's agreement to share and where the system is genuine, current wives have power of veto. Under matriarchy, its purpose is to satisfy the intimate needs of women without adultery and restore balance to the ratio of sexes, at which point is should be brought to an end. Its retention is an indicator of sexism.

Under patriarchy, where property is more valuable than people – the latent purpose of polygamy (where it is not a necessity) is to further increase the wealth of the husband. To have woman is to have her labour (source of wealth), sex (pleasure of her) and children's labour (new sources of wealth). Each additional wife brings more labour and more pleasure. She also brings more children which equate to even more labour.

Some argue that men can have as many wives as they can afford. This is a red herring. Once food, clothing and shelter are provided, each wife becomes a multiple source of the wealth for her husband. Furthermore, even in the preparation of food, clothing and shelter, women are more likely to play a greater role than men. It follows that in reality women maintain themselves, their husbands and their families and on top of that they create additional wealth for their husbands. Where polygamy has not been brought about by necessity, it contains undertones of sexism.

6.4.6 Calibre of sexism
There was sexism in Afrika before the coming of colonialism, though not necessarily in all parts. Where it existed, it had varying degrees of intensity, but in all cases was less severe than in Europe since:
- It was fundamentally family based and the family in its varying forms tends to recognise the importance of mothers;
- Afrika's predominantly communal social systems tended not to permit individual land or people ownership;
- Afrikan societies were predominantly matriarchal, inculcated with the acceptance that people are more important than property; and

- There was no great divide between rich and poor. In a sense, everyone was poor together, with disadvantaged women a little poorer. It is the widespread impoverishment of everyone that caused some to argue that there was no sexism in Afrika. These advocates failed to take account of the relative degree of women's impoverishment.

6.5 Colonial invasion and occupation
6.5.1 Colonialism and the slave's slave
To conquer a nation is to take charge of its land, society and women, symbolized through: (i) colonization; (ii) an imposed state; and (iii) rape:

- Colonization is the physical theft of the conquered people's land and the resources contained on and in it;
- The state is imposed for management and administration of society, but remembering that the state is highly organised violence, its fundamental role is to oppress conquered people, who must not under any circumstances be allowed to rise up and take their freedom; and
- Rape is always an outcome of war as conquered men leave their women totally unprotected from unrestrained rampant patriarchy. Raping them produces new people, loyal to conquerors.

This is what happened to Afrika as a result of European imperialism's invasion, the final phase of which was planned and coordinated at the Berlin Conference of 1884/5. This retrograde intervention for Afrika was calamity for Afrika's unprotected women. Samora Machel explains the calamitous impact in Mozambique as follows:

> " ... the oppression of women is the result of their exploitation; oppression in society is always the result of imposed exploitation. Colonialism did not come to occupy our country for the purpose of arresting us, flogging us and beating us with the *Palmatoria*. It invaded and occupied our country for the purpose of exploiting our wealth and labour. In order to exploit us, in order to quell our resistance to exploitation and prevent us from rebelling against it, it then introduced the system of oppression; physical oppression, through the courts, the police, armed

forces, imprisonment, torture and massacres; and spiritual oppression through obscurantism, superstition and ignorance, designed to destroy the spirit of creative initiative, to kill the sense of justice and criticism, to reduce the individual to passivity and make him accept his exploited and oppressed state as a normal thing. Humiliation and contempt came into being in the process, since he who exploits and oppresses tends to humiliate and despise his victims, regarding them as inherently inferior beings. And then racism appears, the supreme form of humiliation and contempt." (Machel, 1973, p. 26)

Though undoubtedly present, sexism wasn't pronounced in Afrika. It wasn't that Afrikan men were less sexist than European men per se, rather they were content with being family boss and had not organised their sexism to state level exploitation and oppression. Sexism was therefore not yet deeply ingrained. The sexism of Afrikan men was constrained by the fact that they were living in tribal societies.

The tribe is a family unit, the largest possible. Each member claims descent from a single common ancestor. In a family based society it is more difficult, though not impossible, to devalue women. Women are the foundation of family and where family is the basis of society, there is the possibility of their being valued for the fact of their womanhood. Women were therefore valued in Afrika despite their men's sexism.

European men by contrast had achieved state power via their feudal system. They had long since put that violence into effect upon their women. They even organised witch hunts issuing special tortures with built-in heads men win, tails women lose outcomes to justify their savage misogynistic attacks.

It was when European men physically conquered Afrikan men in their own land, that state mechanisms overrode tribal ones and the entrenchment of sexism in Afrika regressed towards its current condition. It is the state – all be it colonialism's external one – that concretised sexism in Afrika. The social transformation to colonialism further degraded Afrikan women, reducing them to what Sekou Toure describes as 'the slave's slave' (Toure, Undated, p. 9).

6.5.2 Triple oppression

Capitalism seeks control of labour by denying workers ownership of their surplus. Detachment from labour brings exploitation. Capitalism entered Afrika as colonial conquest. For the Afrikan woman, on top of her husband boss was his new boss the coloniser, both extracting wealth from her labours and oppressing her to keep her in place. Added to this was the racism of the coloniser which like colonialism, impacted them jointly. However in her case, it degraded her to the lowest of the low – she became even the servant of her children. This was a triple blow for Afrikan women who found themselves exploited by:

- Their husband boss - gender oppression
- European conquerors - nation oppression
- Colonial thieves - class oppression

Triple Oppression

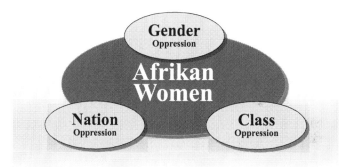

Brother Omowale

Colonialism actively prevented Afrika from industrialising, preferring instead to steal its natural resources. It used them to provide work for people in its heartlands and actively wasted Afrika's capacity to produce. Afrikan women's triple oppression put them amongst the worst affected by this wastage. Their underutilisation showed itself in their complete marginalisation from decision making. They were excluded from all important societal decisions leaving them with no control over their lives. They were also handed menial often irrelevant tasks to keep them occupied and distract them from even thinking about bettering their situation.

6.5.3 Matspiritual oppression

In order to maintain the exploitation and oppression of women or any oppressed group, it is necessary to establish an ideology that justifies it. It will come from the philosophical masculine principle driving capitalism/colonialism which translates into exploitative principles at the ideological level i.e. Exploitation (money/property before people), Individualism (me before we) and Elitism (respect your betters). The object is to dissolve actual and potential resistance by extinguishing the very idea of emancipation from the minds of the colonised and winning them over.

That ideology must be supported by an education system, other state structures and mass media that systematically indoctrinate society. The purpose of these instruments is to train and remould the victims ideologically so they internalize exploitation, accept their oppressor as good/positive and 'enjoy' their oppressed situation as 'right'. Victims must be tricked into receiving the oppressor as their 'defender', with whom they are not only satisfied, but intensely loyal. Instruments are used to diffuse the oppressor's preferred norms and modes of behaviour for imitation, acceptance and quelling of oppressed people's natural resistance.

Their latent task is to crush victim's self-awareness/self-esteem by painting their type as bad, negative and woefully inadequate. Some signs of internalisation include attempted cessation of struggle where women: (i) believe 'There is no other way', 'Change is impossible', 'Do as their master instructs' and 'Accept their lot in life'; (ii) suffer their discrimination silently and retreat into focusing their energies on supporting their families; and (iii) accept their allotted inferiority, blaming their 'inadequacies' for their problems whilst attacking their sisters and themselves. Self-destruction in the form of suicide is an intense example.

The victims, reduced to mere objects, cease in their own minds to be human beings and must dissociate from their true identity to achieve human status. This condemns them to the status of 'beast of burden' attempting to grow in a system designed precisely to stifle their full human development – in fact reinforcing their bestiality. This level of oppression has to be planned, developed, implemented and refined over years until it becomes deeply ingrained. In the case of Afrikan women, the desired outcome is their complete alienation from their labour. They produce abundance including new labour sources, but none of it belongs to them.

> "The process of alienation reaches its peak when the exploited person, reduced to total passivity, is no longer capable of imagining the possibility of liberation exists and in turn becomes a tool for the propagation of the ideology of resignation and passivity. It must be recognised that the centuries old subjugation of women has to a great extent reduced them to a passive state, which prevents them from even understanding their condition." (Machel, 1973, p. 28)

This level of docility is not enough for colonial and now neo-colonial exploitation where the idea of freedom, if it emerges at all, is to be totally rejected and crushed. If this element is done 'successfully', reality is turned upside down in victim's heads. They internalize their exploitation as good, maintain their own dominance and see resistance, emancipation, liberation and freedom as negatives to be avoided. Fully trained and immersed in counter-revolution and satisfied, even delighted with their oppression, freedom fighting organisations now perceived as 'enemy' and synonymous with 'doomsday', are left trying to liberate victims against their will (Preiswerk, 1980, p. 3).

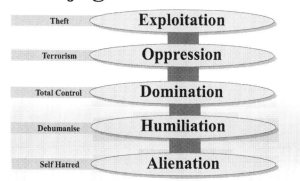

Brother Omowale

Neo/colonialism brainwashes its victims to conform to a sliding scale where they sink further and further into a mentality designed to destroy their desire to be free. It trains them to: (i) Tolerate, accept, 'enjoy' and be thankful for their oppression; (ii) Believe that they can't exist successfully without their oppressors, whom they must emulate, defend, support and champion; and (iii) Actively contribute to their own oppression and attack any entity that dares to try to liberate them from it.

The objective of this elaborate system is explained by Sekou Toure. Culture created, the gun; it is more powerful and superior to ballistic and other physical weapons. An oppressed people's culture is therefore capable of overthrowing foreign military conquest. Imperialism understood this weakness, recognising propaganda as a better tool for subduing Afrikan and other dominated peoples. It used its education and other systems of communication to dull their senses and quell their desire for freedom and the return of all that is rightfully theirs. Propaganda was used to indoctrinate them into accepting the theft of their land, people and resources as something to be grateful for; to expunge the desire for liberation.

It was the transformation from one type of society to another – from communal to the embryo of feudalism that dragged women from equal status into slavery. It was another societal transformation - this time into colonialism - that further entrenched the enslavement of Afrikan women, heaping triple oppression upon them. Yet another transformation, to neo-colonialism, intensified *matspiritual* oppression. The solution to women's inequality lies in a revolutionary transformation to a new progressive society, based on feminine and humanist principles. Women's emancipation requires nothing less than revolution – they are inseparable.

6.6 Women nurturing and educating for Afrika's advancement
6.6.1 Women do more to nurture life
All unborn children are totally dependent upon their mothers during pregnancy, but it doesn't end there. If a baby is laid down and left to fend for itself, it will die. The baby will complain by crying, but will be incapable of taking the actions necessary preserve its life. The baby is totally dependent upon others for its survival. It follows that the nurturing role is absolutely vital to the survival and development of young people and through them, humanity.

The nurturing role is not equally distributed between women and men. An intimate interaction lasting for as little as one minute for the man can bring 20 or more years of responsibility for the woman. This underpins the general tendency for new and young lives to remain with women. There is never any doubt that the new born child is the woman's, whilst a true father can have no idea of his child's existence. The bond between mother and child is therefore generally greater.

This stronger bond helps to explain why women generally assume a primary role in the nurturing of children. In doing so she habitually makes personal sacrifices, putting the needs of her children before her own. Her circumstances generally force her to be more in tune with the principle of collectivism: i.e. putting 'we' before 'me'. Men's focus tends to be on satisfying of their own needs which breeds individualism: i.e. putting 'me' before 'we'. This is why educating women equates to educating the family, community and nation, whilst educating men only to individuals (Clark, 2003, p. 265).

6.6.2 Afrikan women, nurturing and primary education

Biological processes involved in reproducing human beings impose certain distinct roles on women and men and this provides the fundamental basis for gender relations. However, the majority of gender roles have developed as a result of learnt behaviours taken from the dominant ideas of particular societies. Despite the ultimate dominance of learnt behaviours, biological reproduction processes remain crucial initially. Women are biologically closer to children and generally play a greater role in nurturing. They are the foundation of children's lives, their first teachers.

The Afrikan woman inherits the longest education and teaching heritage, meaning Afrika has the benefit of the world's most experienced primary teachers. It must harness this revolutionary bonus since Afrika cannot afford to underutilise the world's most experienced primary teaching force. This role gives Afrikan women a real source of power through which they can directly shape society:

- Women nurture and educate future women. They can either support or confront the systematic oppression which dampens women's consciousness. Their role is to develop women of the future who will not accept a position of subordination, but fight it;
- Women also nurture and educate future men. They can train them to:

o   Oppose the systematic oppression which dampens women's consciousness;

o   Understand the benefits to women, men and society of eliminating the oppression of women; and

o   Actively work towards the achievement of women's equality in their chosen areas of production.

Through their nurturing role, women are the most important and powerful teachers. They have virtually total control of the grass roots of every child's education. Effective organisation of their primary teaching role can positively shape future society. The power to correct internal wrongs is already in Afrikan women's hands. Their task is to consolidate, coordinate and organise it.

6.6.3 Role of Afrikan women's consciousness

We are in the neo-colonial phase of Afrika's history. Afrikan women's ignorance of **neo-colonialism** and its intrigues preserves their exploitation. Ignorance destroys their resolve to fight for emancipation and liberation, fosters the illusion that society is impossible to change and instils in them an attitude of passivity and servility.

Conscious educated Afrikan women are vital to the process of creating a just society. Their contribution will involve fighting the ideology imposed by **neo-colonialism** - the current form of the exploiting system, making a qualitative leap towards their own emancipation and an improved society for the next generation of women and men.

Through lack of consciousness many men will resist, so will some women. Women must be able to practically demonstrate to men and unconscious women:

- The variety of ways in which **neo-colonialism** causes great harm and damage to Afrika and her people.
- How men and others benefit from the emancipation of Afrikan women.

They must be able to explain how:

- Men need women's victories in order to win.
- Men who hate women ultimately hate themselves. They hate the very place from which they came i.e. the womb that distinguishes women from men.

6.6.4 Liberating women's productive capacity

There are clear benefits to everyone in educating girls. This is a fact well known to capitalism:

> "... Countless studies have shown that countries, like those in East Asia which have invested in primary education, including education of girls, have done better." (Stiglitz[13], 2002, p. 76)

It nonetheless blocks their development. In Afrika colonialism's wilful undermining of women's consciousness through inadequate educational provision denied the continent of the benefits of their full participation. Afrika suffered a double loss; Afrikan women were denied personal development whilst Afrikan society was robbed of their contribution. The losses were further entrenched by denial of industrialisation, which meant inefficient utilisation of even the limited labour employed.

Any social construct that prevents the conscious participation of any individual or sector of society will operate to inhibit both the achievement and maintenance of revolutionary society. This is especially so in the case of women, who constitute more than half. No society can function effectively with 50% of its productive capacity by-passed. Systematically educating girls will be Afrika's first step in bringing the doubly underutilised half of society more fully into production.

It will be a requirement of revolutionary Afrikan society that all members, consciously and fully participate. This means Afrikan women must be actively encouraged to learn and develop, through the receipt of appropriate, high quality education. This will put them in a position where they can give back to their people, contribute fully and effectively participate in the advance of Afrika. That process must begin immediately.

---

[13] Stiglitz is an arch capitalist – awarded its Nobel prize for economics

Afrikan women must win emancipation - it will not be given to them. They must put forward their own demands, mobilise to fight for victory against *sexism* and *neo-colonialism*, maintain and sustain it and actively organise to fight for victory and be on the front line. Their genuine emancipation will include their being: (i) entrusted with wider and varied responsibilities in productive life; (ii) substantially involved in societal decision making; (iii) substantially involved in solving the major problems confronting society; and (iv) being truly respected by all men, bringing about a major shift in the behaviour of men towards women.

This implies the need to join and create organisations that are fighting *sexism* and *neo-colonialism* and are committed to the revolutionary transformation of their society. Through these organisations they must ensure that society recognises and corrects: (i) all practices that demean women; (ii) the negative role played by *neo-colonialism* in intensifying and multiplying those practices. Afrikan society must systematically eliminate the *neo-colonial* system as a women's emancipation initiative.

6.6.5 Afrikan women need revolutionary organisation
Afrikan revolutionary political organisation must develop a clear vision of Afrika's future with a political line leading to it. This will generate revolutionary ideas in the form of a plan to fight *sexism* and *neo-colonialism* and transform society to the advantage of female and male Afrikan agricultural and industrial workers.

The organisation, its vision and political line must be constructed by Afrikan women, supported by Afrikan men, focused on leading the fight against capitalism – the exploiting system (in its *sexist* and *neo-colonial* forms) and defend the interests of Afrikan agricultural and industrial workers.

Afrikan women must organise around those revolutionary ideas (political line), internalise them and through permanently engaging and immersing themselves in organisational tasks, engage in production and continuous cultural education. Marriage and family life must not prevent their engagement in revolutionary activities. Their family duties must form an integral part of Afrikan women's productive and educational duties in the revolutionary process, rather than replacing them.

It is their revolutionary duty to do more than solely focus on family – important as it is. Family as a unit is too small an aggregate to challenge the system of **neo-colonialism** that exploits Afrika. All Afrikan people must organise on a scale large enough to challenge and defeat it. That scale is **Pan-Afrikan** which means worldwide. If women assume wider and varied political, economic, social and cultural responsibilities, the liberation of Afrika will be massively accelerated.

6.6.6 Unifying role of Afrikan women and their bitter pill

Generally Afrikan women are the most exploited, oppressed, dominated, humiliated and alienated section of humanity. They find themselves on the wrong end of oppressive practices of virtually all other groups. These destructive phenomena contribute to their triple oppression and double oppression of Afrikan men. However, their fundamental contradiction is not with any of these groups. It is with the capitalist social order. They must understand this point in order to progress, since they must swallow the bitter pill of uniting and allying with others who contribute to their oppression.

As mentioned in chapter 1, neutrons generate an inward pulling force and protons expansive, potentially explosive and destructive. The expansive forces are masculine in character and tend towards division of the atom. The pulling forces are feminine, uniting the atom and holding everything together in tension. If the feminine force is inadequate or fails, there is an almighty explosion destroying the atom and everything in proximity.

This suggests land, society, tribes and women which also operate on the feminine principle, are fundamentally uniting forces holding people, culture and nature together. Should they fail, there is catastrophe. Women therefore have a crucial uniting role in holding people, family and society together and in balance. On the social plane, they are the uniting force of the world.

Afrikan women have a special uniting role because they are confronted with more oppressive constraints than virtually any other group. They share nation oppression with their men; gender oppression with other women; and class oppression with other workers. They are positioned to understand everyone else's pain, even if others don't fully understand theirs.

Afrikan men oppress Afrikan women, but despite this they are obliged to unite because to do otherwise would mean extinction. They must love and struggle with their men simultaneously, compelled to unite with their men to change/improve them. They must also build contradictory alliances with other women and workers in the capitalist heartlands who indirectly benefit from its exploitation of them, with the aim of winning from them a deeper commitment to liberation. It is for Afrikan women to teach others how they can commit more deeply.

There will be no true liberation for any group in the world until the position of Afrikan women is not inferior to any other. In the process of liberating themselves, Afrikan women simultaneously contribute to the removal of the constraints placed on virtually all other oppressed people. By helping themselves they help others and all others whilst simultaneously contributing to their oppression, help themselves by supporting the struggle of Afrikan women – the mothers and true leaders of world revolution. This is the motivation for uniting under the leadership of Afrikan women who must overcome this contradiction to assume their role. Ultimately, the progress of Afrika and to a lesser extent worldwide revolution will be gauged by the condition of Afrika's women.

6.6.7 A Strategy for solving oppression of Afrikan women

An essential element of liberation strategy will be to find others suffering similar oppression, build links, share ideas and resources and fight the common enemy (capitalism in its *neo-colonial* form) on different fronts. This is necessary to mobilise broad fronts of exploited and oppressed people to make a successful revolution. This means Afrikan women being receptive to experiences of others as a basis for effective engagement in revolution. In the words of Samora Machel, Afrikan women must:

> " ... form the broadest possible front mobilising, organising and uniting all the women who until now have remained outside the process of transformation." (Machel, 1973, p. 33)

They will need to establish a power base internally and build alliances with other oppressed groups despite contradictory oppressive tendencies. This revolutionary sacrifice will help them prepare for and overcome oppressive barriers confronting them. They will be aware that all other groups that they build alliances with contribute in some measure to their oppression, but must do it anyway. The ultimate aim of revolution is to end all exploitation and oppression for everybody in the world. Revolution will give triple relief to Afrikan women and double to Afrikan men. It will also give varying degrees of relief to other people in the world.

Afrikan Women Aligned

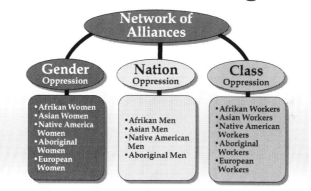

Brother Omowale

The first point of unity for Afrikan women is to unite amongst themselves as an essential component for tackling male domination. The second is unity with Afrikan men to confront nation domination. These are internal fronts of their liberation struggle. In nature the complementarity between the sexes is primary for survival, but in the struggle for emancipation that primary grouping forms part of the oppression they face. When sexism is defeated, that primary allegiance will resume, but not before. The third internal element is unity as workers to defeat *neo-colonialism*. Implementing a strategy aimed at solving the problem of *triple oppression* will require internal unity and external alliances:

- *Gender oppression* – other Afrikan women, Asian women, Native American women, Aboriginal women, European women;
- *Nation oppression* – Afrikan men and through them: Asian men, Native American men, Aboriginal men;
- *Class oppression* – other Afrikan workers – Asian workers, Native American workers, Aboriginal workers, European workers.

6.6.8 Revolutionary progress and Afrikan women

The purpose of revolution is to advance humanity from one phase of history to the next. We are currently in the capitalist phase which manifests as **neo-colonialism** in Afrika. The next for Afrika and the world is scientific socialism. In Afrika its form will be Pan-Afrikanism. Revolution and with it emancipation means progression to this improved system of living. This is the objective of genuine women's emancipation.

Our current condition is we have family members who no longer behave like family. They are **neo-colonialists** who actively exploit other members on behalf of outsiders and themselves. Under socialism we will be obliged to have a state to constrain wayward members on behalf of the majority. The role of the state will be to keep them in order for recovery and progress. The state must stay in place until wayward characteristics are vanquished. Rendered redundant, it is abolished.

The advance of Afrika to this new phase – scientific socialism (formed as Pan-Afrikanism) - will require further sacrifice from women. Women who have sacrificed so much already and one of the principal targets of oppressive states, are asked to campaign and work for the achievement of a unified continental state capable of more effectively oppressing them. This new state will be a requirement for the achievement of socialism.

To counter this contradiction it will be necessary for Afrikan men to make an 'unthinkable' sacrifice. They will need to humble themselves, stand down/aside to allow women to lead management of the state. This is their equivalent to what Amilcar Cabral called "Class suicide".

The profound violence of the state in the hands of men creates a situation where the nation's most violent masculine tool is in the hands of masculine beings, leaving masculine orientated oppression unchecked. The solution is to create balance by allowing the necessary masculine state to be run predominantly by feminine beings.

Women are the givers of life, who sometimes give their lives in order to bring forth new life. They have an understanding of the value of life far deeper than men. Violence of the state in their hands is less likely to be unleashed, resulting from their greater reluctance to take life.

Women's sections of revolutionary organisation will co-opt/veto men to manage the state alongside them in proportions to be agreed. As the holders of men's secrets, they are best placed to make this calibre of decision. As a general rule, men approach women for sex. They therefore know the true character of men through their approach and conduct in this private area.

Women's ultimate role will be to manage the state to extinction, guiding Afrika through scientific socialism - where there must be a state, to communism - where there must not. They will lead Afrika back to its original feminine/humanist principles, to a new updated version of communalism, where new technology extends human boundaries to ever higher heights. Communalism combined with high level technological development operating in harmony with nature, is communism. The object is the achievement of a condition where human beings and nature are treated respectfully, married with the advantage of the most effective and efficient tools.

.

Pan-Afrikanism
Resolves Racism

Chapter 7

7 Pan-Afrikanism resolves Racism
7.1 Material and matspiritual elements of Racism
7.1.1 Land - material base of Racism

Racism must have a material base to be real. Modern racism has its origin in the enslavement of Afrikan people. It required the physical theft of Afrikan people's bodies and labour to ignite this scourge. Imperialism was in effect pregnant with the foetus of racism during the enslavement era. It was during this era the scientific racism school and other apologists for racism developed the body of ideas that would attempt to dehumanise Afrikan people and justify racism.

It was not until the end of slavery, the birth of capitalism and more precisely the colonisation of other people's land that racism became fully grounded on its material base. Land is the material base of racism. It is the base upon which the main components of racism (power over others; the group or nation; and elitist notions of superiority) are founded. Whenever a people own and control their land, they are powerful; whenever a people do not, they are powerless.

European imperialism went to the Americas and stole that land from Native Americans. The result was European imperialist thieves became powerful and Native Americans powerless. It went to Afrika and stole Afrikan people's land. The outcome was, it became powerful and Afrikan people powerless. It went to Australia and stole Aborigines'' land. The same thing happened again, it became powerful and aborigines powerless. It went to India and stole Indian people's land. The same pattern ensued, it became powerful and Indians powerless.

Zionists went to Palestine, stole Palestinian's land, became powerful and Palestinians, powerless.

Everywhere the result is the same. If a people's land is stolen, the thieves become more powerful. They on the other hand, become powerless and with powerlessness comes the scourge of racism, initially from the thieves, but not necessarily limited to them. Land is the material base of racism. Indeed, land is the basis of all power, including the power element of racism.

If further evidence is necessary, consider the Chinese. European imperialism went to their land and stole some of it, but couldn't quite get enough to accomplish grand theft. Though seriously disempowered, Chinese hold on their land was sufficient for them to regroup and in 1997 they successfully expelled British imperialism from its last foothold – Hong Kong.

The Chinese are now a powerful people and notions of anti-Chinese racism are an historic memory. They couldn't care less whether you or I like them because we don't have the power to thwart their destiny even if we wanted to. Even those who hold anti-Chinese elitist ideas cannot be racist towards Chinese. They simply do not have the power to implement anti-Chinese policies that would have anything greater than minimal impact on them as a people. They most certainly cannot take away their land and corresponding power. Anti-Chinese racism is now a relic of the past.

7.1.2 Principles underlying Racism

Racism can also be materially evidenced at the atomic level. We can infer racism as the social equivalent of part of neutron expansion forces driving the atom towards explosion if left unchecked. It is no co-incidence that its modern manifestation began and expanded in sync with the beginning and expansion of European imperialism i.e. the expansion of European enslavement of Afrikan people and land theft, from which it derives its powerbase.

Land theft is fundamentally underpinned by the principle of exploitation. From this base the thieves, having disempowered their victims developed an attitude which saw them as superior and their victims inferior. Their fabricated inferiority served as justification for the thieves' inhumanity and a rationale for maintaining their evil slavery/colonial systems. For the thieves the bogus idea of victims' inferiority sooths their consciences whilst they perpetrate abuses. For the victims, acceptance encourages dissolution of actual and potential resistance, extinguishing the idea of a right to be treated humanely and with it any notions of liberation.

Exploitative Principles Hierarchy

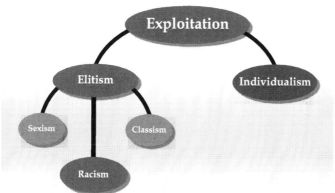

Brother Omowale

A position can be found for the attitude of racism amongst the exploitative family of principles, as a sub-category of elitism [I'm better that you]. Along with sexism and classism it forms a branch of that principle, with elitism forming a branch of exploitation. All of this is of course derived from theft of land as its material base the principle of which is exploitation. If we think of exploitation as a cake, elitism is its marzipan; racism, sexism and classism its different coloured icings. Exploitation is the essence, racism one of its forms.

7.1.3 Race 'Race' Racism contradictions
Justification of racism can only be achieved by turning reality upside down. The following is an explanation:

> "Contrary to popular belief, there is no such thing as race. Race is a false construction which was created by Europeans ... to differentiate themselves from ... other people ... The concept of race was created by scientists and scholars at Gottingen University in Germany between 1775 and 1800. During this 25 year period, these "scholars"

invented the word *Caucasian*, divided humanity into races, and contended that the white race was superior." (Browder, 1996, p. 3)

If it is true that there is no such thing as race, on the basis the difference between the various branches of humanity are too small to constitute differing races that is not the same as saying there are no discernible biological differences. There are obviously discernible biological differences.

Origin of 'Race'

"Contrary to popular belief, there is no such thing as race. Race is a false construction which was created by Europeans ... to differentiate themselves from ... other people ... The concept of race was created by scientists and scholars at Gottingen University in Germany between 1775 and 1800. During this 25 year period, these "scholars" invented the word *Caucasian*, divided humanity into races, and contended that the white race was superior."

Anthony Browder,
From the Browder File Volume 2, Page 3

Brother Omowale

The Afrikan person typically comes with high melanin content. There will be variations around this central theme, but nonetheless remains correct. By contrast, Europeans come with low melanin content as standard. Whilst there may be lighter and darker tones of European, low melanin content is what they have in common. The difference is almost as clear as black and white. Similar analyses can be made with other 'racial' groups in the human family. 'Racial' groups are best categorised, not by their extremities where the lines between them are blurred and there may be overlap, but by their cores where the differences between what is typical of each are pronounced and clear. 'Race' in the sense of discernible differences within the human race, really does exist – it is underpinned biologically/scientifically/materially by melanin, which impacts the hue of humans. However, despite the best efforts of the scientific racism school, there is no credible evidence that abundance/lack of melanin in any way confers superiority/inferiority.

In addition to the allegation that 'race' is not real, there is also an argument that racism is not either. The evidence above finds against the suggestion: Firstly, the 'race' element of racism can be scientifically demonstrated to exist on the basis of varying melanin levels; the power element is scientifically founded on land and the theft and deprivation of it; and the attitudinal element can be clearly and objectively established among the exploitative family of principles as a sub-category of elitism.

Like everything else, racism changed over time. At one point in history its material base was the theft of Afrikan people's bodies. At another, it was European imperialism's theft of other people's land. Currently, it is based on the continued theft of subjected people's resources from their land, whilst granting them the illusion of political independence. The common theme is exploitation – its base principle. The material basis of racism can be variously described as: (i) Biology + Geography supported by Ideology; (ii) Melanin + Land supported by Actions (incorporating ideas informed by principles). Semi-detached from its material base it may be referenced as 'Colour' + Nation supported by Culture.

7.1.4 Components of Racism
It is the material base of racism which gives substance to theories of it. That said, there are a number of elements that should be considered. A broader idea incorporates 5 interrelated and overlapping components that combine to make racism. The 5 components are as follows:

- **The group**: Racism operates at *group* level - it is a requirement of racism that one group is dominated by another. Individuals can manifest racism (i.e. be racist), but individuals can never be the source of racism because no individual is powerful enough to hold an entire people in subjugation. Individualism is the underlying principle with one 'individual' sub-group setting itself apart from the rest of humanity, perpetuating the illusion of 'white supremacy'.
- **Ethnicity**: For their actions to qualify as racist the perpetrating group must be of a different *ethnicity* to the dominated. Where one group dominates another of the same *ethnicity*, their behaviour may be bad, it may even be evil but it is not racist because racism requires that perpetrators and victims come from different biological and cultural groups.

- **Power**: One group must be *powerful* enough to dominate the other. The dominant group must then force the dominated to submit to its will, ill-treating and humiliating members in the process. Prejudice, hatred, dislike and detestation without the use of *power* designed to subjugate different cultural groups are not sufficient to constitute racism. So long as those distasteful emotions do not hold another group from developing their people's welfare, they are not of themselves racists. Driven by more than mere dislike or hatred, its underlying principle is exploitation.
- **Superiority**: The powerful group imposes the idea of its *superiority* on the dominated who are made to feel inferior. Sometimes members of the dominated group accept the idea of inferiority. If the element of *superiority* is removed then racism cannot exist because we are left with two groups that are merely different and difference cannot constitute racism by itself. Its underlying principle elitism is indispensible to racism.
- **Systematic**: Racism is part of a *systematic* process of oppression that has capitalism as source. Racism cannot and does not stand alone; it emanates from something greater than itself i.e. a *system*. Groups are more powerful than individuals and systems are the ultimate expression of group power. It is the power of the capitalist system that gives strength to racism. Without the power of the system, racism is reduced to prejudice which by itself is relatively harmless in its effect.

Components of Racism

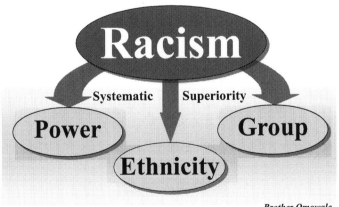

Brother Omowale

Racism is constantly present in the daily lives of everybody in the world; but despite this some people may be genuinely unaware of its existence. Racism is part of the force used by the capitalist system to hold back the development of Afrikan people and others it has disempowered. Racism is also a part of the force used to threaten and attack peoples that have successfully resisted capitalism's attempts to subjugate them.

7.2 Solutions to Racism
7.2.1 Group problem
The defeat of anti-Afrikan racism will not be achieved through Individual, family, community or even national level anti-racist initiatives. Whilst they can contribute, they cannot solve the overall problem. Racism cannot be solved at any of these levels because its source is capitalism, which operates globally. Its trans-national business corporations steal wealth from virtually all parts of the world, supported by its international political/economic institutions such as IMF, World Bank, WTO and UN. It maintains military bases around the world coordinated through the likes of NATO. This is what gives racism its power. To counter this, Afrikans must **group** at the **international level** i.e. the **Pan-Afrikanist level**. This includes building alliances with progressive non-Afrikan forces.

7.2.2 Power problem
The most destructive part of racism is the **power** element which is used against dominated groups. Afrikan people must develop **power** equal to or greater than that of the racists to defeat it. The defeat of slavery, colonialism and neo-colonialism is the defeat of racism. The solution to racism is regaining control of land and resources by subjugated peoples. This is the political outcome of scientific socialism, where state power is brought firmly into the hands of previously subjected people. It is supported by its economic outcome industrialisation, which allows previously subjected peoples the capacity to meet and satisfy their needs.

Controlling Afrikan land is the central issue in solving anti-Afrikan racism. When Afrikan people take control of Afrika, they will become the richest and the most **powerful** people on earth. Capitalism's job is to prevent this. Afrikan people must take control of Afrika to re-establish themselves as a **power** in the world. When we do this anti-

Afrikan racism will entre rapid decline leading to its death. Nobody will be able to enslave Afrikan people in their homeland because they will organise to defeat any such attempt. Nobody will be able to practice racism against Afrikan people in the Diaspora, because Afrika's centre of gravity (i.e. Afrikan people at home) will be so **powerful** that messing with any Afrikan person anywhere will be too foolhardy a risk.

7.2.3 Critical actions
Afrikan people must make control of Afrika reality. This means:
- Joining or creating organisations orientated towards Afrikan liberation;
- Networking with other organisations that support Afrikan liberation;
- Uniting and organising with other Afrikan liberation organisations on a worldwide basis to regain control of Afrika (1st stage of **power**);
- Building alliances with other oppressed peoples to defeat capitalism the common enemy:
  - This will contribute to destroying racist tyranny wherever it exists in the world;
- Fighting and defeating the capitalists at all levels (2nd stage of **power**)
- Recapturing control of Afrika's land; and
- Placing Afrika's resources under the sovereign control of Afrika's masses.

This outcome is Pan-Afrikanism the of achievement which marks the death of Anti-Afrikan racism. Genuine anti-racists will inevitably support Pan-Afrikanism. It is the yardstick by which genuine anti-racism can be measured.

Afrika's Solution
Scientific Socialism

Chapter 8

8 Afrika's solution – Scientific Socialism
8.1 Relationship between Scientific Socialism and Pan-Afrikanism
8.1.1 Scientific Socialism – outcome of Pan-Afrikanism
Scientific Socialism and Pan-Afrikanism are for Afrikan people one and the same. The essence of Scientific Socialism is the same everywhere, whilst its form varies from time to time and place to place. Its essence is derived from its higher level ingredients i.e. its materialist philosophy - respect for nature, humanist ideology - respect for people, state run politics - how we govern ourselves and industrialised economy – how we produce what we need. The next phase of history – Scientific Socialism – will be experienced by the whole of humanity, but only Afrikan people will experience it as Pan-Afrikanism. Other sections of humanity will have their particular manifestations.

In Afrika its form is determined by the particular characteristics of Afrikan people in their particular environments (parts of nature occupied). In combination, this produces Afrikan people's unique history, culture and identity underpinning their unique route, requiring unification, liberation and development of their homeland and themselves. This equates to Pan-Afrikanism, the form Scientific Socialism will take in Afrika. The Afrikan revolution will result in Afrika becoming Scientific Socialist in essence and Pan-Afrikanist in form.

8.1.2 The material ingredients of Scientific Socialism
Scientific Socialism is a term which describes the way a society or nation is run – it is a form of governance. On the face of it terms such as

"society", "nation" and "Scientific Socialism" are abstract – they exist largely in the realm of ideas. We may have an idea of what they are, but when it comes to clinically explaining, we can't necessarily put our finger on them.

The first step in clarifying apparently abstract terms is the identification of their material base. One part of the material base of "societies", "nations" and "Scientific Socialism" is nature. Societies and nations cannot exist outside nature. They are therefore founded on and contained within it. Nature is composed of elements: air, fire, water and earth. It follows that these elements constitute the material base of all that is contained in nature, including societies, nations and the Scientific Socialist expression of them.

The force of gravity draws on everything in the earth's atmosphere. Together they prevent air, fire and water floating into space. They are drawn to earth making land the most solid element, the base of nature. The equation is simple no land equals no foundation, no society, no nation. Land is their fundamental material base. This is especially important in the case of the Afrikan nation, since Afrikan land is by far the wealthiest/most valuable in the world.

Neither land nor nature, solely constitute the entire material base of a society/nation. Societies and nations also contain living things. Plants are alive. If we place plants in a darkened area with a pinhole of light, they will grow toward the light. They realise that sunlight is essential to their lives and by moving towards it, they preserve and extend their lives. However, despite being alive, plants are not capable of creating societies or nations.

Animals are also alive. If their lives are threatened, they adopt one of three modes of defence: fight, flight or freeze. Despite being alive and operating in a higher realm of life than plants, animals are also incapable of creating societies or nations. They can create herds, spools, flocks etc. but not societies or nations.

The one exception is the animal known as human being. Human beings have a higher level of consciousness than other creatures and a correspondingly more sophisticated culture. Human beings are distinguished from other animals by their mastery of fire. Whilst all other animals literally run away, humans have learned to control it and put it to use in their service. Fire is scientifically applied to run cars, heat homes, cook food and power energy plants etc.

Humans are also distinguished by their ability to create tools. This is important because tools can have an exponential impact on people's ability to apply their labour with increased effectiveness and efficiency. For instance, I might find that I can walk 20 miles in a day. With the assistance of a bike, I might be able to cycle 60 in the same period. Assisted by a car, I might be able to drive 600; an airplane 24,000 and a space ship hundreds of thousands. The more potent the tool, the greater is its enhancing impact on human abilities. This also illustrates how the application of science can enhance and improve the quality of our lives if applied in a principled, caring, thoughtful, conscientious and nature loving manner.

These distinctions make humans capable of creating societies and nations. Our higher level consciousness comes from our enhanced ability to interact with nature and apply tools scientifically to it. People are the other critical material ingredient forming the basis of a society/nation. People and nature (fundamentally land), are the material ingredients of societies/nations – if they are removed, societies and nations cannot exist. All other aspects of a society/nation i.e. the *matspiritual*[14], are founded upon and derived from people and nature with land as their base.

8.1.3 People and nature relations – Towards Matspiritual ingredients
People and nature simultaneously represent the material (physical) ingredients of societies, nations and the methods by which they are run – including Scientific Socialism. By scientifically examining interactions between these lower level material ingredients, we are able to identify locate and assess their related higher level *matspiritual* ones.

---

[14] *Matspiritual* denotes Afrikan culture's nature based approach to "spiritual" matters. "Spirits" come from nature, are inseparable from it and cannot exist independently of it. All "Spirits" have material as their base. "Spirit" is anchored in and by material.

Amilcar Cabral in his book *Return to the Source* explains economics at its essence is the relationship between people and nature, whilst politics is the relationship between people and people (Afrikan Information Service, 1973, p. 41; Mc Culloch, 1983, p. 84). It is the relationship between people and nature that fundamentally determines the relationship between people and people. At the same time, the relationship between people and people gives direction to the relationship between people and nature. All social systems produced by human beings are fundamentally based on the relationship between people and people on the one hand and people and nature on the other. Together these two sets of relationships determine all other types or categories of human relationship. In other words, all human relationships are reducible to some permutation of economics and politics i.e. political economy.

Relations & Derivatives

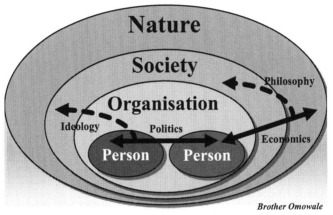

Brother Omowale

Nature is older than people, it existed before people. People were created out of nature and are completely contained in both time and nature. Since people are contained in nature, politics must be contained in economics. In other words all politics is economics; however because the rest of nature exists outside of people, the rest of economics must exist outside of politics - therefore not all economics is politics. Economics is bigger than politics; politics is really a part of economics, but it is the critical part that determines the direction and levels of success of economic activity.

At the same time as surrounding people, nature also fills people – at the atomic level it is inside people and therefore their interactions. This means wherever politics is found it has economics inside. Furthermore at the higher level of ideas where ideology (people based) is ordinarily inside philosophy (nature based), wherever ideology is found it has philosophy inside. Externally, nature's movement acts on people stimulating nature's movement inside them, driving them to produce ideas from within.

As people interact with others i.e. politics, their relationships develop a particular calibre, which in turn produces particular principles. If the tendency is for others to be honoured, treated with innate dignity, respect and valued above private property, the principle of humanism develops – humanism simplified is respect for people. If on the other hand, they are devalued and used like private property, the opposite principle of exploitation occurs – disrespect of people.

Similarly, if the tendency is for people to club together to solve their problems, the principle of collectivism develops. By contrast, if people consistently put their personal interests first i.e. before those of the groups to which they belong, individualism becomes dominant. Furthermore, the tendency to treat fellow human beings as equals develops egalitarianism. If others are adjudged superior/inferior on the basis of sex, race, class and the like, elitism develops as the norm.

Principles at the level of society produce ideology at the level of culture. They are in essence the same, but operate at different levels. The manner of our interactions with others produces our ideology. We can observe that people are the base for politics and politics the base for ideology.

Human beings come from nature, are part of it and must extract from it in order to survive - we must breathe, drink and eat. The question is do we give back, or more precisely what do we give back i.e. replenishment or pollution? Are we sustaining or killing it? Do we seek to live in harmony with or dominate it? Do we treat nature as an end i.e. worthy of respect in its own right or is it merely one of our tools? Do we respect or disrespect nature? The manner of our interactions with nature determines our philosophy.

Since people are a part of nature and principles remain consistent in all situations, we can extrapolate ideological principles predicated on people relations, into the broader realm of nature to assist our philosophical examination. This process brings the following results:

- The philosophical equivalent of humanism translates to **nature before spirits** and its exploitation equivalent becomes **spirits before nature**;
- The philosophical equivalent of collectivism translates to **spirits inside nature** and its individualism equivalent becomes **spirits outside nature**;
- The philosophical equivalent of egalitarianism translates to **nature and spirits are equal** and its elitism equivalent becomes **spirits are superior to nature**;

Humanism, collectivism and egalitarianism are core principles of both Afrikan culture and Socialism. Their extrapolation points to a philosophy characterized by its recognition of equality of spirit and physical nature, where spirits reside in nature and nature is starting point from which spirits are to be understood. They are both materialist, meaning implicit within them is respect of nature.

Opposing Cultures

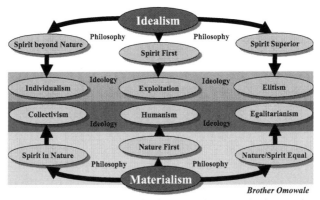

Brother Omowale

If we investigate nature in order to understand the unknown, our philosophy is materialist, logically explainable and is therefore underpinned by scientific methodology. If we investigate the unknown via spirits, we apply philosophical idealism and our methodology takes on a magical/mystical character. Spirits that are outside nature and thereby beyond our capacity to locate are abstract and therefore scientifically inexplicable. We can only explain spirits logically if they are rooted and identifiable in nature. People and nature form the base for economics and economics the base for philosophy.

As an aside, the relationship between nature and nature is ecology – a **matspiritual** ingredient. As nature interacts with nature, it brings life into being, sustains it, but dialectically it also actively kills. This is perhaps indicative of a "Godlike" capacity producing what some people might refer to as "spirituality". There is a genuine difficulty here because different people mean so many different things when they use the terms "God" and "spirit" in the abstract. This latter point is proffered as stimulation for thought rather than an objectively proven fact.

These different levels of operation can be categorised into what Kwame Nkrumah explains as logical types. He says:

> "Matter belongs to one logical type, properties and qualities of matter to a higher logical type, properties of properties to an even higher logical type." (Nkrumah, 2009, p. 90).

In his sense people and nature i.e. the material foundations of societies and nations are one logical type. The interactions between them produce politics, economics and ecology, another logical type. The manner of those interactions produce ideology, philosophy and what some might mean when they use the word "spirituality", a third logical type. The second and third types founded on the first, are **matspiritual**.

8.2 Scientific Socialism and the 4 Dialectic analysis of Afrikan culture

8.2.1 Matspiritual ingredients of Scientific Socialism

In the first instance, Scientific Socialism refers to the material or lower level ingredients of societies and nations i.e. people and nature. It recognises that both of these ingredients are continuously varying from time to time and place to place. It further recognises that no two people or groups are the same, nor are any two locations. A plenum of interactions between them is also ongoing on a continuous basis – they are always in motion and therefore constantly changing.

Material interactions between people and nature produce **matspiritual** outcomes and together they produce unique/distinct peoples with distinct identities, derived from their unique biology, environments, histories and cultures. This means despite the fact the *matspiritual* ingredients of Socialism will be identical for all peoples and societies, the manifestation of Scientific Socialism will be different in each case precisely because of the people's unique identities, derived from their unique biology, environments, histories and cultures.

Scientific Socialism:
Fixed & Variable Factors

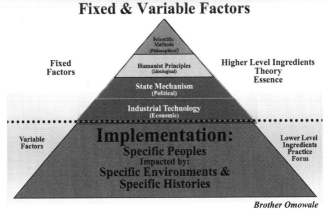

Brother Omowale

Scientific Socialists adopt the position that there is no separation between material and *matspiritual* ingredients i.e. no separation between people, nature, society, nation, economics, politics, ideology and philosophy. All of these aspects are totally integrated, forming one unified whole, represented in time and space by particular people's unique/distinct identities and cultures. Scientific Socialism is therefore a particular outcome of how a people manage their distinct/unique identity and culture using their own resources in their own space.

8.2.2 Identifying the economic dialectic

Our economic activity is the sum total of our interaction with nature and that ability is profoundly impacted by the calibre of tools we deploy. The most potent economic tool in a society/nation is industrialisation. Human beings in an industrial setting are able to produce far more than their counterparts in a pre-industrial (i.e. agricultural) one. From this is derived the *economic dialectic* i.e. does the society/nation *have/not industrialisation*? Industrialisation is an absolute requirement of Socialism - if it hasn't got it, it is not/cannot be Socialist. Imperialism has debarred Afrikan society from

industrialisation.   Socialism   cannot   be   achieved   until   Afrika's
industrialisation void is filled.

8.2.3 Identifying the political dialectic
Similarly, national/societal scale political activity is the sum total of
people's interactions within its borders.   Again the potency of
interaction is profoundly impacted by the calibre of tool deployed. The
most powerful political tool is the state. The state is violence. It is the
most violent tool in a society/nation, with the primary function of
empowering one section of society/nation by oppressing the remainder.
Despite pretences to the contrary, it is always bias.

The state is never a 'nice' tool and ultimately humanity's objective must
be to get rid of it. It is nonetheless intrinsic to certain types of society as
the principal tool for maintaining that social order, meaning **the state's
existence/non existence** provides the basis for the **political dialectic**.
The Socialist society/nation must have a state – any nation/society
which does not, is not/cannot be Socialist.   Imperialism has broken
Afrika into a multiplicity of non-functioning jigsaw puzzle pretend states,
thereby blocking her political path to Socialism.   Afrika must form a
single unified continental super-state governing the affairs of Afrikan
people at home and abroad as an indispensible first step towards the
achievement of Socialism.

8.2.4 Identifying the ideological dialectic
Our ideological activity is a qualitative development on our politics. It
boils down to how we treat other people. It rests fundamentally upon
whether our engagement is humanist or exploitative in character;
whether   we   put   people   before   money/profits/property   or
money/profits/property before people; whether we treat other people
as ends in and of themselves, or merely as a means to our owns ends;
whether we respect their dignity and inherent worth as human beings
or use them as tools; whether we respect or disrespect fellow human
beings.

The overarching opposing principles i.e. humanism and exploitation are
part of broader families of principles. The others include whether our
actions are governed by collectivism (we before me) or individualism
(me before we); and egalitarianism (we're all equal in essence) or
elitism (I'm better than you). Sexism, racism and other illogical notions

of human superiority/inferiority are rooted in the elitist principle and are therefore in ideological opposition to Socialism.

Ideology & Principles

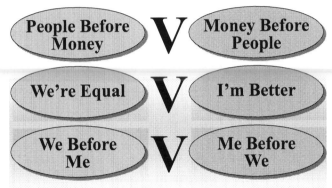

Brother Omowale

The *ideological dialectic* is fundamentally the conflict between the *humanist and exploitative families of principles*. The Socialist society/nation requires humanist principles. Humanism, collectivism and egalitarianism are a precondition for Socialism. If a society/nation doesn't operate on the basis of humanist principles, it is not/cannot be Socialist. Afrika is already ideologically adapted to Socialism since, particularly in its villages, humanist principles remain dominant. Ground has been lost in the various jig saw puzzle pretend state structures and cities where capitalist principles have been imposed from outside, but this transgression nonetheless remains recoverable.

8.2.5 Identifying the philosophical dialectic

Finally, our philosophical activity is also qualitative. Built on our economics it boils down to how we treat nature, which in turn is predicated on whether we believe that material or spirit is the source of nature. Fundamentally there are only two philosophies. A belief that nature comes from material is known as *philosophical materialism* and generates as principle, a *scientific* response to the investigation of nature – experimentation and analysis are among its tools; or a belief that spirit is source is referred to as *philosophical idealism* and generates *mystical/magical* principles as opposing methodologies for the pursuit of new knowledge – prayer and meditation form part of its tool kit.

From the two fundamental approaches, we can extrapolate five philosophical outlooks/categories which incorporate any and all possible philosophies. These are derived by mapping out the different permutations of possible relationships between the fundamental categories material and spirit. The five secondary categories are here labelled as follows:

- **Nothingness (Idealist)**: Refers to the belief that neither material nor spirit exist. There is no such thing as the universe, because nothing whatsoever exists. Everything codified as nature or mind, including ourselves is fictitious/nonexistent.
- **Spirit Only (Idealist)**: Refers to the belief that only spirit exists. Anything resembling material is only an illusion. The universe is composed only of spirit. Nature is imaginary, an activity of mind.
- **Prime Spirit (Idealist)**: Refers to the belief that both material and spirit exist. The universe is composed of both. To understand the universe one must begin with the investigation of spirits. Spirits/mind are the source of nature.
- **Prime Material (Materialist)**: Refers to the belief that both material and spirit exist. The universe is composed of both. To understand the universe one must begin with the investigation of material reality. Nature is the source of spirits/mind. Afrikan philosophy resides in this category.
- **Material Only (Materialist)**: Refers to the belief that only material exists. Anything claiming to be spirit is at best imaginary. The universe is composed only of material. Nature is exclusively material, mind doesn't exist.

Of the five categories three are idealist. In varying degrees, they are imbued with disrespect for nature and therefore stand in opposition to Afrikan philosophy. Two, **Nothingness** and **Spirit Only** deny material. In them nature is so unimportant it doesn't even exist. These branches of idealism cannot respect nature, since it is impossible to respect something believed to be nonexistent.

In **Prime Spirit**, nature is de-prioritised to a position behind "spirits" and their ideas. It loses importance as it is literally reduced to afterthought. Its respect for nature is tempered to the extent it treats it as secondary to spirit. These uncaring approaches to nature flow and transform into capitalism at the political level.

Two **Prime Material** and **Material Only** are materialist and are bases for Socialism. Since materialism is predicated on the existence of material i.e. nature, all branches start from the point that nature exists and to that extent at least must respect nature. Materialists respect nature, though there may be variations in degree.

Since Afrikan philosophy will not countenance the exclusion of spirit, only **Prime Material** provides a basis for Socialism in an Afrikan setting. **Afrikan philosophy** is **Prime Material** which is fundamentally **Materialist** making it compatible with **Socialism**. In it, material is primary and spirits (found in nature) are rooted in material, thereby giving them materialist qualities and the foundation necessary to make scientific investigation of them possible.

5 Philosophical Possibilities

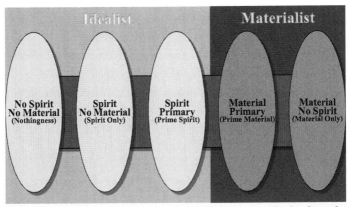

Brother Omowale

The term **Matspirit** is used to denote this special characteristic of "Afrikan spirituality." It illustrates three things:

- Firstly, in Afrikan philosophy "spirits" are rooted/grounded/anchored in the material i.e. nature, making the material i.e. nature the starting point of all things "spiritual";
- The material i.e. nature and its "spiritual" dimensions are absolutely inseparable, at all times forming one unified whole.

They are both infinite and therefore present in all situations; and

- In so far as they are detectable, 'spirits' are inside material i.e. nature.

These special characteristics distinguish **Afrikan Matspirituality** from abstract idealist notions of "spirit". It reminds us that there is no place in the universe where spirits reside independently, separately or detached from material, thereby placing them firmly in the materialist philosophical camp where they can be scientifically scrutinised. **Matspirit** can be scientifically examined via its material ("Mat" – "terial") base. **Matspirit** supersedes the term "A-Material" (Pert-em-Hru, 2017c, p. 277-282) by grounding it in the material.

8.2.6 Outcome of 4 Dialect Analysis

The **4 dialectic tool** focuses specifically on the **matspiritual** i.e. higher level ingredients of societies and nations. It identifies **matspiritual** categories and opposing ingredients contained within them struggling for domination. These are:

- Philosophy, comprising either scientific or magical/mystical engagement with nature - methodologies;
- Ideology, comprising either humanist or exploitative treatment of people - principles;
- Politics, comprising either no state or a state mechanism - governance;
- Economics, comprising either an industrial or a pre-industrial (agricultural) production - economy.

At the lower i.e. material level, the achievement of a Scientific Socialist society/nation requires people with their distinct identities, operating in their distinct parts of nature, applying their distinct biology and environments, producing distinct histories and cultures to solve their particular problems. This is achieved through deployment of the following fixed **matspiritual** higher level ingredients:

- Respect for nature and scientific methodology at the philosophical level;
- Respect for people through humanist principles at the ideological level;
- A state mechanism for governance at the political level; and

- An industrially driven economy at the level of economic production.

4 Dialectic Categories

Brother Omowale

The ideological level determines the people's sovereign control/ownership of state and production is focused on meeting the people's needs. The philosophical level determines industrial production is in concert with nature.

"What then is scientific socialism? Socialism's philosophy requires **scientific methodology**. Its ideology requires **humanist principles**. Its politics requires **a state mechanism** collectively **controlled by the majority** in their interest; and its economics requires **industrialisation** collectively **owned by the majority** in their interest. It requires the above ingredients to be managed via **democratic centralism**. These are the high level ingredients of **scientific socialism**. **Scientific socialism** is the above combination of ingredients infused in societies in different locations on earth, producing different outcomes for respective peoples based on their environment and corresponding culture. It is also a phase of history.

The fact that there are a specific set of ingredients which *must* be present means the ingredients are actually the principles of socialism. Socialism can therefore be expressed as a hierarchy of principles, which gives socialism the second part of its scientific character. The required ingredients mean that socialism can be written as a formula in much the same way that the ingredients and process for baking a cake can be codified.

The third part of socialism's scientific character comes from the fact that when the formula for a socialist society is achieved, its combination of both constant and variable factors produces different outcomes in different locations. The outcomes cannot be precisely the same as a result of key variables such as local environment and the respective peoples' culture.

When the ingredients are scientifically applied, socialism takes on the particular character of the society applying it in its environment. This is scientifically consistent with the manner in which water boils at slightly different temperatures when heated at different altitudes ... Whilst we cannot be certain about the details of how socialism will operate in all situations, we can be certain about some of its bigger higher level, universal characteristics. Socialism everywhere will fit the above ingredients and criteria. If it doesn't, it isn't socialism – it is disqualified. It is this certainty that forms another important part of socialism's scientific character.

Incidentally, uncertainty at the level of socialism's detail brings with it an important positive. It means scientific socialism cannot and will not be prescriptive. The most it can do is issue a set of methodologies and ethics (principles) that set the philosophical and ideological context for the institutions and rules by which respective peoples choose to run their society.

This latitude means scientific socialism comes with a built in safeguard protecting the collective freedom of choice of the people practicing it in their localities. Socialism's operational details will be decided by the people in their own society within the parameters of the higher level ingredients. Socialism essentially amounts to a series of choices about how we choose to run our societies" (Pert-em-Hru, 2017c, p. 232-4).

Afrika has operated with correct philosophy and ideology for Scientific Socialism since human life began. This means the core elements of Scientific Socialism are already deeply imbedded in Afrikan culture. Our culture and Scientific Socialism are and have always been at home with one another. However, our culture's current political and economic retardation are barriers preventing Afrika and her people from achieving Scientific Socialism and enjoying the fruits of modern living.

The very highest tiers of Afrikan culture i.e. philosophical and ideological have long since been waiting for the tiers immediately below i.e. political and economic, to catch up. This updating problem must be solved if our threatened culture is to be rescued and made fit for the modern era. We will then have a just social system protecting our people's humanity and equality, genuinely emanating from Afrikan culture.

8.2.7 Afrika's expression of Scientific Socialism will be unique
Scientific Socialism's higher level *matspiritual* formula when applied in differing lower level situations i.e. in different parts of nature, by different peoples with distinct biology, environments, histories and cultures, produces different results which are scientifically explainable. The essence i.e. the higher level ingredients will be the same everywhere, whilst the form i.e. the lower level ingredients will differ according to people-space-time.

This means the calibre of Scientific Socialism that will develop and grow in Afrika, though imbued with the same higher level ingredients as everywhere else, will operate differently from anything experienced in the world to date. Afrikan people will uniquely adapt it to best suit our own particular needs and circumstances. Scientific Socialism provides the essence of Afrika's next historical phase and Pan-Afrikanism, its unique specific form. This is Pan-Afrikanism - the characteristic that preserves guards and maintains Afrikan culture by modernizing outdated elements.

8.2.8 Are we ready for Scientific Socialism?
Afrikan people everywhere have become impoverished because the political and economic parts of our culture have been interrupted, dominated and retarded, rendering them outdated. As a result history

has in a sense, moved forward without us, resulting in tremendous suffering for our people. Our current state of political and economic backwardness leaves us with no choice other than to modernize if we are to survive.

Our prospects for achieving this are good.   Firstly, our 1.6 million growing population is testimony to our indestructibility in the face of adversity.   Even at our weakest, a determined enemy cannot exterminate us. As we organise and strengthen we become invincible. Secondly, our average age of 18 on the continent makes us the youngest people in the world, best able to adapt to latest technologies. Thirdly, Afrika is by far that richest continent in the world.   Our abundant youthful population and wealth filled land positions us the people of the future.   Our task is to effectively organise these attributes/assets for a glorious future.

Updating Afrikan Society

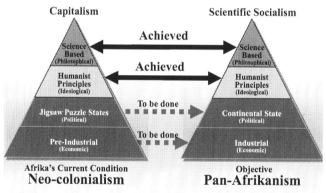

Brother Omowale

The adoption of Scientific Socialism will update our mode of governance, making us truly independent and self-determining politically. Our new self-determining status must then be directed towards updating our scientific capacity to produce what we need, lifting us out of our economic slump. These changes will ensure the survival of Afrikan people and our culture. At the same time it will be the guardian of our philosophical methodology and ideological principles, maintaining and upholding the highest and oldest aspects of Afrikan culture for future generations.

Each of us has a duty/role in the updating and saving of our culture, which we will either fulfil or betray. In this regard, the **4 dialectic analytical tool** provides a framework and acid test for us as individuals. It helps us better understand our personal position on the question of the liberation of Afrika and her people and target our efforts accordingly. For instance, you are a Scientific Socialist if at the personal level, you want:

- Respect for nature and the scientific approach inherent in Afrikan philosophical methodology as practiced since the beginning of time to remain, recuperate and grow as our means of engaging nature;
- Afrika's respect for people manifested through humanist principles to flow through our dealings with each other and the rest of the world;
- Afrika to have a single unified state governing the entirety of our land, controlled by all our people worldwide; and
- Afrika and her people to enjoy the benefits of producing via our own industrial means in concert with nature.

The blows undermining Afrikan culture came from capitalism in its gestation. Its defence and restoration will come from Socialism. **Scientific Socialism in the hands of Afrikan people is Pan-Afrikanism - simultaneously the modernization and guardian of Afrikan culture.** If you are an Afrikan person conscientiously and systematically working towards the achievement of the above four dialectical outcomes in the context of a genuine Afrikan liberation organisation, you are an active Scientific Socialist — a guardian of Afrikan culture modernized for our survival. If you are not, then your personal liberation objective is to become one.

Mentioned Sources

1. Africa Information Service, (1973), *Return to the Source: Selected Speeches of Amilcar Cabral*, Monthly Review Press
2. Anderson. SE, (1995), *The Black Holocaust for Beginners*, Writers and Readers Publishing Incorporated
3. Brietman. George, (2002), *Malcolm X Speaks*, Pathfinder
4. Brietman. George, (2003), *Malcolm X: By Any Means Necessary*, Pathfinder

5.   Browder. Anthony, (1996), *From the Browder File Vol II: Survival Strategies for Africans in America: 13 Steps to Freedom*, The Institute of Karmic Guidance

6.   Cabral. Amilcar, (1971), *Our People are our Mountains: Amilcar Cabral on the Guinean Revolution*, Committee for Freedom in Mozambique, Angola and Guine

7.   Cabral. Amilcar, (1974), *Revolution in Guinea: An African People's Struggle*, Stage1

8.   Cabral. Amilcar, (1979), *Unity and Struggle: Speeches and Writings of Amilcar Cabral*, Monthly Review Press

9.   Clark. Steve, (2003), *The Final Speeches: Malcolm X*, Pathfinders

10. Davis. Angela, (1983), *Women, Race and Class*, Vintage Books, New York

11. Diop. Cheik Anta, (1974), *The African Origin of Civilization: Myth or Reality*, Lawrence Hill Books

12. Diop. Cheikh Anta, (1991), *Civilisation or Barbarism: An Authentic Anthropology*, Lawrence Hill Books

13. Garvey. Amy Jacques, (1986), *The Philosophy and Opinions of Marcus Garvey*, The Majority Press.

14. Hay. Margaret, Jean and Stichter. Sharon, (1984), African Women: South of the Sahara, Longman

15. Hill. Robert (ed.), (1983a), *Marcus Garvey and the Universal Negro Improvement Association Papers: Volume I, 1826 – August 1919*, University of California Press.

16. Hill. Robert (ed.), (1983b), *Marcus Garvey and the Universal Negro Improvement Association Papers: Volume II, 27th August 1919 – 31st August 1920*, University of California Press.

17. Hill. Robert (ed.), (1984), *Marcus Garvey and the Universal Negro Improvement Association Papers: Volume III, September 1920 – August 1921*, University of California Press.

18. Hill. Robert (ed.), (1987b), *Marcus Garvey, Life and Lessons: A Centennial Companion to the Marcus Garvey Universal Negro Improvement association papers*, University of California Press.

19. Hill. Robert (ed.), (1991), Marcus Garvey and Universal Negro Improvement Association Papers: Volume VII, November 1927 – August 1940, University of California Press.

20. Machel. Samora, (1973), *Mozambique: Sowing the Seeds of Revolution*, Committee for Freedom in Mosambique, Angola & Guine

21. Mackie. Liz, (2008), *The Great Marcus Garvey*, Hansib Publications.

22. M'buyinga. Elenga, (1982), *Pan-Afrikanism or Neo-colonialism: The Bankrupcy of the OAU* Zed Press

23. Mc Culloch. Jock, (1983), *In the Twilight of Revolution: The Political Theory of Amilcar Cabral*, Routledge and Kegan Paul

24. Montgomery. Bernard, (2000), *A Concise History of Warfare*, Wordsworth Edition Limited
25. Nkrumah. Kwame, (1974), *Neo-Colonialism: The Last Stage of Imperialism*, PANAF Books Limited
26. Nkrumah. Kwame, (1980), Handbook of Revolutionary Warfare, PANAF Books
27. Nkrumah. Kwame, (1980a), *Class Struggle in Africa*, PANAF Books Limited, reprinted; first printed in 1970
28. Nkrumah. Kwame, (1980b), *Revolutionary Path*, PANAF Books Limited, reprinted; first printed in 1973
29. Nkrumah. Kwame, (1981), *The Struggle Continues*, PANAF Books Limited, reprinted; first printed in 1968
30. Nkrumah. Kwame, (1998), *Africa Must Unite*, PANAF Books Limited, reprinted; first printed in 1963
31. Nkrumah. Kwame, (2009), *Consciencism*, PANAF Books Limited, reprinted; first printed in 1964
32. Padmore. George, (1963), *History of the Pan-African Congress*, The Hammersmith Bookshop Limited
33. Pert-em-Hru. Omowale, (2017c), *Pan-Afrikanism: From Programme to Philosophy*, Ukombozii
34. Pert-em-Hru. Omowale, (2017d), *Pan-Afrikanism: The Battlefront*, Ukombozii
35. Preiswerk. Roy, (1980), *The Slant of the Pen: Racism in Children's Books*, World Council of Churches
36. Sankara. Thomas, (2004), *Thomas Sankara Speaks: The Burkina Faso Revolution 1983-87*, Pathfinder
37. Sons of Garvey Press Association, (1990), *Selected utterances of Marcus Moziah Garvey: Africa for the African*, Cleage Group Publications.
38. Stiglitz. Joseph, (2002), *Globalization and its Discontents*, Penguin Books
39. Toure. Sekou, (Undated), *Women in Society*, All-African People's Revolutionary Party
40. Toure. Sekou, (No. 88), *Revolution, Culture & Pan-Africanism*, African Democratic Revolution
41. Toure. Sekou, (1977), *The Strategy and Tactics of the Revolution*, The State Office, Republic of Guinea, English 1st Edition, Volume XXI
42. Van Sertima. Ivan, (1996), *African Presence in Early Europe*, Transaction Publishers

Internet references:

1. Desjardins. Jeff, *The median age of continents*, Visual Capitalist, 15th February 2019, https://www.visualcapitalist.com/mapped-the-median-age-of-every-continent/
2. Kiprop. Victor, *Continents by Population*, WorldAtlas, 12th June 2019, https://www.worldatlas.com/articles/continents-by-population.html
3. Sawe. Benjamin Elisha, *Which Continent Is The Richest In Natural Resources?* WorldAtlas, 20th August 2018, https://www.worldatlas.com/articles/which-continent-is-the-richest-in-natural-resources.html.

Index

Author: Brother Omowale

Spoke some home truths in Britain's Parliament on 17th January 2017. Some sections of the media went berserk as a consequence. Click link for presentation:
https://www.youtube.com/watch?v=Sp-ylYnzbg8

Omowale Ru Pert-em-Hru
07933 145 393
Ukombozii@gmail.com

Author of
The Pan-Afrikanism Series

Publications written by
Brother Omowale

Pan-Afrikanism
From Programme to Philosophy:
An outlook on Liberation

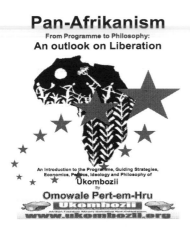

Pan-Afrikanism
The Battlefront:
Afrikan Freedom Means Defeating Neo-colonialism

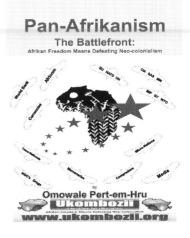

Pan-Afrikanism: From programme to philosophy

"Pan-Afrikanism: From programme to philosophy" is the only book in the world to provide clear lucid and simple explanations of the liberation strategies of Marcus Garvey, Kwame Nkrumah and Malcolm X. Historians have been naturally concerned with reporting facts of the lives of these great Pan-Afrikanists, but it is for activists to contextualise them in liberation strategies and action plans - a process kick started in it. In addition:

1. It provides a clear succinct explanation of international capitalism's parasitical dependence upon Afrikan people;
2. It provides a clear simple explanation of scientific socialism, relating it to Afrikan principles and culture;
3. It introduces the notion of the greater cycle of revolution which examines and locates revolution not as an incident, but as a process in the context of the entirety of human history;
4. Through an examination of universal principles, it locates the material base of the two opposing sets of ideologies driving human activity and identifies the natural position of Afrikan culture in that milieu; and finally,
5. Through a newly devised set of dialectical tools, it provides a powerfully clear philosophical analysis of matter as a basis for uncovering and understanding the universal laws required for Afrika's liberation.

"Pan-Afrikanism: From programme to philosophy" is a long overdue and much needed source book on the theory of Pan-Afrikanism. For people new to Pan-Afrikanist activism or those who simply want to understand what Pan-Afrikanism is, this book provides clear theoretical guidance. For seasoned cadres and veterans of the Pan-Afrikanist movement, it is a checkpoint/frame of reference for assessing, orientating or even refocusing the trajectory of their activities. Ideally should be studied collectively in groups, particularly those genuinely working towards the liberation of Afrika and her people in the context of worldwide revolution.

Pan-Afrikanism: The Battlefront

When we (Afrikan people) were oppressed under slavery and colonialism our ancestors knew it; they knew that they had to remove these oppressive systems in order to be free. Now we are living in the neo-colonial phase of history and most of us don't know what it is. If we don't know it, we can't understand it; if we can't understand it, we can't consciously do anything to challenge it; if we can't do anything to challenge it, we can't get rid of it; if we can't get rid of it, we're stuck in it; if we're stuck in neo-colonialism, Afrika can't be liberated and we won't be a free and self determining people. The critical task before us therefore, is to raise our collective consciousness of neo-colonialism and how to defeat it in Afrikan communities everywhere. *"Pan-Afrikanism: The Battlefront"* raises our consciousness to better equip us for Afrika's liberation.

"Pan-Afrikanism: The Battlefront" provides a thorough analysis of neo-colonial mechanisms and processes by which the capitalist system arrests Afrikan development in the contemporary world. By facilitating a grounded understanding of how those mechanisms hold us back, it lays the foundation for Afrikan people's corrective actions. It seeks to enhance our understanding by:

1. Introducing readers to some basic concepts of war;
2. Explaining how Afrika's resources was the hidden reason behind World Wars I and II;
3. Linking neo-colonialism to its roots in the enslavement and colonisation of Afrikan people, exposing it as their modern manifestation;
4. Examining the origin, development and intricate workings of neo-colonialism and its adverse impact on Afrikan people;
5. Exposing how a wavering neo-colonialism is altering its form in a desperate and increasingly vicious attempt to increase its life span;
6. Exposing the appointment of President Obama, as an act of counter-insurgency and containment against Afrikan people in quest of liberation; and
7. Exposes Zionism as settler colonialism and genocide, which whilst operating as a junior, but powerful partner in imperialism, actively undermines the interests of Afrikan people.

"Pan-Afrikanism: The Battlefront" should be treated as an introductory and grounding text, laying the foundation for a fuller understanding of the essence of the economic and political problems confronting Afrikan people in the world today. As with the other books in the series, it should be studied collectively in groups, particularly by groups genuinely working towards the liberation of Afrika and her people in the context of worldwide revolution.

Pan-Afrikanism: Material Based Concepts

"Pan-Afrikanism: Material Based Concepts" applies materialist philosophical tools to raise understanding of key Pan-Afrikan concepts such as history, culture, identity and the role of women in Afrika's liberation. Methodologically, Pan-Afrikanists use historical facts rather than imagination as basis for developing theory. *"Pan-Afrikanism: Material Based Concepts"* supplements this working from nature as material base to interpret those historical facts for clearer understanding of Afrikan people's problems and improved strategising. In addition to contextualising and explaining Pan-Afrikanism, it:

1. Clarifies what Pan-Afrikanism is not, referencing dangerously undermining distortions about religion, sexuality and biological make up, wrongly associated with Pan-Afrikanism. This lays the basis for distinguishing it from neo-colonialist and Divisionist imposters misleadingly labelling themselves "Pan-Afrikanists" and clears confusion, allowing Pan-Afrikanism to be properly defined and explained;

2. Explains history contextually, facilitating its proper application for achieving Pan-Afrikanism. History is more than a collection of facts. Historical phases and how they are derived must be understood, if revolution is to be achieved;

3. Explains culture contextually and its proper application for Pan-Afrikanism. At one level, culture is a people's total experience and the failure to understand its source, operation and derivation hinders liberation efforts;

4. Explains identity contextually and its proper interpretation for unity and Pan-Afrikanism. Identity removed from its material base triggers identity confusion as it reduces to 'opinions' and transforms destructively into a source of deep rooted disunity;

5. Takes feminine and masculine principles, locates them in the context of nature as base and uses this to examine and highlight the role of Afrikan women in the liberation process;

6. Succinctly explains the context and basis of racism;

7. Clarifies and explains the symbiotic relationship between Afrikan culture, Pan-Afrikanism and scientific socialism.

"Pan-Afrikanism: Material Based Concepts", is the third in a trilogy of books demystifying and explaining Pan-Afrikanism. For people new to Pan-Afrikanist activism or seeking greater understanding, it adds clarity and theoretical guidance. For seasoned cadres and veterans, it provides a frame of reference for assessing, orientating or even refocusing the trajectory of their activities. As with the others, it should be studied collectively in groups, particularly those genuinely working towards the liberation of Afrika and her people in the context of worldwide revolution.

Drug Economy attack on Afrikan Youth: We Fight Back!

"Drug economy attack on Afrikan youth: We fight back!" uncovers a world where state agencies including bankers and police, manage Britain's dirty money and drug economy hand in hand with Afrikan and other pushers as fronts. This results in the criminalisation of targeted Afrikan youths contained in internal colonies. It:

1. Critically examines state mechanisms and their operations, exposing their inherent violence and the British State's disproportionate violence against Afrikan youths in its home based colonies;

2. Exposes the origins and development of 'Low intensity Warfare'. Widely deployed against Afrikan youth in Britain and other capitalist centres, it was designed by Britain's then leading general Frank Kitson against Afrikan freedom fighters during decolonizing struggles in the 1950's;

3. Unearths underground workings of the multi-billion dollar international drug economy operating in service of capitalism's elite, exposing the corrupt role of banks, police and even governments that impose drug economies on Afrikan youths contained in internal colonies;

4. Reminds of real life cases where Scotland Yard went overseas to recruit known murderers and rapists as mercenaries, paying them handsomely to unofficially police Britain's drug economy attack on contained Afrikan youths. It was no surprise when they raped and murdered whilst 'on duty' in Britain. Police mercenaries' murderous activities are the root source of spiralling gun and knife crime in targeted Afrikan communities;

5. Clarifies Malcolm X's use of the phrase 'by any means necessary'. Criminals posing as freedom fighters abuse the phrase, misleadingly suggesting he supported smuggling drugs to fund 'Afrikan liberation'. This is a lie. His opposition to the drug economy was uncompromising. Some social commentators even suggest he was assassinated by 'the mob' because of it.

Criminality created by the British state's drug economy is used as justification to unleash police terror campaigns in Afrikan internal colonies: Police budgets increase; Gun toting SAS killer soldiers are said to operate on Britain's streets disguised in police uniforms; Unprovoked murders of Afrikan people by police and their agents become increasingly common; Afrikan youths are routinely stopped and searched several times more than any other group; and drug induced state violence is wilfully perpetrated against siege ridden law abiding Afrikan communities. These claims may sound sensational but inside the covers of this book there is compelling evidence to support them.

Publications written by
Brother Omowale

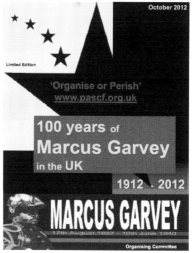

Conceptions and misconceptions of Garvey and Garveyism

In 1914 Marcus Garvey and his fiancée Amy Ashwood co-founded the UNIA – an organisation destined to become the largest international grassroots Afrikan organisation of the 20th century. At its low there were only 13 members following a split in 1917; in 1918 Garvey was calling meetings attracting 3, 5, 7 and over 10 thousand people. By 1919 the UNIA boasted a membership of over 2 million. In 1920 its convention brought 25 thousand into New York's Madison Square Garden's. In 1923 Garvey assessed the membership of the UNIA at 6 million and later reported 11 million.

Its success impressed, not only the minds of Garvey's followers, but their hearts. Years after death he elicits incredible pride and loyalty from Afrikan communities around the world. Unable to erase his legacy, imperialism's intelligence agencies set about distorting it by creating and cascading myths designed to dampen his popularity. *"Conceptions and misconceptions of Garvey and Garveyism"* challenges a number of popularised myths distorting Garvey's legacy:

1. The myth that Garvey was anti-Christian when in fact he was a Christian publicly objecting to the way Europe's elite misused his religion;
2. The myth that Garvey was anti other races and opposed to working in inter-racial solidarity when in fact such alliances were nurtured when deemed appropriate;
3. The myth that it is not possible to simultaneously be a 'Garveyite' and 'Marxist', when in fact the UNIA was a broad grouping which brought together wide ranging political ideologies including the 'Marxists' who brought 'Race First' ideology into the organisation;
4. The myth that Garvey was the prophet of Ethiopia's emperor Haile Selassie despite the fact they developed into bitter ideological enemies, with Garvey brutally and publicly castigating the emperor and the emperor silently plotting his political destruction;
5. The myth that Garvey sought to repatriate all Afrikan people when in fact targeted collective repatriation of some (not all) was an implicit part of the UNIA's liberation strategy; and
6. The myth that Garvey was anti-socialist when in fact he opposed European's racist misrepresentation of socialism.

Whilst historians have reported facts of Garvey's life, it is for activists to deepen understanding of his tremendous contribution by contextualising them into liberation strategies and action plans. *"Conceptions and misconceptions of Garvey and Garveyism"* concludes by outlining the Afrikan liberation strategy of Marcus Garvey and the UNIA.

Strategically selected quotes from Marcus Garvey

"Strategically selected quotes from Marcus Garvey" is intended as a handbook for members of Pan-Afrikan organisations, other activists and students to assist them in the speedy assimilation of Garvey's key strategic ideas. Beyond that it is hoped that it will also contribute by performing a similar role in the wider Afrikan community and among friends and supporters of the wider Afrikan liberation struggle, popularising his ideas in the process.

Centenary of World War, the UNIA and 'Race First'

As its title implies, *"Centenary of World War, the UNIA and 'Race First'"* was written as a commemoration of those 3 important events in Afrikan people's and broader humanity's history. It presents evidence supporting the thesis that Marcus Garvey was the greatest Afrikan grassroots organiser of the twentieth century. It exposes a fake debate which occurred in Britain shortly before the centenary year which misleadingly claimed - in opposition to the historical record - that 'Marxists' cannot be members of the UNIA. It concludes by identifying the origin of 'Race First' as an idea and term, demonstrating that it was brought into the UNIA by what the fake debate wrongly labelled 'Marxist members' of the UNIA.

100 years of Marcus Garvey in the UK

Written to commemorate the 100th anniversary of Marcus Garvey's first arrival in Britain, *"100 years of Marcus Garvey in the UK"* contains Garvey's autobiographical account of his organising activities. It summarises and recounts aspects of his history whilst there. It briefly summarises the essence of Garvey and the UNIA and shows how he successfully married his Christian beliefs with his Pan-Afrikan vision. Finally, it recounts the early history of the Marcus Garvey Organising Committee, set up in Britain in the early 2000's.

Special note:

The following titles have been incorporated into *"Conceptions and misconceptions of Garvey and Garveyism"*: (i) *"Strategically selected quotes from Marcus Garvey"*; (II) *"Centenary of World War, the UNIA and 'Race First'"*; and (iii) *"100 years of Marcus Garvey in the UK"*

Publications written by
Brother Omowale

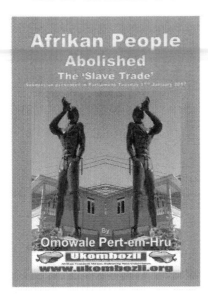

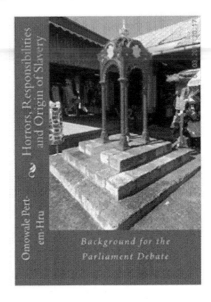

The Beautiful Black Afrikan People

Went for a walk

© Omowale Pert-em-Hru, 1998
Reprinted, 2019

Afrikan People Abolished the 'Slave Trade'

British imperialism owes each and every Afrikan person in the world a whopping £615,598,559 Billion first instalment i.e. six hundred and fifteen million, five hundred and ninety eight thousand, five hundred and fifty nine billion pounds - each. The premises/assumptions, formula and calculations are openly stated in *"Afrikan People Abolished the 'Slave Trade'"*.

By combining economic, political and military analysis on the geographical plane, *"Afrikan People Abolished the 'Slave Trade'"* introduces the new *Abolition Matrix tool*, which revolutionises the readers ability to accurately and properly analyse and assess the impact of forces leading to the defeat of slavery. The *Abolition Matrix tool* is supported by a gender balanced, contextually rich rendition of the Haitian revolution. In addition it:

1. Provides a brief insight into the glorious history of Afrikan people before the enslavement era, illustrating how Afrikan genius advanced humanity;
2. Graphically outlines the outrageously inhumane treatment issued to Afrikan people by the wicked enslavers of European imperialism;
3. Examines the thesis that Afrikan people's enslavement was self-inflicted, providing evidence of Afrikan resistance usually excluded from that debate;
4. Exposes evidence indicating William Wilberforce was an anti-abolitionist subversive government agent, tasked with undermining the whole abolition movement and process;
5. Provides lucid, clear and succinct examples of named Afrikan warriors, whose actions forced the abolition of slavery and the misnamed 'Slave Trade';
6. Contextualises slavery as the origin of imperialism's colonisation and neo-colonisation processes; and
7. Identifies the origin and core principles of slavery and anti-slavery social systems, proving that slavery has no implicit connection with Afrikan people and their culture.

"Afrikan People Abolished the 'Slave Trade'" should be treated as an introductory/grounding text, laying the foundation for a fuller understanding of the primary and critical role of Afrikan people in abolishing slavery and the misnamed 'Slave Trade'. As with the other books in the series, it should be studied collectively in groups, particularly by groups genuinely working towards the liberation of Afrika and her people in the context of worldwide revolution.

"The Horrors, Responsibilities and Origin of Slavery" has now been incorporated into *"Afrikan People Abolished the 'Slave Trade'"*.

271

The Beautiful Black Afrikan People Went for a Walk

Written for children and adults alike, *"The Beautiful Black Afrikan People Went for a Walk"* gives a simple, cogent and clear account of the early history of Afrikan people and humanity, presented as metaphor. Potently written, it clears the fog of centuries of misinformation, turning the perspectives of 'orthodoxy' upside down.

It may come as a deep shock to some but allowing for a little artistic licence, *"The Beautiful Black Afrikan People Went for a Walk"* is a truthful history of humanity made simple. The impact of the ice age on the human family has, for some time, been theorised by anthropologists and related academics. It is widely recognised as instrumental in the diversification of humanity.

Understanding this corrects a plethora of racist distortions, the sum total of which result in Afrikan people being place as a sub-ordinate grouping outside the human family. By identifying Afrikan people as the first inhabitants of all parts of the world and the source from which all other branches are descended, it places them in their correct historical and geographical position as the mothers and fathers of humanity.

By exposing new minds to this truth of history, Afrikan people are presented as a critically important part of the human family and the process of dismantling racism from its root is begun. *"The Beautiful Black Afrikan People Went for a Walk"* is an important learning tool for people of all races, pointing all in the direction of hidden historical truths. A must read for all children of the world, their parents and grandparents, it makes an ideal gift.

For further information about publications contact:

+44 7933 145 393 or

Ukombozii@gmail.com or

Visit the website

Omowale
Ru Pert-em-Hru

Omowale Ru Pert-em-Hru is committed to the restoration of justice for Afrikan and other oppressed people of the world. He is founder of Ukombozii, the Pan-Afrikan Society Community Forum (PASCF) and Marcus Garvey & Haitian Revolution Annual Memorial Lectures.

He has been involved in student and community activism since the 1990's, is author of the *Pan-Afrikanism Series* of books and presents the *Pan-Afrikan People's Phone-in* — produced as educational tools for those genuinely interested in the liberation of Afrika. He is Education Coordinator of *Sankofa360ºLtd*.

In acknowledging the primacy of matter he is a philosophical materialist, seeking to contribute to the unification, liberation and development of Afrika and her people under Scientific Socialism — Afrikan people's contribution to worldwide revolution.

Pan-Afrikan People's Phone-in

Presenter

Omowale Ru Pert-em-Hru

Mondays 8-10pm

Phone - On air Number:

+44 (0) 203 290 1138

Skype – On air Link:

Panafrikanpeoplesphonein

The Pan-Afrikan People's Phone-in is a space for themed interactive guest based discussion conducted on internet radio. Dealt with from a Revolutionary Pan-Afrikanist perspective, themes focus on issues affecting Afrikan people locally and globally.

Spread the word: Please tell all of your family friends, fellow organisation members, colleagues, associates and other networks about this show.

Printed in Great Britain
by Amazon

62931729R00173